SOME NECESSARY ANGELS

ॐ

ESSAYS ON WRITING AND POLITICS

Jay Parini

WITHDRAWN

COLUMBIA UNIVERSITY PRESS   NEW YORK

Columbia University Press

Publishers Since 1893

New York   Chichester, West Sussex

Copyright © 1997 Columbia University Press

All rights reserved

Library of Congress Cataloging-in-Publication Data

Parini, Jay.

    Some necessary angels : essays on writing and politics / Jay Parini.

      p.   cm,

      ISBN 0–231–11070–7 (acid-free paper)

    1. Parini, Jay—Authorship. 2. Politics and literature.

    3. Poetry—Authorship. 4. Poetry. I. Title.

PS3566.A65Z475 1997

809.1—dc21   97–25379

Casebound editions of Columbia University Press books

are printed on permanent and durable acid-free paper.

Printed in the United States of America

c 10 9 8 7 6 5 4 3 2 1

iv

For Devon, this and all

CONTENTS

Contents

INTRODUCTION

Since 1968, when I arrived in St. Andrews, Scotland, as a student on my junior year abroad, I've considered writing to be my daily work. By 1970, as a graduate student at St. Andrews, I was able to spend at least half of each day at my writing table—a habit that has stayed with me. In those days I occupied the top flat of a tall granite house near the North Sea; from there I watched the changing sky through a cold blue window as I wrote poems, essays, and fiction. I remember the thrill when, in 1971, my first poem—a translation from Ovid's *Amores*—was accepted by *Scottish International,* a now-defunct periodical. I ran through the damp streets of St. Andrews with the letter of acceptance in my pocket, convinced that the world was mine.

It has not, of course, always been so easy. It was many years until, in the late seventies, I was able to place poems in *The New Yorker* and *The Atlantic*. But I did rather quickly realize that the point of writing was not publication. I wrote poems because I found them forming on my lips as I walked the streets or lay in the bath. I could hardly read a volume of verse in those days without scratching lines of my own in the margins, often writing first drafts of poems in the blank pages at the back of a book or on any scraps of paper I could lay my hands on quickly. Words called to words.

I still write poems when I can, but I also enjoy writing prose, and this volume contains the best of my work in the essay format during the past twenty-five years. The essay on the poetry of Alastair Reid, who was my mentor in St. Andrews, is the earliest piece here, a review-essay commissioned by *Lines Review,* a Scottish journal. It was the first critical piece of writing that I did in which I felt my voice emerging. I still reread it occasionally, hoping to skim off a little of that freshness: the buoyancy of beginnings.

My graduate thesis at St. Andrews was about the poetry of Theodore Roethke, and my essay here on Blake and Roethke is a product of those years, though written later, when I was teaching at Dartmouth. It is more formal than most of the other essays: like most critics in the academy, I began in a traditional mold, adhering to the conventions. Only gradually did I feel at liberty to discard the more constricting trappings of scholarship. Purposely excluding from this collection most of my early academic pieces, which were somewhat dry studies of influence, I have included only essays that seem to carry in them the life of an individual voice and sensibility. I've written with greater keenness about poets I admire deeply: Frost, Roethke, Warren, Heaney, Reid, and Charles Wright. These are the poets (there are others, such as Philip Levine, about whom I've written but never at length) who played a large role in my development; they were, and remain, spiritual guides.

Some work here is very personal. The first part is devoted to autobiographical writing. "Mentors" traces my friendships with three older writers—Alastair Reid, Robert Penn Warren, and Gore Vidal. The seven essays that follow are all autobiographical in some way. "Town Life" and "My Life in Baseball" are in a way Thurberesque. "On Being Prolific," "Poetry and the Devout Life," and "Writing in Restaurants" are reflections on the writing life. "Reflections of a Nonpolitical Man" concerns my wary, sometimes passionate contact with the world of politics—a theme developed in several essays in the third part of this collection.

Although I have written a good deal about novelists as well, I have chosen to focus on poetry in part 2 of this collection. I have done my best work in this area, and I wanted especially to preserve in this format these particular essays—most of which are not easily available elsewhere. The essays on Warren's later poetry and Charles Wright are, in fact, printed here for the first time.

Part 3, The World and the Word, contains a sampling of recent essays. "The Lessons of Theory" takes an aerial view of literary theory over the past two or three decades, isolating what seems to me important in the post-structuralist movement, and it might be thought of as the results of a senior seminar on theory that I taught several times at Middlebury College. "The Imagination of Politics" is based on a lecture on this subject for the Salzburg Seminar in Austria in 1993, and it concerns the vexed relationship between literature and politics. "Literary Theory and the Culture of Creative Writing" was also a lecture, delivered at Dartmouth College. In its earliest form, "Fact or Fiction" was the Fowler Hamilton Lecture at Christ Church College, Oxford, in 1994. I presented "Poetry and Silence" as a seminar paper at Oxford in 1993.

This book is full of ghosts: friends and texts, many of them sunk in memory. I found myself biting my nails as I reread them, remembering past lives, passions long spent, ideas now substantially revised, often transmogrified beyond recognition. Nevertheless, this collection offers a fair account of my thinking in the years since I haltingly began to put my thoughts on paper, to discover in the crabwise scrawl across the blank page some image of myself, some picture of the world.

Some Necessary Angels

1. Personal

MENTORS

There may be deep psychological reasons for my obsession with mentors and mentoring, but they don't interest me. The fact remains that I've been much influenced by my friendships with Alastair Reid, Robert Penn Warren, and Gore Vidal. Their literary styles, approaches to the craft of writing, even their ways of being in the world, have framed my own development.

I met Alastair Reid in Scotland in 1970. I had first arrived in St. Andrews, an idyllic coastal town on the East Neuk of Fife, in 1968. It was the "home of golf," as their tourist brochures claim, but also the home of Scotland's most ancient university, founded in 1312. The medieval city walls are still, here and there, intact, and the university's granite towers dominate this town beside the North Sea. I spent seven years there, and I still dream about its cobbled byways, steamy pubs, and windswept vistas.

Hearing that I wanted to be a writer, a tutor of mine named Anne Wright said, "Ah, then you should meet Alastair Reid." She and Reid had been students together at St. Andrews in the forties, after the war. It was a heady time, with so many veterans (like Reid, who served in the Pacific with the Royal Navy) returning to student ranks. These men did not feel constrained by the in loco parentis mode characteristic of British higher education in those days, and this made for complex, combustuous relations between administrators and students. "Alastair was a cut-up in those days," Anne Wright recalled, no doubt understating the matter. "You will like him."

I telephoned, and he said to meet him at a pub, the now-defunct Central Tavern, in Market Street. I still remember how tremblingly I went to see him. I had never met a "real" writer. Already, I had checked his books—the slim volumes of idiosyncratic, pellucid, gorgeously musical verse, the collections of essays on travel and ideas—out of the university library. I had never encountered a prose manner like that before, so deeply personal in syntax, image centered, at times almost singing. The tone was so infinitely worldly wise, with a flicker of Celtic charm at every crucial turn. I knew at once that I wanted my poetry and prose to look like that.

Alastair sat at the bar, a man in his mid-forties with a broad ruddy face, big hands, and a whimsical grin. He sipped a pint of bitter with easy familiarity and smoked tobacco as though it were grass, sucking in, holding, then blowing out. His eyes turned on me like headlamps, and I was swept away.

I learned that Alastair lived with his young son, Jasper, at Pilmour Cottage, a house above the West Sands that overlooked the sea. It was nestled in a grove of tall oaks, where hundreds of sooty-winged rooks gathered—"my rookery," as he called it. The house was rented, and Alastair was spending a year or so in St. Andrews after being away for decades. After his graduation (in classics) from the university, he had gone to the United States, where he found a job teaching classics at Sarah Lawrence. After several years, his poems and prose pieces began to appear in *The New Yorker*, and he decided to live by his pen. In the early fifties, he bought a farm in Mallorca, where he apprenticed himself to Robert Graves and became the great man's amanuensis.

He told me about how he learned to write from Graves. He was set the task of bringing into rough English the *Lives of the Noble Caesars* by

Suetonius. (Graves had acquired a commission for the translation from Penguin, one of an endless series of small literary tasks that brought in enough money to support his vast family.) At first, Alastair was vaguely offended. He, after all, knew how to write. But when he took his work to Graves, Alastair sat beside him with amazement, watching as weak adjectives disappeared, gathered into the trunks of sturdier nouns, as adverbs evaporated, as verbs grew stronger. He watched the swift hand of the master as he cut and pasted, drawing Alastair's syntax in tightly, as a father might lace a child's boot.

Alastair learned more than the details of a particular craft, although that would have been enough. He learned a way of living, of being, that involved, foremost, a dedication to the job of writing, a commitment to a kind of daily rhythm in which words are cast like a net, gathering and transforming "reality" in a web of prose or verse. He shadowed Graves each day, becoming familiar with his routines. Ever since, he has preferred houses by the sea, and a habit of writing near a kitchen, so that he can keep a pot of soup boiling while a poem or piece of prose boils on the desk nearby. Alastair has found cooking an appropriate analogue to writing: a way of bringing together disparate elements, subjecting them to the heat of imagination, letting them meld, set. The satisfactions of these arts are not dissimilar.

I took to visiting Alastair at Pilmour Cottage in the afternoons, pedaling out along the West Sands to his isolated house through what seemed like perpetual rain. A mug of tea was always waiting, and I would take my poem of the day from a damp rucksack and put it on his kitchen table. Between stirrings of soup, he would sit beside me and do what Graves did for him: add or chop a word, a phrase. Sometimes whole stanzas would disappear or get moved up or down. Once he crumpled a whole poem without a word. He said little. I watched and learned. (This way of teaching reminds me now of those traditional Japanese masters of calligraphy who teach by having a student simply repeat certain patterns, following their brush strokes exactly.)

My poems, not surprisingly, began to sound extremely like Alastair's. I knew this, of course, but it did not worry me. I knew that one day, if lucky, my voice would blend with his, would gradually separate and become distinct. This happens naturally. I think it took longer than I imagined it would, and I can still find myself—decades later—slipping into an Alastairian mode. Yet I don't mind. It's a worthy line, a verse heritage that includes within its folds the voices of Alastair's masters: Graves, Yeats, Hopkins, the anonymous Anglo-Saxon poets.

Alastair also guided my intellectual life. Though I have spent much of my life in the academy, I was never one who could learn from schools. The very idea of a syllabus and reading list put me off, and I always went out of my way to read only those books that were not required. I resisted the formal authority of the classroom and determined to go my own way. But I needed a model, an example of someone who had sought *his* own way and found it. I wanted to know what Alastair was reading, had read. And he obligingly turned me in the direction of certain poets and prose writers whom he admired. Quite literally, he introduced me to the two Latin American writers he was at that time busy translating: Jorge Luis Borges and Pablo Neruda. We met Neruda in London; it was only a year or so before he died of cancer, but the great spirit was there. Borges came to stay in St. Andrews, and my contacts with him—in Alastair's kitchen, mostly— were memorable. With Alastair's help, I made my way carefully through Borges's intricate metaphysical tales and through the poems of Neruda, whose greedy pleasure in the world's alphabet of sensations has been a perpetual light in one corner of my mind.

Alastair's way of being in the world is another matter. He is, as he likes to say, a cat person, moving without dog loyalty from house to house, country to country. His only permanent address since 1953 has been *The New Yorker*, and he has usually lived in other people's houses. The constrictions of conventional marriage have held no appeal for him. As he says in one poem, "Change is where I live." I find this admirable but terrifying. I quickly realized that my own instincts worked against Alastair's here and that I preferred a doglike existence: one house, one wife, a permanent landscape, which for me is always northern New England. But the cat person still calls to me, and—perhaps in obeisance to something I learned from Alastair—I can't resist my forays into the larger world. My wife, Devon, and I regularly go abroad, to Italy or England, where we rent a house for a month, a year, at a time. I entertain fantasies of villas in Mexico or Sicily. I too am drawn to the exhilaration of impermanence, though I retreat for daily life to my wood-frame farmhouse on a hill overlooking the Green Mountains. Unlike Alastair, I want it both ways—a mistake, perhaps.

Alastair embodies, for me, the Taoist way, although he would laugh at this notion. He lives in the moment, utterly, and does not excessively fear mutability. I often think of this verse from the *Tao te ching* as his credo:

Do not be concerned about your place in the world.
Accept misfortune as part of what it means to be human.

What does this mean, to not be concerned about your place?
It means to accept being nobody,
and not to overburden yourself with loss or gain.

What does it mean, to accept misfortune?
Bad luck is natural, part of what it means to have a body.
Without a body, there could be no misfortune.

Give in, with humility.
Then you will be trusted to look after the things of this
world.
Consider the world a part of yourself.
Then you will truly love the things of this world.

Alastair has never cared to own things; in fact, most of his clothing is "portable property"—to borrow a phrase from *Great Expectations*. He finds the idea of landownership laughable. He moves lightly in the world, taking no more than he needs. He is attentive to everything, everyone. He listens better than anyone else: taking in what you say, teaching you how to use what you know. Everything in his life is absorbed into an ongoing narrative, and people like his company because he includes everyone in this process of making. No phrase or happening goes unattended, is left dangling; everything is sewn into the larger fabric of a day, a week. He has a childlike sense of play about him.

His dust-jacket note for *Passwords* (1964) best catches this sense of being in the world:

> I saw the light in Scotland, and the sharp contrasts, rough and gentle, of its landscape and climate still haunt me strongly enough to keep me from returning. I left Scotland first during the war, when a spell at sea in the East gave me my first taste of strangeness and anonymity. Afterwards, following an irrelevant education, I crossed to the United States out of curiosity, and lived there off and on until the same curiosity propelled me back to Europe, to Spain in

particular, which I discovered to be a cranky incarnation of the whole human paradox, joyful, harsh, loving and violent, all at once. I have lived peripherally in France, in Morocco, in Switzerland; the list I hope is not complete—a kind of wistful dissatisfaction keeps me on the move. I have been in and out of trouble; have taken great pleasure in games of all kinds, in friends, in children, in languages, in talking, in running water; and have tried above all to keep a clear eye. Although I am in love with the English language, I have no noticeable accent left. My passport says I am a writer, which has proved a useful cloak for my curiosity. Poems are for me the consequences of the odd epiphanies which from time to time miraculously happen. Prose I keep for a calmer, more reflective everyday attention to the world. I think I have always been a foreigner.

One hears the tone and manner of the man in the syntax, the subtle figuration, of the passage. One can learn a lot from someone like this, and I have. But it remains true of all mentoring relationships that one must take some things and discard others. Mere imitation never lasts. The point of mentoring is that one has an example to follow. One can temporarily "follow the brush," then—ideally, and quite mysteriously—find oneself alone, paradoxically bound to the mentor yet freed from him (even by him) as well.

The passage beyond the mentor relationship is rarely easy, and I found it particularly difficult in this first crucial relationship to move into a more adult form of friendship. It took many years, in fact, and had some difficult passages. Once, for example, we shared a flat in Puerto Rico together (in 1980) for several months. I was just beginning to move into the realm of the published author, and there were strange tensions in me that I took out, like a Prodigal Son, on my literary father. It led to some awkward scenes. But we ironed these tensions out over the next decade. I see Alastair regularly in various places (England, the Dominican Republic, New York, Vermont). Devon and our three boys have come to think of him as a member of the family, and—of course—he is.

I moved from St. Andrews to Hanover, New Hampshire, in the fall of 1975, taking a job at Dartmouth College. Robert Penn Warren had a summer house nearby, in West Wardsboro, Vermont. Before now, I had read only his most celebrated novel, *All the King's Men*, plus a handful of his poems, but I deeply liked what I'd read. After reading through his *New and Selected Poems* (1975) in 1976, two friends and I went to interview him for *New England Review*, and a friendship began that lasted until his death, at eighty-four, in 1989.

Warren had left his native South long ago, although it remained the setting for most of his fiction and much of his poetry. You do not leave the South, of course. It goes with you. But Warren had found a congenial home in New England, moving between a stone barn in Connecticut that he and his wife, Eleanor Clark, had converted into a house soon after he began teaching at Yale in 1950 and a rustic house in Vermont, where he spent every summer and most winter holidays. Red (as he was called by his friends) and Eleanor invited me to their annual New Year's Eve bash that year, and the tradition continues to this day (carried on by Warren's children, Rosanna and Gabriel).

In my mid-twenties, I was looking for a way to marry teaching and writing. As a writer, I was trying to find a mode of working that allowed for the making of poems, critical essays, and novels. There were few models on the horizon for writers who moved easily between the empires of poetry and fiction, and these were mostly European. Goethe and Victor Hugo came to mind, as did Thomas Hardy and D. H. Lawrence. Beckett wrote just a little poetry but was able to write plays and poems with equal success. For the most part, writers stuck to one genre. I worried that a kind of hubris would bring me down, that I might not develop as a poet or novelist or critic if I kept trying to work in different genres.

What first attracted me to Warren was his example. I saw that he had managed to have a teaching career, to write poems seriously for many decades, and to continue to publish novels well into his seventh decade. He was an old-fashioned man of letters of a type now rare. I knew instinctively that I could learn from him, and I deliberately sought his company.

Fortunately, Red was an extremely accessible man. He and Eleanor actively liked the company of younger people, and it was easy to see them. Devon and I became a part of their regular circle, visiting them whenever they were in Vermont, sometimes venturing south to Connecticut. I always looked forward to these visits, as much for the tactile feel of their house as the good company.

Their place was buried deep in the woods behind Stratton, up an unmarked gravel drive. The house was many-angled and roomy with a huge stone fireplace in the living room and several decks and balconies. We had lunch on a screened-in porch above a deep-throated brook. Drinks, at sundown, were on another porch with mountain views. Dinners were held at a long country table, and the conversation ranged dizzyingly from politics to literature. (Eleanor had once been Trotsky's secretary, and she held her opinions firmly and defended them with rare force of conviction.) One did not speak lightly in their company.

Red and Eleanor each worked in separate "shacks" some distance from the house. Red's shack overlooked a cold pond in which he would swim each afternoon from late May through early September. It was amusing to watch him, a bathing cap drawn tightly over his ears, as he swam, using a peculiar crawl. "Swimming is a regular, boring activity, which makes it ideal for meditation," he told me. "Poems come to me when I swim or walk in the woods. Any form of regular repetitive exercise stimulates the unconscious mind." When he stepped from the water, he looked like some prehistoric monster, his skin loose, his face immensely craggy. He talked rapidly in a high-pitched voice in a barely comprehensible southern accent.

His rituals were important, part of his creative life. These involved getting up early, a round of exercise (lifting weights, even into his eighties), a small breakfast, then several hours of isolation and work before lunch at one. Lunch always began with a glass of sherry on ice, which in summers he often took at the pond. The meal itself was convivial, informal. He usually had a rest after lunch, a solid nap, then a long walk in the woods or a swim, sometimes both. Late afternoon was "a good time for revision," Red told me. He would retreat to his shack for an hour or so before cocktails. Dinner was late, at seven, and—when he had visitors—a visit was always paid to the musty well-stocked wine cellar. Red enjoyed conversation, and dinners would stretch to eleven or so, with long stories by Red about the Old South. He had a perfect memory for Civil War battles and historical details in general. I remember one evening when the conversation (mostly a monologue by Red) ranged from Julius Caesar to Napoleon to Jefferson Davis.

After dinner, I would sit by Red on the ancient yellow couch in the living room and quiz him about the past. I wanted to hear about the Fugitives, the school of poets he once belonged to at Vanderbilt in the twenties. He had known so many writers well: John Crowe Ransom, Randall Jarrell, Allen Tate, Katherine Anne Porter, Eudora Welty, Saul Bellow, on and on. His was a lucky life, with friends galore, with good conversation usually at his elbows. He often repeated himself, but I was glad to hear his stories again and again.

Red was unstinting when it came to advice about writing. I once asked him if writing poetry, then turning to fiction, had posed any problems. "Poetry is the great schoolhouse for fiction," he said. "Think of Hemingway, Faulkner, Fitzgerald—they all began as poets. Most writers do. Some keep at it, like Lawrence, and the poetry keeps the fiction fresh, supplies details, images, metaphors." He had turned to fiction, he said, "because there is so much pleasure in narrative, in making a whole world." He claimed to have "five or six novels complete" in his head, "if only there were time, and energy." At seventy-five, he had reluctantly abandoned fiction. "I'd be trying to write a novel and the poems kept creeping up in the margins. I couldn't avoid them." In this he resembled Thomas Hardy, one of his great loves. "Hardy gave himself over to poetry in the end," Red said. "But he was a poet in the novels too." In his last years, Red would often reread his favorite writers: Hardy, Eliot, and Shakespeare. "At a certain age, you return to old familiar texts," he told me. "And you see things in them you hadn't noticed or weren't ready to notice."

Red would read my poetry and fiction and make detailed suggestions, offering encouragement and suggesting directions. He urged me to keep a broad view. "It's easy to get lost in details," he said, "but a writer has to think about the shape of his work as a whole—that has to stay at the back of the mind." He also urged me to keep the audience in mind. "Readers are very precious," he said, "and you mustn't disappoint them." He argued that teaching kept one in touch with actual faces and voices. "Too many writers become isolated and lose that immediate relationship with people," he said. "It's lonely work, and the isolation is dangerous." Teaching, as long as it didn't cut too deeply into one's writing time, was an ideal way to maintain contact with a live audience.

Once, when I was going through a dreadful slump and unable to write well, he gave me an essential piece of advice: "Cultivate leisure. That's the best thing a writer can do for himself. Good work never comes from effort. It comes easily. If it doesn't, it isn't ready. Go for a walk, swim, read a book. Learn to wait." He explained that he, like me, was prone to overworking and that his imagination would become "ragged and thin." He said I should actively create an atmosphere of ease and leisure, "a space in your life where nothing special happens but where the ground is fertile, and seeds can take root." He suggested that "empty hours are like water on these seeds." When working, I should "hurry slowly." "It's important to feel the silences in a poem, in a paragraph of prose. Make the white space part of the line or sentence."

Red's manner with people was fetching. He was warm and encouraging to everyone, though one could intuit that he had a high standard. He behaved by the strictest codes of gentlemanliness and expected similar behavior. He never bad-mouthed anyone, although he could deflate pretensions with a wisecrack or sly aside. There was nothing even remotely narcissistic about him: his mind was directed at the world, and ideas were the meat at his table. He read poetry and fiction, history, and philosophy, but history continued to have a great pull on him, and one saw Gibbon and Momsen at his bedside table. "The truth of poetry is greater than the truth of history," he said, "but one depends upon the other. History is an invention that we can't do without. Without it, we'd be like the somebody who wakes up from a deep sleep and can't think where he was." He always refused to think of himself as a "historical novelist." "That phrase would cover just about anybody," he said. "If memory is involved, as it always is, then the work is 'historical.'"

The advent of literary theory in the late seventies and eighties was at times nettling. The New Critics were in bad odor, and Red was considered a founding member of that school. "There was no school," he insisted. "You couldn't possibly see much of a connection among the work of critics as diverse as Cleanth Brooks, [I. A.] Richards, Maynard Mack, [W. K.] Wimsatt, Louis Martz, and so many others. I suppose the one thing we had in common was a wish to look closely at a given text, but the deconstructionists do that, almost to a point of madness." He said that the notion that the New Critics wanted to divorce literature from life was nonsense. "I'm a biographer at heart. It's life that matters, and literature is a part of life."

I read Warren's later poetry with special interest. It was moving to witness a man of his stature as a poet confronting the end of life and using poetry as a way to get a grip on this experience. His poems were philosophical, deeply so, almost religious, if one thinks of religion in its root sense (*religio*), as an attempt to 'link back' to some infinite reservoir of power and being. Warren was able to focus his attention on language as the supreme source of knowledge in this later work, which began with *Audubon: A Vision* (1969) and continued through his final volume of *New and Selected Poems*. But the manner is fully present in *Audubon*, as when he asks: "What is love?" The answer comes: "Our name for it is knowledge." But this is heart knowledge, a kind of visceral understanding of the world's ruthless, dispassionate blend of truth and beauty. In *Audubon,* and successive volumes, one sees what Dave Smith has nicely called "the human need to prevail by witness."

Warren became, in effect, a relentless namer: of memories, experiences, natural objects. He looked around him with childlike wonder, seeing everything fresh. Again and again, he said to himself:

> Think hard. Take a deep breath. As the thunder-clap
> Dissolves into silence, your nostrils thrill to the
>
> Stunned new electric tang of joy—or pain—like ammonia.

He had a strong desire to see things in their raw glory, including the self and its involvement with fate. As in *Audubon,* where narrator wishes

> To wake in some dawn and see,
> As though down a rifle barrel, lined up
> Like sights, the self that was, the self that is, and there,
> Far off but in range, completing that alignment, your fate.

There was something breathtaking about Warren's last push into language, in the nobility of his stance, in the brightness of those sunny particulars that crowd his poems. His language was, like the man, raw boned, expansive, talky, and occasionally nostalgic. He hurled big abstractions like Time and Fate and Knowledge around with abandon. This was ambitious poetry, reaching high for some combination of complete understanding and spiritual grace. Few poets ever try so hard or achieve so much.

Mentors are important in different ways. They can teach by the example of their life or their work or some mixture of the two. I think I got more from Red Warren than even I realized at the time. Some years after his death, I find myself circling back to him, to his work, repeatedly. And I hear his voice in my ear: "Cultivate leisure." I can actually see him, his broad-brimmed hat pulled low, a walking stick in his hand, following a trail through the woods near Stratton. We once stood together on a cliff, looking westward across several mountain ranges, and he said, "That's what we're here for, to look."

In 1985, I spent part of the academic year in Italy, in a small village on the Amalfi coast. Our villa, a white-baked house with colorful tile floors and vaulted ceilings, had a lovely rooftop terrace from which we could see the whole coastline from Salerno to Amalfi. On a clear day, the foothills of Calabria winked in the distance. Above us, through a dense lemon grove, was Ravello, and we could see a magnificent villa clinging to the cliff above. I asked my neighbor (the owner of a local bookstore) who lived there, imagining some Italian nobleman or captain of industry. "Gore Vidal," he said, "an American writer."

I told him I knew Vidal's work well and asked if he ever came down from his perch. "He comes every afternoon to my store to buy the English papers," I was told. I left a note saying that I hoped to meet him one day, if that was agreeable. I gave him my number, and that very evening the phone rang. "Come to dinner," the famously patrician voice said. "Tomorrow night would be fine."

Devon and I were awed by Vidal's villa, La Rondinaia, meaning Swallow's Nest. One walks from the center of a village piazza to a cliffside path with dazzling aerial views. At the end of a private walk, one encounters tall iron gates that are opened electronically from the house. Inside, the garden lures one forward through a walkway of cedars, past a dark blue swimming pool and cabana with a travertine deck, through a loggia, down steep stairs, along another narrow path to the villa itself, which is built into the side of the cliff on five levels, with countless balconies and terraces. "Welcome to the most beautiful view in the world," Gore said, with an undercurrent of irony that made it sound unpretentious.

We met Howard Austen, his companion since the late forties, and settled into the study for drinks. That first night stays in my head, the lively banter, severe politics, the vast social world of high-level Washington pols, Hollywood stars, and writers—all of whom Gore seemed to know intimately. Having come, like most people, from an ordinary background (I did, at the age of twelve, once meet the mayor of Scranton, Pennsylvania, in a hotel lobby), I was impressed and a little frightened but skeptical as well.

Any skepticism toward Gore soon vanished. Despite the glittering world into which he happened to be born, he actually lived in relative isolation. He and Howard were pretty much self-sufficient, and Gore spent most of his time reading and writing. How else would one get so many words down on paper? By 1985, he had published some twenty novels, as well as a half-dozen books of essays. He had written several immensely popular plays for Broadway, a dozen or more screenplays for Hollywood, and countless original scripts for television. His fiercely sardonic commentaries appeared everywhere from *Esquire* to *The New York Review of Books.* "Work, work, work," Gore said to me. "That's my life. The rest is illusion."

I was taken by Gore's wit, of course, but also moved by his clear signals of friendship. Before long, we met almost every day at a local bar in Amalfi for a drink. We often had dinner together, usually at his place but sometimes at mine or in a restaurant. A friendship grew that has stretched far beyond that year on the Amalfi coast. We have, indeed, become close friends.

Gore's example as a writer is complex. As he has said, "The obvious danger for the writer is the matter of time." He quotes Goethe: "A talent is formed in stillness, a character in the stream of the world." Gore has managed, it seems, to achieve both, although most writers should probably be wary of appearing on television too often or running for public office. One should, however, remain engaged with the world on some level. Perhaps my generation, which came of age during the Vietnam War, takes this for granted.

I remember reading Vidal in college in *The New York Review of Books.* His radical politics were highly persuasive then, as now. Gore argues that the United States has only one party, the Party of Business. That is, the difference between Democrats and Republicans is laughably slight. (There is, for example, no real labor party in this country—something that Europeans find incomprehensible.) Our democracy is a partial affair, because politicians are essentially paid for (if not bought) by special interest groups. It should surprise nobody that less than half the eligible voters actually turn up at the polls; there is deep apathy, even cynicism, everywhere: a natural result of our monolithic politics. What keeps Gore's political analysis from being utterly depressing is the constant wit, as when he called Ronald Reagan "a triumph of the embalmer's art." The situation can't be so bad if it's so funny.

Writers do, in fact, have a responsibility to society. They should actively seek to represent the public conscience. Those who have language and analytical skills at their command have an obligation to use them. A democratic state can function fully only when its people have wide access to a healthy, complex, public discourse—a situation that has been sadly lacking in the United States, where the spectrum of opinion found in most mainstream periodicals is surprisingly narrow. "If I see a pothole in the road, I point to it," Gore once told me. He often alludes to Alfred North Whitehead, who said that one got to the essence of a culture not by looking at what is said but by looking at what is not said, the underlying assumptions of the society, too obvious to be stated. Truth—or some crucial aspect of truth—resides in those silences.

The private job of the writer is another matter, although even here one has responsibilities to what the Romans called the res publica, and to history—that "necessary angel of reality," as Wallace Stevens called it. Gore's work in the historical novel was, for me, a particular inspiration, and my third novel, *The Last Station* (1990)—a novel about Tolstoy—owes something to our conversations about his *Lincoln* (1984). He urged me to put Tolstoy at the still center of the novel and to revolve my characters around him as in a cubist painting. I did as he suggested, and it worked.

The problem with writing fiction that also trades in ideas is how to keep the reader's attention. I recall sitting by Gore's pool one summer and talking about a short story I was writing. I asked him if he thought it possible to hold the reader's attention while two characters discussed Kierkegaard for ten or twelve pages. Gore replied, with a barely restrained smirk: "Only if your characters are sitting in a railway car, and the reader knows there is a bomb under the seat." Now, I always try to keep that bomb under the seat. It's a sure way to create narrative compulsion.

Another tip from Gore that stays in my head concerns reviewing. One often hears that Vidal is the "best reviewer since Edmund Wilson." What is meant, I suppose, is that Gore writes engagingly about books and that he knows a lot. Once I was stuck with reviewing a book that, for reasons now happily forgotten, defeated me. I called Gore to complain, and he said, "Describe the book, that's your job." That advice returns to mind whenever I'm stuck with a difficult book. The work is to describe the textual object coolly and clearly; everything else follows from that.

Gore's reviews, or "bookchat," provide a good model for any novice reviewer. He often begins with a personal anecdote, one related to the subject at hand. His criticism has a vivid sense of the relation of literature to life. He is learned, but he wears this learning lightly. For instance, an essay on Barry Goldwater (*Rocking the Boat* [1962]) opens,

> Julius Caesar stood before a statue of Alexander the Great and wept, for Alexander at twenty-nine had conquered the world and at thirty-two was dead, while Caesar, a late starter of thirty-three, had not yet subverted even his own state. Pascal, contemplating this poignant scene, remarked rather

sourly that he could forgive Alexander for wanting to own
the earth because of his extreme youth, but Caesar was old
enough to have known better.

The sweep of this is breathtaking, and it makes a point about worldly power
that is useful throughout the piece.

Whereas Red Warren was, like me, a teacher as well as a writer, Gore is
basically anti-academic. Whenever I feel mired in the academy, I call Gore
for refreshment. His wit is always sobering. "Teaching has ruined more
writers than alcohol," he once told me. "Beware of the scholar-squirrels," of
"the hicks and hacks of academe." Having held a professorial job for two
decades, I should take offense, but I don't. Gore is a satirist, and satire works
by hyperbole. The ideal readers of Gore Vidal should have no personal
attachments whatsoever. They should delight in seeing fun poked at any-
one, especially those in power.

I was sitting with Gore one summer in the piazza of Ravello, drinking
wine, as the cathedral threw a long shadow across the cobbled square. He
recalled a visit he had made years before to a nursing home in Rome where
George Santayana was living—the husk of the man, one should say. Gore
admired the Spanish-born philosopher who had taught generations of
Harvard students what aesthetics is all about. "I don't remember anything
he said, not specifically, but there was something about him that had an
effect," Gore said.

I knew exactly what he meant.

Mentors have an aura, an indefinable yet alluring presence that affects the
person under their spell. I have been, to varying degrees, under the spell of
Alastair Reid, Robert Penn Warren, and Gore Vidal. Their energies have
charged me in different ways. I have benefited from their examples, some-
times defining myself against them. Their styles of writing, subjects, ideas,
prejudices, fears, and fondnesses have played into my own. I have some-
times swayed from their headlamps, ducked. Other times, in a dark wood,
I have looked for their glow at the edge of the forest; more often than not,
it was there. My gratefulness to all three is boundless, and my admiration
perpetual.

TOWN LIFE

I seem always to find myself living in small towns. This once bothered me, because I hoped to become a poet, and "real" poets, like Robert Frost, lived in country settings, where the woods were "lovely, dark and deep" and neighbors were something to be fenced out. If they could not live in the woods, poets, such as T. S. Eliot, took to cities, where streets followed "like a tedious argument / Of insidious intent." Town life struck me as a painful compromise between two splendid extremes, sharing the poetic advantages of neither. But gradually, perhaps with maturity, it came to me that town life has its own aesthetic, and I have given up longing for woodlands or subways.

I grew up in a moderate-sized Pennsylvanian city that was really a small town in disguise. Scranton was once, in the early nineteenth century, a village called Slocum's Hollow. (Why on earth would anyone prefer Scranton to Slocum's Hollow as a place name?) By the time I came along in 1948, the coal companies had gone, leaving a residue of burning culm dumps, abandoned breakers, and houses whose basements were liable, at any moment, to fall through to Red China. (A small boy in my neighborhood once fell through a crack in the sidewalk and was never recovered, according to my mother.) The fever of economic boom passed with the mines as well, and my neighborhood of West Scranton settled into a low-keyed, unambitious routine. The shabbiness of the Lackawanna Valley, which is really the northern extreme of Appalachia, didn't bother me much as a child. The fumes blowing off the culm dumps weren't lethal; that was simply how air smelled. But the oppressiveness of what I considered the small-town mentality, where you could never escape your family's aura, began to rankle when I hit my teens. My mother went to the same elementary and high schools I did, and we shared a fair number of teachers, most of whom were neighbors. My grandparents, who lived more or less next door, had always lived in West Scranton, and their reputation for religious seriousness and moral rectitude preceded me wherever I went. The corner grocery store, owned by Joe and Mary Genova, was a favorite hangout, with its windows full of penny candy and coolers of Coke. But the Genovas acted in loco parentis; they parsimoniously meted out candy and Cokes with dutiful concern for our cavities and appetites, which—come hell or high water—mustn't be "spoiled."

Our mail carrier, Willard Thomas, was more than simply a government functionary. He took the matter of our mail seriously. Whenever the monthly letter from my pen pal in Bolivia was more than three days late, he worried obsessively, searching the newspapers for reports of "trouble" in Bolivia; he was also my Sunday school teacher when I was eight and, later, my Little League baseball coach. Then there was Miss Forgen, my first grade teacher. She took immense personal credit for having "brought jay out of his shell." I lost track of her after leaving elementary school, but not long after I published my first book of poems, a perfumed envelope arrived in the mail; inside was a card with "Congratulations!!!" scrawled in the margins by Miss Forgen. She had also enclosed a crisp five-dollar bill.

In 1968, I decided to go as far from home as possible and went off to St. Andrews, the oldest university in Scotland, on the suggestion of a young British student I met, quite by chance, at the Scranton YMCA swimming pool. He filled my head with visions of professors in black robes and mortarboards, students in scarlet academic gowns, medieval buildings with flying buttresses and high Gothic arches. That St. Andrews had fewer than ten thousand residents and was wholly as provincial as Scranton, if not more so, did not occur to me. At least it was *not* Scranton.

I seem able to recall every detail of that evening, close to midnight, when the train pulled into the St. Andrews station. I was two weeks early for the autumn term, and the train was empty. As I stepped from the railway car, a slantwise drizzle hit me in the face. Undaunted, I left my suitcase at the station and ran, exhilarated, through the small gray town that would be my home for the next seven years. The streetlamps glowed yellow in the sea fog. St. Andrews, with its medieval city walls still intact, its ruined cathedral and castle overlooking the sea, its romantic gardens and Gothic cloisters, was everything I hoped for.

The reality principle took hold quickly. With two other students, I rented a cottage called The Garioch, not far from the sea. We had to cook for ourselves, and within weeks I realized that the green grocer, ironmonger, postmaster, used bookseller, and local bank manager were crucial to my daily existence. I felt disconcerted but at home. Anonymity seemed impossible to achieve.

My main college tutor was a wizened little English professor who had been a naval commander during the Second World War. He was convinced—indeed, had devoted decades of scholarship to proving—that William Shakespeare must have been an officer in the Royal Navy during his famous "lost years." How else could he have known so much about naval protocol (as in *Anthony and Cleopatra* and elsewhere)? His classic study, *Shakespeare and the Sea,* is rivaled for eccentricity only by a similar study published by an American professor at the same time, entitled *Shakespeare the Lawyer.* Once, after several years in St. Andrews, I met my old tutor in the college quad. He said, in his usual barking manner, "I say, can you come to tea next Wednesday? I'd like you to meet a young American who, like yourself, writes poetry." I said I'd love to come but wondered who this student so like myself could be. "His name," the professor said calmly, "is Jay Parini." "But Professor," I said, "*I'm* Jay Parini." He was completely unruffled, saying, "Augh, no matter. Come anyway."

The British tolerate levels of eccentricity far greater than we do, and I came gradually to love the way, in the fishbowl of a small Scottish town, humanity swims about in bizarrely varied colors and patterns. The physical place too is surprisingly varied. I think I know every cobblestone, close, and cranny in St. Andrews. Like Henry David Thoreau, who claimed to have "travelled much in Walden," I have been everywhere in St. Andrews, from its craggy beachheads to its windblown, rabbit-infested golf courses (golf was "invented" in St. Andrews). The town's layout, with three main streets coming to a triangular peak at the ruins of an old cathedral, has become a permanent part of my mental terrain.

Returning to the United States, I instinctively sought out another small town, taking a job at Dartmouth College in Hanover, New Hampshire. But the romantic notion of living as a poet-farmer still attracted me, and I wasted months looking for an appropriately rustic farmhouse; somehow, the prospect of living on twenty-five or so acres, with the dark woods surrounding me like bandits, left my feet invariably cold when time came to close a deal. I wound up in the center of the village, where I could walk briskly to the bank or post office in ten minutes, no matter how much snow had fallen the night before. A pattern not unlike my life in St. Andrews took over, with early morning walks across the golf course that invariably ended at Lou's, a local diner, by eight-thirty. Lou reserved a small table for me in a back corner. He had been in business in Hanover since the early fifties, and portraits of two dozen local worthies hung in state above the lunch counter. It was my secret hope that, if I should live in Hanover and eat breakfast at Lou's for long enough, my portrait too would some day hang above the coolers and coffee pots. My waitress, a staunch but unpolemical Christian Scientist called Eleanor, did not approve of caffeine but nevertheless kept my coffee mug full as long as I sat there. I was sensible enough to leave after an hour or so if for some reason there was a rush on Lou's. There usually wasn't, and I sat quite guiltless for as long as three hours, writing in my notebook. I began to wonder if it were possible to write anywhere else.

I never stayed in Hanover long enough to make Lou's rogues gallery. Seven years of residence counts for little in a New England town, where the real natives often trace their family lineage in one place back to the eighteenth century. I began all over again, in Middlebury, Vermont—an hour and a half over the Green Mountains from Hanover. I live there with my wife, Devon, and children in a quirky white house with blue shutters, built circa 1910, on a broad oak-lined street full of other quirky shuttered houses not unlike ours. The routines founded in St. Andrews and Hanover seem well suited to Middlebury life. There's a golf course across the street, for early morning walks. And I have a choice of diners a few blocks away. I love the walk uptown, past familiar houses and public buildings to the village green, where I sit with a notebook in hand, waiting for poems to strike or not strike, as the muse will have it. As anyone who has lived in New England knows, the village green is a symbolic center of town life. The essential buildings—churches, banks, post office, bookstore—circulate around this organic hub, which often sports a picturesque gazebo used only for infrequent and intolerably dull summer band concerts.

Given my experience with town life, Middlebury's geographic and emotional terrain seem to fit snugly. I think I would desperately miss the intimate daily contact with people like my mail carrier, Larry, who lights up when I see him if there's definitely a check amid my usual bundle of junk mail. He passes bills across my doorstep with proper chagrin. A friend who visited me from New York was quite startled when I waved Larry's official Jeep over to the curb last summer to inquire about his recent operation. Unabashedly, he dropped his trousers to his knees to show me the putrid scar running the length of his inner thigh. That same day I took my urban visitor to the local diner where I write; a tall man at the next table, whom I vaguely knew, asked if he could sit down and demonstrate a recently acquired skill. He had learned how to play a facsimile of the *William Tell Overture* on his teeth. (Indeed, he has since displayed this remarkable talent on Vermont Public Radio.)

As middle age begins to overtake me, I have become almost embarrassingly a burgher, mowing my lawn with assiduous regularity, providing everything from soup to watermelon for the hordes of local children, and doing my bit in July when the Peasant Market—a charity fair—overwhelms the village green with baked goods and white elephants. Last year, during Peasant Market, I was responsible for borrowing a dozen picnic tables and setting them up before 7 A.M. on the green. The town loaned me a large truck—the first of its kind I had ever driven. Dutifully, I set off at sunrise toward the home of a neighbor whose love of his lawn is exceeded only by that of his wife and children. It had been raining all night, but the day broke sunny and mild, and I assumed that the lawn had soaked up the night's precipitation. Blithely, I drove straight across his wide front lawn, where the picnic table was conveniently sitting beside the porch. Not thirty feet onto the lawn I knew trouble had found me. The truck, like a rhino, sank to its hips in the lawn. Panicked, I threw the truck into four-wheel drive and revved the engine. When I popped the clutch, the truck swirled madly, churning up what remained of my neighbor's lawn. I can still see him gazing dejectedly from his bedroom window as I shrugged my shoulders and waited for someone to *do* something.

Town life is such that grudges, by necessity, fade in time. I live in the fond hope of regaining this neighbor's respect. And I am quite certain that, if I purchase enough objects from his antique store, I will fall again into his good graces before the year 2000.

As I should have realized before I fled Scranton as a barely postadolescent romantic in search of civilization, there is nothing quite like town life. It has the bustle and glow of an urban existence without the extremes of noise and activity that lead to exhaustion. It offers a plausible variety of experience without the faintly nauseating smorgasbord of big-city life. And there is a lovely sense of communal responsibility in a place where you depend daily on the same people to fulfill your needs, and where your misdeeds are indelibly recorded for future retribution. As for the countryside, it seems close enough. On a wintry day, the Green Mountains (blue for most of the year) are just visible from my bedroom window. In summer, the town seems like a clearing in the woods, and the woods are close enough to smell. The loneliness and isolation of country life, where your own thoughts and inner voice dominate the landscape, have no place here. Town life is, I think, more than a compromise. It is a synthesis.

AMALFI DAYS

Ten years ago, my wife, Devon, and I spent the better part of a year in Amalfi, a coastal town in the Naples region of southern Italy. Life there had not changed substantially in many centuries, and the peasant mentality was, indeed, alive and well among our neighbors.

My paternal grandmother was a peasant woman much like them. She lived in a tiny house in a rural part of Pennsylvania, and her daily rituals for decades had included gardening and canning food and making her own pasta and wine. So I felt at home.

We had been partial to Italy for years, having spent the first summer of our marriage—1981—in a little town in the Umbrian hills, an hour or so north of Rome. This time we hoped for something near the sea, having fallen in love with the peculiar shade of blue that seems possible only beneath a bright Mediterranean sun.

Serendipity led us to an old stone villa on a steep cliffside overlooking the sea. The house belonged to the friend of a friend, and it came fully furnished. A family of caretakers lived nearby. This family, it turned out, was willing to clean the house, look after our two small boys, Will and Oliver, replace lightbulbs, or do anything else that needed doing. From the first day, we knew we'd landed—miraculously—on our feet.

It was impossible not to love this house. Its crisp white walls and vaulted ceilings recalled a medieval monastery; we could almost hear the monks chanting as we sat in the living room with the shutters open and looked out to sea. The house was tiled throughout with colorful hand-painted tiles typical of the region, which proved irresistible to our children, who could run and slide on them when their feet were wet. Devon and I slept in a big room in a bed that could easily have fit our two small boys as well; a huge wooden crucifix hung above our bed, adding to the religious aura of this house. The boys, fortunately, had a room to themselves. Both bedrooms had balconies with gasp-making views of the sea.

Better than the little balconies off the bedrooms, however, was the amazing rooftop terrace. The view of the sea from up there was nothing short of damaging to the eyes: a dazzle of light reflecting off the sea, with a distant view of the Calabrian hills across the water. For shade, there was a grape arbor, a cozy little niche on the south side of the terrace where we would eat at a garden table or sink into a chair to read. Because the house was built into a cliff, the back of the terrace looked out to a steep hillside that was crammed with lemon trees, their brilliant yellow globes like tiny suns. The hill turned into a limestone cliff about halfway up, with the Villa Cimbrone—a landmark piece of Italian domestic architecture—enthroned high above our heads in Ravello. We could also see the alabaster walls of La Rondinaia, a five-story villa clinging to the cliffside like a spider web and owned, since 1972, by Gore Vidal, the American novelist who would soon become a good friend as well.

Looking from the northern wall of the terrace, we had a fine view of Amalfi itself—one of the most entrancing places on earth. The russet roofs and amber stone walls of Amalfi make a haunting vision of medieval town planning, with so many narrow winding streets converging on a sequence of elegant public squares. Legend has it that Amalfi was founded by Hercules, who was in love with a beautiful woman called, of course, Amalfi.

She died a tragic death; heartsick, Hercules buried her at this magnificent site, calling the place after her. Myths and legends aside, we have positive proof that Amalfi was a going concern in the early Middle Ages. From the ninth to the eleventh centuries, it was an independent republic with influence over a large territory along the coast. It adjoined the powerful dukedom of Naples. Having a wonderful natural harbor, Amalfi became a center for ships and trading, and its fleet sailed to such destinations as Tripoli, Alexandria, Tunis, and Constantinople. Amalfi soon became one of the most powerful maritime republics of Italy, rivaling Genoa and Venice. Standing on the steps of its magnificent cathedral—begun in the ninth century and finished two centuries later—one can almost imagine the sense of worldly power that must have fueled such grand projects as this one. And one begins to understand the Latin proverb: sic transit gloria mundi—so pass the things of this world. Which is to say that Amalfi has long since passed its prime: the ships are gone and so is the access to wealth and power. It has become a small village with a glorious past; apart from tourism, which makes the place bustle in the summer, not much is going on here in the way of commerce or industry (the only "factory" in town makes hand-made paper).

It takes a long time to get the feel of a new place from the inside. I'm by nature a small-town person, which is to say I adore the feeling of community that can only be had on a neighborhood scale. I like it when I go into a drugstore and the pharmacist knows my name and wonders how I'm doing with my allergies. I am delighted when the bank teller doesn't have to look up my name on the computer to see if he should cash my check. The servers in the local restaurants should be acquaintances if not friends, ready to bring me a cup of coffee the way I like it without asking whether I take sugar. In the modern world, of course, these little luxuries are almost unobtainable, but in Amalfi all of the above pertained. Devon and I, with the boys, were taken into the life of the village with open arms.

Nevertheless, Amalfi remains a medieval place, and this has its down side too. For instance, our younger son woke up one morning with a high fever. We became quite panicky and rushed him to the emergency room of the local medical clinic. The place was hardly more than a dark hole in the wall with a cramped waiting room and a drowsy nurse at a bare desk. She did most of the routine work, which consisted of dispensing Band-Aids and cough syrup. The doctor, I was told, was not available (he was at the local bar, I later discovered—his usual hangout). But the doctor's mother was on duty, and she would be glad to see us. The nurse said this without blinking.

A little apprehensive, I said, "Is she a qualified doctor?"

The nurse looked at me queerly. "A doctor's mother," she said, "is as good as a doctor. Maybe better."

We had no choice but to see the doctor's mother—a large woman in her mid-seventies with a big bun of gray hair at the back of her massive head. And we were, in fact, satisfied with her help. She took the sick boy into her arms, put her palm on his forehead, then kissed him on the lips. "A virus," she said, as if she had smelled it on his breath. She gave us a packet of suppositories and sent us happily on our way, reassured. The boy, I should add, recovered beautifully.

One aspect of community—or communal—life in Amalfi that struck us quickly was the way that the town deemed children a common possession. In the United States children are often treated like private property. One hesitates, for instance, to scold a stranger's children in a public place, no matter how badly they are behaving. In southern Italy, which remains a peasant society for the most part, everyone feels responsible for the care of children. They are part of the social fabric, and any tear in that fabric affects everyone. I was at first horrified when a local restaurateur in Amalfi wagged a finger at my elder boy for slurping his pasta. The boy was, however, behaving rudely, and it was my fault for not jumping on him earlier. Devon and I found ourselves quite relieved that the responsibility for tending them was not placed so squarely on our shoulders. We were the primary caretakers, of course, but we had a feeling of general public support. Children were, above all, welcome; they were acknowledged as real people; they were cheered on, scolded, listened to, and taught. By everyone.

Wherever one lives, one gradually etches a particular groove in the earth's surface, a familiar network of paths that one plies daily and only rarely alters. Before long our daily ritual in Amalfi was set. Devon and I are both writers, and we prefer to write in the morning, when our minds have been swept clean by a night of sleep and our energy levels are at their peak. So we arranged for the family attached to our villa to babysit the younger boy during the morning hours—from 9 till 1. The older boy attended a little grade school run by the Sisters of Mercy. (He didn't know a word of Italian when he started; in a couple of months he understood nearly everything.) I would drop the elder son off at school, then proceed to a small cafe beside the sea. Devon would make her way to another cafe. All morning we would sit and write, undisturbed, drinking cappuccini. It was lovely. I wrote poems in a spiral notebook, poem after poem. Devon was working on a novel, and because she likes to write on a typewriter, she carried with her a portable, battery-operated electric model that fit neatly into her beach bag. Eventually, the padrone of what we thought of as her cafe suggested that she simply leave the typewriter behind his cash register; that way she wouldn't have to lug it down the steep path into the village every morning.

When the clock struck one, we expected to sit together with the boys at the big oak table in our dining room. Frequently, Elvira, the housekeeper, would have made a spectacular pasta or meat dish; sometimes we just ate cheese and fresh fruit with a loaf of bread from the nearby bakery. We never ceased to marvel at the variety of vegetables available in the local market. Once, having had many salads of arugula in local restaurants, we tried without success to buy some of that wonderfully tangy green-leafed plant. We asked Elvira where we could buy it, and she looked at us with astonishment. "Nobody in Amalfi buys arugula," she told us with mild disdain in her voice. She took us outside, where the hillside was literally overgrown with the stuff. "You want arugula," she said, "and you got it."

When in Amalfi, do as the Amalfitani. That was our motto. So we took greedily to our beds after lunch. Even the boys seemed quite happy to sleep for an hour or two after eating. In the States, I almost never take naps because I always seem to wake up feeling worse than before I fell asleep. But in Amalfi I could sleep blissfully for two hours after lunch and wake up as fresh as the surf itself. After our siesta, we'd all stroll into town for whatever the season offered by way of amusement. In the dead of winter, there wasn't much to do apart from sitting in cafes or taking chilly hikes into the countryside. We'd occasionally take a bus to Salerno or, more rarely, Naples, where we'd go shopping or simply walk about. On a day when we felt especially adventurous, we'd take the ferry to Capri—only a couple of hours away. In late spring or summer, we'd go to the beach, where we could rent small paddle boats or just swim. The swimming is heavenly, though one occasionally worries about tales of pollution. Rumor has it that the Mediterranean is not what it used to be, and I'm sure that a lot of work will have to be done to restore this bit of paradise to its legendary pristine self. Still, the water along the Amalfi coast from Amalfi to Positano—the only stretch I know intimately—puts on a good show ; it seems pellucid, full of fish, and dazzling.

Southern Italy is still full of little restaurants that don't overcharge for a plate of pasta and a bowl of fruit, so we tended to eat out in the evenings. Our favorite restaurant was called Zaccharia. It hung out precariously over the sea, and one was invariably served a marvelous pasta full of dime-sized clams. There was no menu. Zaccharia himself—a taciturn man in his fifties with black eyes and hair—decided what everyone should eat. The meal usually began with a plate of garlic bread and fresh anchovies, all on the house. The pasta with clams came next. You could stop there or continue onto something weightier: lobster, perhaps, or swordfish. The wine was always the same unbelievably dry and crisp white wine typical of region— *vini locali,* as it's called. According to local legend, Zaccharia's mother made all the wine for her son's restaurant by treading on the grapes in her bathtub. Even if this were true, it didn't matter. I'd walk many miles in a cold sea fog for a glass of that wine.

After dinner, the entire town of Amalfi gets dressed up for the nightly parade. About nine o'clock the fun begins. Lovers, arm in arm, compete for space on the sidewalks with ancient widows, priests and nuns, local worthies, ne'er-do-wells, teenagers, and a genial mix of European tourists. Everyone's out for a stroll, for gossip and storytelling, for idle chit-chat. We tended to gather at the Bar Sirena, which has a grand view of the harbor and the chief promenade. The boys would play with the children of the padrone, and Devon and I would discuss world as well as local events with any one of a dozen people we had come to know. Quite often, Gore Vidal himself—known to everyone as *Lo Scrittore* [The Writer]—would join the assembled company and hold forth in his inimitable style.

We left Amalfi on a hot summer morning with watery eyes and our suitcases full of gifts from local friends. Our time there had, quite simply, run out. Much as we liked to pretend otherwise, we were not Amalfitani; we were Americans, and our lives—our "real" lives—lay elsewhere. Our friends in Amalfi, of course, couldn't understand this. "You should move here for good," one of them said, explaining excitedly how I could get a job at the university in Salerno. There were many days when, in my fantasy, I imagined pulling up stakes in the United States and becoming an Italian. But this was impossible, as I knew only too well. You can't become something you're not. Even in the midst of this little town's extremely warm welcome, my family and I remained foreigners, full of crazy ideas and misconceptions about how to cook pasta and how to dress our children.

As one does in such cases, we swore we'd return—again and again. But we knew the truth: that one can have new adventures in familiar places, but that the past is always past. History repeats itself only in the textbooks. Unless we were willing to become permanent expatriots—and we weren't about to do any such thing—we would have to content ourselves with occasional return visits, postcards and letters, photographs and souvenirs. Our one comfort was the knowledge that we had known firsthand this amazing town, this bright and cheerful place that was full of human depth and medieval strangeness, and that we had somewhere to go to when—as Wordsworth said—"the world is too much with us."

MY LIFE IN BASEBALL

Lately, I've begun to play baseball again. It's nothing spe-
cial, just weekend softball, loosely organized: a miscella-
neous gang of men and, yes, a few women. We gather at
a local ball field used on weekday nights by the serious
players: young men who arrive at their games in big-
wheeled pick-ups and Jeeps with fancy roll bars; they all
wear matching T-shirts and hats and have thick mus-
taches. Their wives and girlfriends sit in the little make-
shift bleachers and cheer them on. But on Sunday morn-
ings no one is there, which is why we've chosen that par-
ticular time for our games. And there's something special
about the mornings in summer: the air so sweet and fresh
in Vermont, with a diamond carpet of dew on the out-
field grass and the sun low but rising steadily in the east-
ern sky above the Green Mountains.

What is it about baseball? It somehow calls up in us a kind of nostalgia bordering on sentimentality. My mind fills with images of the dusty ball field near my childhood home in a small town in northeastern Pennsylvania. It was a godforsaken little patch of red dirt with a wire mesh backstop and an outfield where the grass was thinner than my hair has become. But that field occupies a central place in my imagination.

The town, which fed the ball field with its would-be Mickey Mantles and Warren Spahns, was on its last legs. The landscape itself had been severely broken by the anthracite mining industry. Abandoned breakers littered the hillside, and they were strange buildings to behold: huge barnlike husks, weather beaten, with thousands of tiny broken windows with shoots and pulleys dangling from their apertures. Strip mines lay open everywhere like raw wounds that wouldn't heal, while culm dumps clustered around the town's ragged edges—heaps of combustible material akin to slag; they burned all night with a blue-vermilion glow, especially when the wind drew across them, exuding a sulphurous smell that, for me, was what air smelled like until I left that town forever at the age of eighteen.

Dumps surrounded the Pennsylvania ball field where I played a pick-up game almost every morning in summer. Just beyond the right-field fence were railway tracks that once formed a busy artery taking coal west to Pittsburgh and east to Philadelphia. Beyond that was a large junkyard: acres of rusting Chevys and Fords, Studebakers and Nashes stuck in the dirt like deadheads in a dismal swamp. In one corner was a turquoise Edsel with its rear-end crumbled up to the driver's seat. (The grill, an amazing slantwise grin, was left more or less intact.) I used to sit in that Edsel sometimes in the long hot afternoons and pretend to drive away, westward, as far as the land would take me.

The informality of sandlot ball, with its shifting alliances and organic rivalries, excited me, but when I was twelve a couple of eager-beaver fathers decided to formalize everything. They set up a Teener League with official teams sponsored by local businesses and bought us all spanking white uniforms with our teams' names printed on the backs. A flag pole went up in center field and a regulation fence quickly circled the entire outfield so that home runs could be witnessed in the established fashion, with a ball disappearing over the rail. Up until then, a home run was simply the natural result of hitting it where they ain't.

My father grew up in a mining town about ten miles away, a place where sandlot ball was the point of boyhood. I learned from him the requisite lore, the names of the great players and their deeds, the famous teams, and the statistics. The endless statistics. He had been a fine player, and his talents brought him within spitting distance of the Major Leagues. That's what I was told, anyway. The story was that he had tried out for the Phillies but that Granny Hamner had beaten him out for the position of short stop. It's one of those family stories that you don't question, especially when you're twelve and looking for heroes.

I adored everything about baseball, but there was a little problem. I was no good. And I don't say that to brag. I was really no good. My astigmatism put me on the other side of the fence from, say, Ted Williams, whose legendary vision I had come to revere. It didn't matter how slow the pitch, how uncurved, or how fat it hung there in the strike zone like a full moon in August. I couldn't hit the damn thing. Every once in a while, by accident, I would get a piece of it, and that was thrilling. My fondest memory is of a foul ball hit firmly into the left-field stands. On my father's advice, I took to pitching.

As a lefty, I had behind me a lot of positive lore. A lefthanded pitcher has the obvious advantage against a righthanded batter, and because most batters are righthanded, that's a lot of advantage. But I was not by nature a pitcher, however much I loved the centrality and responsibility of the position. My balance on the mound was poor, and I was known as the only pitcher in the Teener League who could hit with any consistency: hit batters. I suppose that's why the coach would let me pitch now and then. Batters came up to the plate with great terror in their hearts, and it affected their judgment. They swung at anything that wasn't coming right at them, and I actually managed to win a few games this way.

For the most part I was consigned to right field. The theory was that because most batters are righthanded, they mostly hit to left field. Right field was a place where poor fielders were put to pasture. And I was the quintessential poor fielder. Pop flies put the fear of God into me. I had seen Willie Mays on TV as he lazily drifted under high-fly balls that seemed to pause in the air till he arrived. It just didn't work that way for me. I never could tell where the thing was heading or where it might land. Ground balls were, at least, comprehensible. I could track their snakelike movement through the grass and throw myself in front of them, hoping for the best.

My career in Teener League ended in right field on an August night in 1963. My team, which bore the ignominious name of ILGWU (it was sponsored by the International Ladies Garment Workers' Union), was tied for the league championship with Spottila's Body Shop—no thanks to me. The game had gone into extra innings, and the air over the field crackled with a tension I can still feel. I was, as usual, marooned in right field. My father, who was probably more excited about the playoffs than I was, stood on a bench near the dugout, shouting encouragement, one of those incomprehensible cheers like "Comma Baby, Comma Baby" or "Hum Boy, Hum Boy" that players shout at each other to keep the team spirit alive. The coach, a pug-nosed guy who worked in a meat-packing factory, had said to us sternly in the dugout before the game: "Remember, fellas: it ain't whether you win or lose. It's whether you win."

There were two outs in the tenth inning, but Spottila's had managed to load the bases, and we did not have another chance at bat. So this was it. I remember being so nervous that cold sweat poured from my armpits down into my glove, which was soaked. My glasses kept fogging up, and I wiped them furiously on my shirt again and again. The game had started late, and it had been a slow one. The moon had begun to rise in the sixth inning. Now the sun had dipped behind the western hills, and the sky was backlit, streaked by fiery clouds. Dusk was accumulating quickly, and the game was on the brink of being called on account of darkness when I heard the tell-tale crack of a bat. Suddenly everything was in motion, with runners running and people screaming. My father was jumping up and down on his seat, waving his arms.

The worst of it was that everyone was shouting at me. "Parini! Parini!" they all cried, and I knew that fate had probably dealt me its worst blow yet; I was determined, however, not to let the possibility of heroism escape me forever. I scanned the violet-colored sky for a ball. Miraculously, I caught sight of the dark speck in the distance as it arced toward the right-field fence. Instinct took over. Caught up in a burst of speed that took me quite by surprise, I chased it right up to the fence itself. In a moment of rashness, I made a flying DiMaggio-like dive for the black speck as it sailed over the fence and seemed to swoop upward into the night and disappear. I hit the fence hard, bouncing back into the red dirt on my back. It occurred to me within seconds that my left shoulder was badly broken.

But that wasn't the half of it. In fact, the ball had been hit to center field, not right field. It had been a ground ball, a hit, and it had ended the game. What I was following in my flight was not a baseball but a bird.

My father, seeing this display of antiheroics, thought I had lost my mind. He bundled me into his car, a black '57 Chevy with fins like wings, and drove me to the emergency room. We said nothing to each other in the car the whole way, and the incident was never again mentioned. The morning after that fateful game, I put my glove into an old wooden trunk in the basement that had been my grandfather's and turned, as they say, to other things.

Since then I have never been a real fan. I don't watch baseball on TV, and I don't read the sports pages. I never even know who is playing in the World Series until the last game, which I occasionally watch if nothing else is going on. But I have often found myself stopping by the road to watch a sandlot game, especially if it's a group of country boys playing a little pick-up game. I'd hate to count the number of times that, in my dreams, I return to the dusty ball field in Pennsylvania to show that I can do it after all. I can hit the ball hard to right center, where it drops sweetly between two fields. I can effortlessly make one of those snazzy shoestring catches. I can throw a sneaky slider or a mind-boggling knuckleball. I can steal home.

One night at the beginning of this past summer, in my forty-second year, a friend suddenly asked if I'd join him and a few friends for a game of pick-up softball.

"Have you ever played?" he asked. The fawnlike innocence of his stare took me aback.

I smiled—rather serenely, I think. "Sure," I said. "I played on a team once, back in Pennsylvania."

"Great," he said, telling me to appear at eight on Sunday morning, only two days into the future.

Those two days seemed like twenty. As soon as I got home, I went up to the attic where that old trunk of my grandfather's languished in a heap of other forgotten things. I'm a pack rat, which means I hang onto stuff such as letters from old girlfriends, favorite hats, faded T-shirts with the name of my summer camp still blazoned on the front, high school pictures, and various objects of sentimental but intensely subjective interest. I knew exactly where to find my glove.

With a little oiling, the glove was fine. It fit perfectly, and I noticed how the web had been repaired in a makeshift way. In fact, I remembered exactly when it had snapped and how, before that fateful game against Spottila's, I had stitched it together myself with a bit of shoelace. It pleased me that the lace still held.

Sunday morning came like the first morning in the history of the world. I got up at seven and, just to warm up, jogged two miles down the country road behind my house. I did a dozen push-ups, put on my sweats, sneaks, and a baseball hat (bought the night before at Kmart), and that was that. I even took my two little boys, Will and Oliver, with me—as witnesses.

I don't think I've ever noticed such a blue sky before or the grass so green. I was sent into the outfield by my friend, along with a couple of other friends—one is a carpenter, the other a computer scientist—and we waited as fly balls were hit our way. I came third, and my breath was tight as I waited. At last, my batting friend yelled, "Parini!" He hit a lofty fly that seemed to linger in the sky just as it had for Willy Mays: a brilliant patch of white ball against a deep blue sky. I found myself drifting, drifting. Without even thinking about what I was doing, I snagged it, tossed it back. Again and again.

The amazing thing was that I could hit. Not wonderfully. But I found that if you really kept your eye on ball—the proverbial wisdom—you could do it. It was better, in fact, not to think about it. Just to watch. Let your arms and wrist do what they were made to do: connect. I realized that my whole problem back in Teener League was that I was watching my father, not the ball. I was thinking about the game. Who was ahead? Was the pitcher too good for me? Was I really a hitter or not? Irrelevant questions, all of them.

What pleases me more than anything is that the boys—Will and Oliver—have no trouble with hitting or fielding. When I throw the ball their way, they hit it or catch it. They take it for granted that a game is a game is a game. That the point of baseball is the sun on the soft grass in the morning, the dirt rising in your nostrils in the lazy afternoons, and the way the backstop throws a long shadow across the mound near dusk. At least that's what I like to imagine that they know.

WRITING IN RESTAURANTS

One always imagines that writers need the solitude of a mountain cabin for creative work, with nothing in the background but the occasional birdcall or snapping twig. One thinks of Thoreau hidden among the foliage at Walden Pond or Robert Frost in his little log cabin in Ripton, Vermont, or—a more extreme example—Marcel Proust buried in his cork-lined study. After all, the merest knock of an unexpected visitor from Porlock brought to a halt the ferocious spell of Coleridge in the midst of writing "Kubla Khan" (or so he claimed). On the other hand, the Left Bank of Paris has always been a favorite spot for writers such as Hemingway or Sartre, both of whom seemed to thrive in the noisy atmosphere of cafes.

For twenty years, I've devoted nearly every morning of my life to writing, and—like most writers, I suspect—

having the right place to work has been terribly important to me. As a graduate student at the University of St. Andrews in Scotland in the seventies, I found a tea shop where I could sit undisturbed for hours on end with books and manuscripts piled up around me. The tea came in shiny metal pots, and the waitress—her name was Fiona—freshened the pot every hour or so. A large plate of scones was always on the table, and you paid only for what you ate. It was a sleepy and, I suppose, unprofitable enterprise—as a business—but for me it provided just the right amount of distraction. I sat there every morning for nearly seven years, composing innumerable college essays, a doctoral thesis, a book of poems, and an unpublished novel in that poorly ventilated but homey tearoom.

When I took my first teaching job, at Dartmouth College in New Hampshire, I was given faculty housing in a quaint faculty apartment building just off campus. A bachelor, I needed a minimum of space—a bedroom with a study seemed positively luxurious. I fitted out the study with a big oak desk, a typing table, a glass-fronted bookcase, filing cabinets, a telephone—the works. Then I sat down to work.

But I couldn't work. It was just too damn quiet. So I wandered uptown, a few blocks away, where I discovered a restaurant called Lou's on the main street in Hanover. It was modeled on the old-fashioned American diner, and I confess to an inordinate fondness for diners. They call up in me an inexpressible nostalgia for a past I never had, a society in which everyone gathered over coffee to chat about everything and nothing, a place where romances kindled, where good humor flourished, and any job could be put off till another day. (I still make a point of stopping at diners whenever I'm even remotely in the market for a sandwich or a cup of coffee on the road.)

Lou's became, for me, the ideal study. I arrived every morning at eight or so, carrying my spiral notebook and assorted texts. I never varied my diet: cups of coffee with dry English muffins (and a scoop of peanut butter at the side, for protein). Lou, the elderly owner of the place, took a liking to me, and he made sure that a particular booth at the back was always empty when I got there. The waiters too became friends; they never had to ask what I wanted. They just brought it. And I would sit there for two or three hours writing poems, scribbling academic articles, underlying my copy of *Paradise Lost*, whatever. I wrote three books in that booth, and I don't think any would have made it into print without Lou's hospitality.

What I liked about Lou's was the distant clatter of dishes, the purr of conversation, and the occasional interruption of a friend. Restaurants provide a kind of white noise, but—unlike real white noise—the sound is human. Noses are blown. People cough. You're reminded of the world of phlegm and digestion. And you feel connected. There is also a strange but unmistakable connection between cooking and writing—writing, like cooking, is a bringing together of elemental substances for transmutation over a hot flame. It seems fitting that writing and cooking should be going on simultaneously under the same roof.

As people are quick to point out, writing is a desperately lonely activity; although writing in restaurants doesn't exactly solve that problem, it somehow softens it. Surrounded by people you don't necessarily have to interact with, you feel free to concentrate. Once I'm involved in the tactile process of writing—the pleasurable transference of emotions and ideas into language—I find that I don't really have to worry about concentration. If I can't concentrate, it means I'm working on the wrong thing or I probably didn't get enough sleep the night before. Whatever the reason for not writing, I don't blame the restaurant.

Restaurant society is still a human web, and if any part of the web is disturbed, the whole fabric shakes. I was fully aware of who else was sitting in Lou's. Every public eating place has its regulars, and the regulars are a tight-knit group, loyal to their spot; they often don't even know each other by name, but they depend upon the tacit assumption of shared good feeling—toward each other as well as toward the place itself. After a year or so, I pretty much knew by name everyone who ate frequently at Lou's. And we often shared the high and low points of our lives. When I got married, for instance, the regulars at Lou's all signed a card of congratulations. I even attended the funeral of an elderly gent who had never said a word to me but who sat for three years in the adjoining booth for at least half an hour every morning. Until the funeral, I had known him only as Herb, the man who liked underdone boiled eggs with a side of dry toast.

As a novelist, I found my time in Lou's an indispensable part of my education. Like Zola, I soon found that local hangouts offer an unbelievably transparent window on any community. Lou's was classless, which meant that taxi drivers, window washers, insurance salespeople, haberdashers, dentists, and professors sat cheek by jowl over coffee and homemade donuts. Looking up from my work, I could take in an array of conversation and dialects, and I learned a great deal about how the United States works from that little booth. I became, alas, a world-class eavesdropper, often

41

scribbling overheard conversations in my notebook and, at a later date, including versions of these dialogues in my fiction.

When I left Hanover in 1982, one of my biggest fears was that I'd never find another place to work that was nearly as cozy. But this was not the case. We moved to Middlebury, a small Vermont town just across the Green Mountains. There we bought a small house from which I could easily walk uptown, where Middlebury offered a dazzling array of alternatives to Lou's. I eventually settled upon an ice cream parlor and soda fountain straight out of Norman Rockwell that goes by the unlikely name of Calvi's. Located on the village green, Calvi's has proved ideal for verse composition. An array of newspapers and magazines lines the left wall. The soda fountain dominates the right, presided over by a large brown photograph of the current owner's grandfather, the Calvi who founded the establishment in the late nineteenth century. In the back are booths and tables, with the stuffed heads of antlered moose and elk staring balefully off the walls. In good weather, one can sit on the screened-in porch off the back that somewhat perilously overhangs Otter Creek and its roaring waterfall—a kind of mini-Niagara that might be thought of as Middlebury's centerpiece. The roar of that waterfall is white noise squared.

Calvi's is sleepier than Lou's, by far. It is dark in the back, and the waiters (who always wear soda-jerk jackets in the old style) are so unobtrusive that one has to stand on the table and dance to get a coffee refill. I don't care anymore. There is just enough clatter to reassure me, and I have found the regulars as interesting and friendly as those at Lou's. I have taken devotion so far as to make Calvi's the setting for a long quasi-philosophical poem about appearance and reality called "At the Ice Cream Parlor."

In the poem, meaning no harm, I refer to the "tacky plastic spoons" that might be considered the hallmark of this particular establishment. I was talking about the relationship between any given plastic spoon and the Platonic ideal of Spoon—one of the great subjects of Western metaphysics, if you will. Assuming—correctly—that Mr. Calvi himself would probably not have read the poem (published in a 1988 book of mine called *Town Life*), a well-intentioned neighbor of mine provided him with a photostat. The padrone found that his gaze stuck upon the fateful adjective: *tacky.* I suspect it will take years—perhaps decades—for me to live down that untoward epithet.

Apart from the vaguely social aspects of writing in restaurants—the delicious sense of being alone within a communal context—there is a further advantage. In a public place, one doesn't normally use a writing machine more complicated than a pencil. In the age of word processing, diners are an ideal place for the rediscovery of this remarkable product of our civilization. The pencil is surprisingly efficient, in fact. You can delete what you don't like with a quick horizontal stroke that both rids you of the unwanted phrase and simultaneously preserves the deletion—just in case it was better than the revised version, which is often the case. Also,the strange visceral connection between hand and brain is somehow lost in the subliminal click of keyboards and the computer screen's unyielding gaze. Furthermore, one misses the slight rustle of paper, the smell of freshly sharpened pencils or wet ink, the ancient and alluring texture of text making.

The habit of writing in restaurants has the added advantage of making one's vocation highly portable. In 1985 I spent a sabbatical year in Italy, for instance, and I found myself quickly adapting to the local scene through my connection to one particular cafe. We were living in a lovely village south of Naples that happened to be rich in cafes. The Sirena [mermaid] was a cafe-bar on the chief promenade that looked out over the old harbor front, with the Mediterranean winking in the middle distance—almost too perfect. It occurred to me almost immediately that this must be the best place in the world for a writer to work. Seated at one of its dozen or so tables, I could take in the baroque spectacle of Italian town life with ease. Eating a fresh pastry and drinking a foamy cup of cappuccino, the muse seemed never too far away. (This was, of course, before the advent of notebook computers.)

My wife, Devon, is also a writer, but her love of the typewriter has usually kept her out of my restaurants. In Italy, however, our little villa on a cliffside overlooking the sea quickly proved inhospitable as a place to work; it was just too damp and cold, especially in winter. So we both made our way to a cafe (usually separate ones) in the morning, me with my notebook and pencil, she with her battery-operated portable typewriter. After a couple weeks, the owner of the cafe where Devon worked—an elderly man whom everyone called Nono—insisted that she actually keep her typewriter behind the bar so that she didn't have to lug it into town every morning.

I wrote most of a book of poems in Amalfi, and when I pick up that volume, I can smell the cappuccino and taste the almond-flavored pastry. I can hear the clinking of cups and low murmur of Italian chatter. It's the same with all my books or essays, even my book reviews. I remember exactly where I wrote them, in what diner or restaurant, truck stop, bar, or country inn. Every word is redolent of some particular cuisine, some idiosyncratic atmosphere that I'll have made temporarily into a kind of home. My only worry is that, in a future filled exclusively with Burger Kings and Kentucky Fried Chickens, both of which clog their atmospheres with canned music, I will have to change professions. The muse cannot stand Muzak.

POETRY AND THE DEVOUT LIFE

The affinity between writing and what St. Francis de Sales calls "the devout life" has always struck me. In particular, the writing of poems—something I've done in a fairly regular way for nearly thirty years—has seemed akin to prayer. Poet and critic R. P. Blackmur put a finger on a central connection between poetry and prayer in a book called *The Expanse of Greatness* (1940):

> The life we all live is not alone enough of
> a subject for the serious artist; it must be
> life with a learning, life with a tendency
> to shape itself only in certain forms, to
> afford its most lucid revelations only in
> certain lights. If our final interest, either
> as poets or as readers, is in the reality

declared when the forms have been removed and the lights
taken away, yet we can never come to the reality at all with-
out the first advantage of the form and lights.

We are all drawn by the promise of this "final interest," the reality behind
the forms constructed by the world and the mind in their daily fruitful col-
lusion.

The problem is that the forms of life present themselves chaotically, and
the easiest response is merely to go with the flow, to let the chaos intervene
and rule. The unexamined life may not be worth living, but it is the most
readily available. For weeks at a time, if not months—especially when cir-
cumstances prevent me from writing poems—I find myself drifting in a
kind of haze. It's often a comfortable haze, but it's a haze nonetheless. I feel
soulless then, cut off from the reality that can only be called a religious real-
ity. Writing about this state in his *Treatise on the Love of God* (1616), de
Sales contrasts the idle, "normal" thought process of everyday life with the
mind in meditative thought: "Every meditation is a thought, but every
thought is not meditation; for we have thoughts, to which our mind is car-
ried without aim or pretension at all, by way of simple musing, as we see
flies fly from one flower to another, without draining anything from them:
And be this kind of thought as attentive as it may be, it can never bear the
name of meditation."

Meditation is more directed: "When we think of heavenly things, not to
learn but to love them, that is called to meditate: and the exercise thereof
Meditation: in which our mind, not as fly . . . but as a sacred Bee flies
amongst the flowers of holy mysteries, to extract from them the honey of
Divine Love."

A contemporary of de Sales's, Luis de Granada, pursued the analogy
between prayer and meditation in a book-length study, *Of Prayer and
Meditation* (1612), in which he observes that "prayer (to define it properly)
is a petition we make unto Almighty God, for such things as are appertain-
ing to our salvation. Howbeit, prayer is also taken in another, larger sense;
to wit: for every lifting up of our heart unto God." He further notes that
"both meditation and contemplation, and every other good thought, may
be also called a Prayer." In this sense, writing, especially the writing of
poems, can be seen as an explicitly religious act, a form of prayer.

I grew up in a fundamentalist household and became familiar with the
language of the King James Bible at an early age. Every morning at break-

fast, my father would read a chapter or so to me and my sister as we crunched our cereal. On Sundays I sat half-listening through what seemed like interminable sermons, but the forms of Christianity grew contiguous with the structures of my brain. I have come to rely on these forms as a kind of falsework, or scaffolding, that holds me upright while I construct, or reconstruct, a spiritual life.

There is, I would guess, no such thing as a devout life without prayer, whatever form that prayer might take. Though I occasionally resort to more traditional forms of prayer—private and public—I have more faith in poetry as a form of prayer. In a lovely essay in *Standing by Words* (1983) called "Poetry and Marriage: The Use of Old Forms," Wendell Berry writes, "In marriage as in poetry, the given word implies the acceptance of a form that is never entirely of one's own making. When understood seriously enough, a form is a way of accepting and of living within the limits of creaturely life." Berry's remarks emphasize the need for a particular kind of faith, a faith in conventions, "old forms." Marriage is one, and poetry is another. Prayer, I would argue, is a third.

All these old forms require discipline, which is another way of saying that one must accept the conventions, the limits, of a given form, whether it be marriage, poetry, or prayer. To succeed in any of these, one must give oneself over to the form with complete fidelity, understanding the artificiality of each. In marriage, for instance, there is no point in thinking about the people one has *not* married. As Berry, with his usual acerbity, says, "Marriage does not invite one to solve one's quarrel with one's wife by marrying a more compliant woman." In other words, one accepts the form of marriage, just as one accepts the forms of poetry and prayer, expecting that good things will come from working within these forms.

One good thing that comes of poetry and prayer, and which makes them, when properly conceived, interchangeable terms, is what Christians call *grace*. Grace is a relation, a point of contact between God and the human mind that is realized only through the direct mental and emotional actions of meditation (whether in prayer or writing). D. H. Lawrence once defined poetry as an "act of attention," and in doing so he laid bare the essence of that form. In the act of composition, the poet's whole being is focused on the concrete reality of the poem. Likewise, prayer or meditation brings the whole of the person into focus on the divine realities.

Ignatius Loyola, founder of the Jesuits, wrote an influential handbook on Christian prayer and meditation called *The Spiritual Exercises* (1536).

Here he identifies the three "powers of the soul": memory, intellect, and the "affective will" (the emotions). He points out that in prayer one has to find a focus, because one cannot contemplate God in the abstract. God has no face and is therefore difficult to focus on, as Milton suggests in Book III of *Paradise Lost* (1667). Ignatius suggests that the praying mind focus instead on a concrete image; the first stage in any meditation, he says, is a "composition of place." Poets, of course, have always known this. Most lyric poems begin with an image rooted in time and space. Through an elaborate process of contemplation, that image is turned over in the mind until it yields something akin to grace for the beholder.

The sacred bee of Francis de Sales flies among the holy mysteries, extracting the honey of divine love. Poets, lifting their eyes to the world's bright substantial forms, likewise fly among the same mysteries, always hopeful that the reality behind the forms might suddenly break through. The discipline required by the writer—the regular hours at the desk, dependence on conventions, the host of limits imposed before the poet begins to write—makes the flight itself possible. Similarly, in prayer or religious meditation the heart and mind combine to "think on heavenly things," as de Sales says. In doing so, those in prayer or meditation create for themselves the possibility for grace, that music, to paraphrase William Wordsworth's poem "The Solitary Reaper," which they will carry with them long after the image they have called up in their minds dissolves.

ON BEING PROLIFIC

One night recently I woke my wife, Devon, with a nudge. "*Now* what is it?" she asked. The question I had for her, urgent though it seemed to me, was a little anti-climactic under the circumstances. But I forged ahead. "Darling," I said. "Do you consider me . . . prolific?" Her response will not bear repetition.

I think I'm not unlike many writers in worrying about my productivity. Indeed, across the nation, writers every-where are talking to their shrinks about this very thing. Like the rest of them, I know in my heart of hearts—I *really* know—that I must never confuse quantity and quality. I remind myself that Chidiock Tichborne, the Elizabethan poet, wrote—or is survived by—only one poem, his famous "Elegy for Himself" (1586), written in the Tower of London on the eve of his execution for treason. I would rather have written that single poem than the *Collected Poems* of most other poets. But the kind of worry I'm talking about goes well beyond reason.

It's probably natural that writers should dwell on this subject, even be obsessed by it. Shoemakers—if any still exist—must take seriously into account the number of shoes they make in a given period as well as their quality. Literature is the last great cottage industry. Every poem or novel is a one-of-a-kind thing, made at home by hand. Not even the word processor can change this. And because quality is less easily measured than quantity, is it any wonder writers like to tot up the number of words or pages—and books—they have written?

When writers get together, the subject often turns to productivity. How does Joyce Carol Oates—whose name is synonymous with productivity—do it? What about Stephen King or Anthony Burgess? Or—among literary critics—Harold Bloom? (The story circulates in academe that a graduate student once telephoned Bloom at home in New Haven. His wife answered, "I'm sorry, he's writing a book." "That's all right," the student replied. "I'll wait.")

The great nineteenth-century writers, of course, set the standards by which we judge productivity. I grow anxious when I think of them: titanic figures like Sir Walter Scott, Charles Dickens, and Honoré de Balzac. They tortured themselves, harnessing themselves to the desk for painful hours, pushing against the natural rhythms of creativity. The wonder is how good their work is, given the amount of it.

Scott, the Wizard of the North, was the first British writer for whom productivity became an issue. His son-in-law and biographer, John Gibson Lockhart, spoke of his "ceaseless pen." Scott's works include a four-volume collection of Scottish ballads, editions of John Dryden and Jonathan Swift, a large *Collected Poems,* twenty-seven massive novels, numerous shorter tales, a nine-volume biography of Napoleon, twelve volumes of collected letters, and a journal that runs to more than seven hundred pages in print. He undertook much of this frenzied writing activity to finance a publishing company that he partially subsidized (shades of Mark Twain and the typesetting-machine company that bankrupted *him*). Scott was also devoted to his house, called Abbotsford. This mock-medieval monstrosity on the banks of the Tweed grew year by year, turret by turret, requiring endless outlays of hard cash. (I have a picture of it on the wall of my study—as a warning.)

The centerpiece of the house is Scott's baronial study, which features a desk of immense proportions with two working surfaces. The ferociously driven author always had at least two projects in the works, and the two desktops helped to keep them separate. "Whatever he wrote met with great acclaim," wrote his modern biographer, Edgar Johnson. "At Abbotsford he rose at five, wrote till noon, and crowded the rest of the long day with physical activity. Plagued with stomach cramps, anxious about debts, teeming with ideas that must somehow be gotten onto paper, he was a hero at his desk—as gallant as Rob Roy or Ivanhoe." A Scottish poet, Iain Chrichton Smith, attended an exhibition of Scott's manuscripts and wrote an affecting poem about the experience that, for me, goes to the heart of the issue here:

> Walking the room together in this merciless
> galaxy of manuscripts and notes,
> I am exhausted by such energy.
> What love he must have lost to write so much.

I associate overproductivity with pain, the anguish of expression (from the Latin *expressus*—pushing something deep inside out into the open air). It hurts. But it heals too. This seems clear in the case of Balzac, who poured out a torrent of books between 1822 and 1848, publishing eight books in 1842 alone. An overweight, ugly man with an overwhelming sense of social inferiority, he would don his monk's gown and write through the wee hours and sometimes into the next afternoon. He described his routine in a letter to a friend:

> I must tell you that I am submerged in excessive labour. The mechanics of my life have altered. I go to bed at six or seven in the evening, like the hens. I am awakened at one o'clock in the morning and work till eight. At eight I sleep for an hour and a half. Then I have something light to eat, and a cup of black coffee, and harness my wagon until four. I receive callers, I take a bath or I go out, and after dinner I go back to bed. I have to live like this for months on end if I am not to be overwhelmed by my obligations. The profits accrue slowly; the debts are inexorable and fixed. It is now

certain that I shall make a great fortune; but I need to go on
writing and working for another three years.

There is a sad, wonderful optimism in the certainty that he was about to
"make a great fortune."

To spur himself on, Balzac used heavy doses of coffee that he prepared
in the Turkish fashion, infusing the grounds in cold water, then heating
them; he gradually used less and less water, creating a brew as thick as
mud—a caffeine riot. Taken on an empty stomach, the effects were
astounding, causing ideas (in Balzac's own words) to "pour out like the reg-
iments of the Grand Army over the battlefield, and the battle begins.
Memories come charging in with flags flying: the light cavalry of compar-
isons extends itself in a magnificent gallop; the artillery of logic hurries
along with its ammunition train, and flashes of wit bob up like sharp-
shooters." In this agitated unnatural way he composed the vast cathedral of
his *Comédie humaine* (1841), a multivolume evocation of French society
that is also an anthology of human emotions and situations.

Dickens, for me, is the quintessentially productive writer. He has much
in common with Balzac, his contemporary: lower middle-class origins, an
overexcitable imagination, a restless nature, and a capacity for inhuman
labor. He had no will to resist taking on new projects. Because his novels
sold exceedingly well, publishers were only too willing to get him to sign on
the dotted line. At several points in his career, he worked simultaneously on
two or three novels for serial publication while editing a journal and man-
aging the affairs of a vast extended family. His energy level was such that he
often took long late-night walks to cool his nerves.

Generally speaking, his early novels came more easily than the later ones,
but he almost always wrote at breakneck speed, entranced by the vivid cre-
ations teeming from his brain. As Edgar Johnson recounted in *Charles
Dickens: His Triumph and Tragedy* (1952), a visitor once recorded for pos-
terity an indelible image of Dickens at work. Henry Burnett wrote,

> One night in Doughty Street, Mrs. Charles Dickens, my
> wife and myself were sitting round the fire cosily enjoying a
> chat, when Dickens, for some purpose, came suddenly into
> the room. "What, you here!" he exclaimed; "I'll bring my
> work." It was his monthly portion of "Oliver Twist" for
> Bentley's. In a few minutes he returned, manuscript in

hand, and while he was pleasantly discoursing he employed himself in carrying to a corner of the room a little table, at which he seated himself and recommenced his writing. We, at his bidding, went on talking our "little nothings,"—he, every now and then (the feather of his pen still moving rapidly from side to side), put in a cheerful interlude. It was interesting to watch, upon the sly, the mind and the muscles working (or, if you please, *playing* in company, as new thoughts were being dropped upon the paper). And to note the working brow, the set of mouth, with the tongue tightly pressed against the closed lips, as was his habit.

With age, it became harder and harder for Dickens to write quickly. During the composition of *Little Dorrit* (1857), for instance—written in his forties—Dickens recalled in a letter the agony of "prowling about the room, sitting down, getting up, stirring the fire, looking out of the window, tearing my hair, sitting down to write, writing nothing, writing something and tearing it up, going out, coming in, a Monster to my family, a dread Phaenomenon to myself." On and on, churning through *Bleak House* (1853), *Hard Times* (1854), *Our Mutual Friend* (1865), right up to the unfinished *Mystery of Edwin Drood* (1865), Dickens refused *not* to write in bulk. Haunted by the specter of bankruptcy, which had sent his father to debtors' prison, he may have wanted to ensure that nothing similar could happen to him. Much like Scott and Balzac, he was driven to possess the outward signs of success too, such as Gad's Hill Place, the magnificent house in Kent that he had often admired as a child. More generally, Dickens wrote because writing—lots of writing—was what being Charles Dickens was all about. The pressure of his imagination required the myriad shapes and forms that emerge in his fiction.

Anthony Trollope, by contrast, was a milder—and probably happier— man. I love to contemplate Trollope, who wrote for only three hours a day but was no less prolific than Dickens or Balzac. His forty-seven novels, several of which—*The Warden* (1855), *Barchester Towers* (1857), *Framley Parsonage* (1861)—might be called masterpieces, are a testament to the fruits of discipline. But the aura of genius that clung to Balzac, Scott, and Dickens was alien to Trollope. In his wonderfully honest and charming 1883 autobiography, he pretty much did himself in with the critics once and for all by describing his working methods. "All those I think who have lived as literary men," he wrote, "will agree with me that three hours a day will produce as much as a man ought to write." He went on, describing his working methods in midcareer: "It had at this time become my custom—and it still is my custom, though of late I have become a little lenient to myself—to write with my watch before me, and to require from myself 250 words every quarter of an hour."

A servant awakened Trollope each morning at five, seven days a week, bringing him a hot cup of coffee (tea came later in the morning). In an English country house in midwinter, this early rising was not an attractive prospect, especially in the age before central heating and electric light. But Trollope had his demons. By 5:30 he was at his desk, rereading the previous day's work and making small corrections for roughly half an hour. By six, he was clocking himself at the usual thousand words per hour. He completed his daily quota of twenty-five hundred words (in today's terms, ten double-spaced typed pages) by 8:30, when he got dressed for breakfast. After eating a hearty meal, he went off to work in the Post Office, where he was a high official. Two weekdays, instead of going to the office, he would spend the day on horseback, hunting foxes. Evenings were spent with his family or at his club. This routine almost never varied throughout his long life.

American writers of the period—Mark Twain, James Fenimore Cooper, and Henry James, for instance—were no slouches when it came to productivity, but somehow productivity does not emerge as a defining characteristic. James, for instance, was astonishingly productive—the New York Edition of his work contains twenty-three volumes, in self-conscious imitation of Balzac's standard edition—but he did not make productivity a point of honor.

Trollope's calmly professional attitude toward writing, however, has been a kind of unspoken ideal for recent British writers like Graham Greene, Anthony Burgess, Iris Murdoch, and A. N. Wilson—all of whom regard productivity as a virtue. Iris Murdoch has gone so far as to chide E. M. Forster for his *lack* of productivity: "Six novels?" she remarked in an interview. "Come on, Forster, you can do better than that!" She has published a novel almost every year without pause since her first novel appeared. When asked what she does when she gets stuck, she replied, "I just keep writing."

And there is A. N. Wilson, who makes me nervous. He is younger than I am by a couple of years, but I will never catch up to him. (Why should I *want* to? Don't ask.) Born in 1950, Wilson has published more than a dozen novels, biographies of John Milton, Hilaire Belloc, and Leo Tolstoy, and Scott; he recently completed lives of C. S. Lewis, Jesus, and Paul, and, I dare say, another novel. A former book editor of the *Spectator,* he contributes countless reviews and essays to major British periodicals. Worse yet, the writing is good. He has commented,

> Writing a book is a full-time occupation. You are thinking about it all the time. Sometimes you will wake up in the morning and realize that the book's problems have been with you even in sleep. Before conscious thought has dawned, even before you opened your eyes in the morning, you realize exactly what is wrong with that chapter you were struggling to finish the day before. Or so it has been with me. Until a typescript is actually out of my hands, and with the printer, I am mulling over it ceaselessly. For this reason, the question of how long it takes to write a book is an unanswerable one, particularly in the case of novels, where years of meditating upon a particular theme will suddenly bear fruit. "It didn't take long to write that," someone will say, upon hearing that the actual *penning* of a story took only a matter of weeks. Well, no it didn't: only about twenty-seven years.

By contrast, contemporary American writers—Saul Bellow, William Styron, and Thomas Pynchon—often harbor long silences, publishing in gigantic well-publicized spasms. A few of our best writers—J. D. Salinger, Ralph Ellison, Grace Paley, and Harold Brodkey—have fashioned whole careers out of the sound of one hand clapping. Their silences seem . . . productive. But then we have Joyce Carol Oates, Gore Vidal, and John Updike, who seem more British than American in their attitudes. "The British tradition of the man of letters insists that writers write a lot, including book reviews," said Joyce Carol Oates. "I think a writer has a responsibility to comment on the culture, to read other writers. I don't know why so many of our writers refuse to write book reviews." Of her own working methods, she said, "I take endless notes before I begin writing a novel, often when I travel. I write on the backs of envelopes, in the margins of magazines, on theater programs."

Alas, Oates—whose work I deeply admire—has paid a price for her prolificacy. Mary Gordon commented on this in the March 2, 1986, issue of the *New York Times Book Review:* "We punish Joyce Carol Oates for the crime of her productivity. A book a year, in some years two—we respond as if she did it just to make us look bad, the A student who hands in for a geography assignment not only a weather map of the Hawaiian Islands, but a papier-mâché model of a volcano as well." Apart from the obvious question about whether a writer can keep to a high standard while writing so much, there is also the fact that Oates is a woman. Does the prospect of a wildly prolific woman frighten male readers?

Two writers whose productivity has intrigued me are Updike and Vidal; they have both written as much as Oates, though reviewers rarely call attention to this aspect of their careers. Updike's frequency of publication is somewhat masked by the sameness of his novels and stories in texture and theme. This kind of productivity makes sense. But Vidal is unpredictable and, worse, his books really *sell.* Beginning as a war novelist at the age of nineteen, with *Williwaw* (1946), he has written everything from historical fiction (*Julian* [1964], *Burr* [1973], *Lincoln* [1984]) to contemporary satire (*Myra Breckinridge* [1968], *Duluth* [1983])—with twenty-two novels to date. He has also had hits on Broadway (*Visit to a Small Planet* [1957], *The Best Man* [1960]) and has written nearly a hundred teleplays. And then, of course, I mustn't forget to mention the six volumes of essays, which many critics regard as his best work. "Yet the reviewers tend to treat every one of my books as though it were my first," said Vidal, talking to me from his home in Ravello, Italy. He refers to this country as "the United States of Amnesia."

Unfairly, I somehow expect writers of genre fiction—John Grisham, Stephen King, Danielle Steel—to churn out lots of books, because they write to something like a formula. (When asked by an interviewer from the *Boston Globe* [August 2, 1987] about the key to his productivity, Stephen King replied, "Nothing in particular. I don't take notes. I don't outline, I don't do anything like that. I just flail away at the thing.") But "real" writers aren't supposed to churn them out. They must agonize. (Do *I* agonize? Sometimes. But the level of agony seems unrelated to the quality of the work.)

What seems true is that serious writers who write a lot of books and who experiment with different kinds of writing will suffer for it. The critics won't keep up with them. Their books will be reviewed in isolation from previous works, and their careers will resist categorization. Overproduction can also damage the quality of a writer's prose. Anthony Burgess, one suspects, would have been well advised to slow down; many of his novels have a frenetic, distorted quality that broadcasts the haste of their composition. Virtually every prolific writer has dull passages, even whole books worth tossing out. Nevertheless, telling these writers to slow down is like telling a bird not to fly. "I write a lot because I'm a writer," Vidal said in his lofty, mandarin voice. "That's what I do."

REFLECTIONS OF A
NONPOLITICAL MAN

My title comes from Thomas Mann, whose *Reflections of a Nonpolitical Man* (1918) was finished, as the author says, "on the day on which the beginning of the armistice negotiations between Germany and Russia is being announced." Mann wrote, "What is this world? It is the world of politics, of democracy; and that I had to take a position against it, that I had to stand with Germany in this war, and not, like civilization's literary man, with the enemy—this necessity stands out clearly to every discerning person in everything I wrote and put together in fifteen years of peace."

Mann thought of himself as essentially nonpolitical by nature, a man who believed that the solution to the perpetual crisis of humanity, the human condition, was finally spiritual and moral, not political.

This is an attractive, even relaxing, point of view, and I'm drawn to it. I don't like to lie awake at night worrying about things beyond the family circle, which provides enough grist for that mill. Abstractly, I really do believe that all solutions to what Wordsworth called "man's inhumanity to man" will be found in a domain that one could label spiritual or moral. Reluctantly, however, I've come to think that the preconditions to any such solution must also be political and probably democratic.

Thomas Mann, of course, lived to eat his words. Even his patriotic blend of romantic theory and German nationalism proved insufficiently illiberal for Adolf Hitler. Push, as it were, soon came to shove, and Mann, on a holiday in Switzerland during the spring of 1933, was warned by his family that he must not return to Munich for fear of his life. At fifty-eight, he found himself in what turned out to be permanent exile from his homeland. Life, for this congenitally nonpolitical man, became painfully, all-consumingly political.

The history of my contact with the world of politics is probably not dissimilar to that of most Americans belonging to the postwar generation, we baby boomers (apotheosized in the human form of William Jefferson Clinton) who now find ourselves pandered to, caricatured, wooed, and mocked by the makers of children's clothing, breakfast cereals, cars, and all manner of electronic gadgetry. We have come to power. But what does this mean?

Like many smart kids of my generation, I went to college and found myself nearly drafted into the Vietnam War. This was my first brush with politics. Until then, I'd assumed that what I'd been told in school was true: America was a nation of compulsive do-gooders. We were the virtual embodiment of democracy, decency, and the good life, the best country on earth. "Wouldn't everyone in the world want to be an American if we opened the floodgates?" my father often asked. The realities of the Vietnam War, so complex and finally degrading to the values we supposedly held, shocked me from my postadolescent, post-fifties drowse. I was not going to drop napalm on villages, bomb cities and jungles and farms indiscriminately, and maim other human beings in support of a puppet right-wing government. I actually admired Ho Chi Minh for his decades of resistance to various colonial powers, and I grew impatient with Lyndon Johnson, who was so obviously lying about what he was doing. Worse, I hated my inability to do anything about the war, though I made some feeble gestures in the direction of political action. I wrote letters to people in power (the sister of the governor of Pennsylvania, William Scranton, was a friend of mine, and I implored her to try to get her brother to do something). I marched on the Pentagon in 1967, joining hands with thousands to circle and levitate that symbolic building. During my junior year abroad, in 1968, I marched on the U.S. Embassy in London. I visited Paris, the seedbed of student radicalism, and met with the many students who had been so visibly active in resisting authority during the spring of that year. Traveling on the Continent, I encountered the worldwide phenomenon known as anti-Americanism for the first time. In 1970, I was once again a member of the huge crowd that marched on Washington, chanting slogans while Nixon watched television in the White House and conducted, by long-distance telephone, further raids into Cambodia. My life seemed amazingly full and vivid. The high was vertiginous.

But the seventies came as a terrible shock. George McGovern was blown out of the water by Nixon, who seemed, even to the undiscerning, the next best thing to a petty crook. How did he manage to fool most of the people most of the time? The U.S.-backed overthrow of the democratically elected Allende government in Chile in 1973 scarcely stirred a ripple of protest on campuses or in the press. I assumed I was in the extreme minority in thinking that democracy was not working well enough in the United States, because we voters were consistently offered such a paltry choice at the polls. Even Watergate seemed not to prove anything to most people except that one man was a bad apple who had corrupted what was otherwise a holy and good system. Gerald Ford (an unlikely figure) came to the rescue. But he was too obviously thick, so it was not surprising that the country turned to a little-known ex-governor of Georgia for hope; Jimmy Carter seemed a decent and intelligent man who could save the system. He had, after all, been educated at Annapolis; he had proved himself a reliable fellow as a member of Rockefeller's powerful Trilateral Commission, and he clearly understood how things worked. I watched, bewildered, as the political energy and idealism of my generation was sapped. (One irony of our time is that liberal administrations, although roughly the same as conservative administrations in basic approaches to policy, have a way of dulling the edge of protest. The Carter administration, for example, set in motion many of the destructive policies in Central America that one associates with Reagan; nevertheless, one assumed Carter was for "human rights" and therefore beyond close scrutiny.)

The chaos that occurred in Southeast Asia following our withdrawal from Vietnam in 1975 was also depressing to watch. "I told you so," those of us who had protested the war were told, as if chaos was not the inevitable result of a brutal war that had left that part of the world devastated. We had driven Vietnam's rural population into urban slums, largely in an effort to weaken the social base of the revolutionary movement. Having left them in an unimaginable mess, we did our best to see that no economic aid or encouragement came their way, knowing we could easily transfer blame for the failure of the Vietnamese to their system. It was depressing to observe the gradual process of forgetting that took place in the seventies, a willed amnesia that nicely prepared the way for what Reagan gloatingly called "the new patriotism."

The unfortunate truth is that I too was eager to forget Vietnam. Like most others from the privileged classes, those who have a choice about what to do with their lives, I went from comfortable situation to comfortable situation. I spent the first half of the seventies in Scotland, where I got a doctoral degree in English. The late seventies and early eighties found me teaching at Dartmouth College, in New Hampshire, where corporations train some of their most efficient managers. I got married in 1981. In 1982, I moved to Vermont, bought a house, fathered children, and published some books. The Reagan revolution didn't upset me as much as I thought it would. Maybe I'd been a spoilsport all along? I began to watch *Wall Street Week* on television, hoping for a tip that would matter, somehow imagining that if I understood the market, I'd gain some control over the world.

But that sense of control did not come, and I soon found myself desperate to travel again, like I had in the old days. Travel has always seemed to me a necessity, not a luxury. The United States is claustrophobic, probably because of its superficial sameness. The Howard Johnsons and Holiday Inns and McDonald's restaurants make every place from coast to coast feel identical. The sitcoms that dominate evening television are look-alikes, unfunny in the same way. The mock-serious news shows are too obviously shows, hosted by the same inanely sincere, mostly male, commentators: Sam Donaldson, Dan Rather, George Will, David Brinkley—perhaps it's unfair to single out Mutt from Jeff, because each is more dourly "tough minded" and boringly glib than the next, constructing commentaries out of prefab concepts. I wanted out.

In desperation, I took several magazine assignments in the mid-eighties just to get away. I went to Thailand twice, then to Sri Lanka and Nepal. I found these countries oddly compelling though scary. These were a few of the countries we lump rather pompously under the rubric of the underdeveloped countries. I had been in the Caribbean before, in Africa, and elsewhere in what used to be called the Third World until the liberal imagination stepped in with an acceptable euphemism. Images gleaned from travels in these countries began to trouble my sleep: the child in Sri Lanka dying of dehydration from simple diarrhea, the misshapen beggar in Katmandu who spit at me when I offered him an insultingly meager gift, the hot little apartment in Bangkok that housed six large families in two rooms, the opium-drugged inhabitants of a mountain village on the Burmese border. The Western traveler has to develop a certain hard-heartedness to survive trips to poor countries. You learn to blame the people themselves, who can't simply shake off their poverty. You learn to blame their government or our government, neither of which seems willing to help except in superficial ways. It seems so hopeless.

Perhaps more frightening is that many of these countries may soon have nuclear weapons. To survive in this not-very-distant future, the United States will have to become a garrison state, with surveillance satellites prowling every inch of the heavens. Returning from my last trip to the Orient in a state of panic and exhaustion, I happened to be at a birthday party for a friend in New York City and was seated next to Lance Morrow, a well-known writer from *Time*. I took this as a good omen and spilled out my concerns, saying that the most pressing issue for Americans had to be "How to Think About Underdeveloped Countries." Americans seemed to understand abstractly that most of the world is living in excruciating poverty, but the political consequences of this situation had not hit home. I described my unoriginal but no less terrifying impressions of what was happening in these countries. Morrow listened dutifully. He agreed that the situation was urgent, and he took down my phone number, saying he might call to discuss it further.

I don't blame him for not calling. My innocence abroad was hardly news, and what else can one say? Americans don't want to hear too much of this kind of thing. They prefer good news, which is why they clung to Ronald Reagan, who had tacitly agreed to tell them only the pleasant things. For those who worried about nuclear war, he provided Star Wars, the perfect fantasy. He gave them clean-cut enemies, the Evil Empire of the Soviets, totalitarian Sandinistas, welfare bums, and Libyan terrorists. It was all very comprehensible, unlike the real world. For those who still wanted to feel that the United States was "standing tall," he offered little sideshows like Grenada and Tripoli: both preludes to the granddaddy sideshow of them all, the Gulf war.

The tranquil fifties became the tranquilized eighties. The population had simply agreed, unconsciously, to turn off for a while, to cultivate its garden and take pleasure in being American. This country has always had a lot to be thankful for, having had the inestimable advantages of geographic isolation: no Goths have landed on our shores to burn our cities and carry off our children. We enjoy ample natural resources. The fact that a tiny percentage of our population controls most of its resources, dominating the political mechanisms of the country by sheer economic muscle, has never seemed to trouble most Americans, as long as the illusion of democracy survives. (According to the Federal Reserve Board, the top 2 percent of the nation's families owned 71 percent of all tax-exempt mutual bonds and 50 percent of all corporate stock in 1985. The gap between rich and poor has only widened in the nineties).

In the mid-eighties, my wife, Devon, and I decided to detach ourselves from the United States temporarily, and we found an eighteenth-century villa on a cliffside overlooking the Amalfi coast in southern Italy. Italy has always been a favorite of mine: the lemon groves, the olive trees that seem to flash silver in the wind, the tangy cheap wine, the endless pasta, the olive oil that tastes like liquid sunshine. I adore the Italian temper too, which seems perfectly guiltless except where Momma is concerned. There is also that Italian sense of style; W. H. Auden, not without reason, called Italy the "land of la bella figura." I thought I could forget the real world in Italy and indulge my taste for the nonpolitical, for la dolce vita.

It would have worked nicely had I not taken to reading *Time, Newsweek,* and the *International Herald-Tribune* with my morning coffee at the local bar. At home, I never read *Time* or *Newsweek,* assuming (correctly) that they are thin gruel, the verbal equivalent of TV, devoted to the status quo, to celebrity mongering, to puffing whatever trash comes down the pike and suppressing the real story whenever it seems anti-American, or (what amounts to the same thing) antibusiness. I had a better opinion of the *Herald-Tribune,* which is published jointly by the *New York Times* and *Washington Post.*

The news, which these publications did their best to make appealing, ruined my mornings. From December 1985 on, it was clear that Reagan was spoiling for a fight with Libya, knowing that it would boost his popularity ratings (though only in the United States, where machismo pays) and provide yet another reason to spend so much of the federal budget on the military. Just before Reagan's attack, *Time* ran a cover story (April 21, 1986) about the coming confrontation with Libya that put the conflict in terms more appropriate for a B western: "As West European allies fretted about the potential consequences," *Time* wrote, "the pilots . . . stood ready for the command, should it come, to attack and destroy." Fretted? The article is a textbook case of prejudicial reportage masquerading as objective journalism. Sitting only a few hundred miles from Libya on the coast of Italy, I was fretting. Perhaps I'd have fretted less in Washington or Dubuque. With good reason, Europe hated what Reagan was doing. But Libya was an easy target, a photo opportunity for our military, nothing more. "Nor was there the expectation that any American attack would depend on whether Libya fired first," *Time* intoned in its best Zane Grey style. "Libya had already fired—choosing the weapon of a terrorist bomb." Even without the hindsight knowledge that Libya was never, in fact, involved in these particular bombings, the sham logic of *Time's* proposition, leading to the dangerous conclusion that because Libya harbored and trained Arab terrorists of one kind or another it (rather than Syria, Iraq, or Iran) must be singled out for state violence by the United States, played on the public's wish to simplify a complex issue at any cost. Reagan, Mr. Lucky, could have destabilized the entire Mediterranean region with his cowboy gesture. He certainly weakened our position in the eyes of Europe and underdeveloped countries.

The day he struck at Libya I was sick all morning, wandering my little village in a daze. I scanned the American papers and magazines, looking for signs of a general uprising; instead, Reagan's approval rating went sky high. At least this is what *Time* told its readers the following week.

I wrote letters to a dozen or so people I thought might be in a position to influence the media. One was Noam Chomsky, the linguist and commentator on international affairs. I remembered his trenchant pieces against the Vietnam War in *The New York Review of Books*. Was it really nearly two decades since I had read those essays? Where was Chomsky now that we needed him? I asked, and he replied:

> You're quite right about what should be done, but, in fact, I
> am in there screaming—all over the place. So are a few other
> people. In fact, the population as a whole is more "dissident"

(I hate to use the term "left" in a depoliticized country like this) than it was during the Vietnam War, I believe. But elites have learned a lot during the Vietnam period. One thing they have learned is that it is a serious error to allow even a minor opening to voices of criticism anywhere near the mainstream. They know better now than to allow that tiny opening permitted in the *New York Review,* for example (the *Review,* since 1973, has been an effective state disinformation journal). What publishing I do, therefore, is in Europe and in marginal journals, or books that you probably don't get to see. You can read what I wrote about Libya in *The New Statesman* or *Il Manifesto* or *La Journada* or *El Pais* or *Covert Action Information Bulletin,* but not in any journal that can reach a real public in the US. Most of my time is therefore spent travelling and speaking: no way has yet been found to stop that. Audiences are very large, very interested, very enthusiastic, but don't know what to do, since everyone feels quite isolated, thanks to the great success of the commissars (the educated classes quite generally) in controlling all organized information flow and public outlet. Actually, things have opened up a bit in the past few months. Thus, after the Libya atrocities, I was actually on radio and TV quite a bit—by US standards. Of course, the situation in Canada and Europe is much different. I have just returned from ten days in Germany, Spain, and Belgium, where I spent many hours on radio and TV, gave many talks, had lots of press coverage including articles and interviews, etc. But I rarely go to Europe, because the problem is here.

Rereading Chomsky's letter, I'm not sure why it came as such a shock to me at the time. I was vaguely aware of everything he said, but the reality of it struck me hard as, from abroad, I examined the mainstream American press. I began to study the press more carefully, trying to learn what interests were offended by certain kinds of stories. One day, for instance, I noticed in the "For the Record" column of the *Herald-Tribune*—not on the front page or anywhere that one might easily see it—a two-line report that several hundred people had been arrested for protesting near an underground nuclear testing site in Arizona. I had thought that nobody was upset when Reagan decided to begin nuclear testing again despite a unilateral Soviet promise not to test if the United States didn't. What if the Soviets were indeed scoring a publicity coup by their unilateral declaration? Was it not in our national interest to welcome any positive gestures made by the Soviets? (This, of course, naively assumed that Reagan really was genuinely serious about reducing the arms race.)

I returned to Vermont in the fall of 1986, just as the contra war against the Sandinista government in Nicaragua was building. I found the hypocrisies of this dirty little war extremely grating. "In a dark time, the eye begins to see," wrote Theodore Roethke, one of my favorite poets. I felt as though, for the first time since the Vietnam War, I was able to peek behind the smoke screen set up by the national press. I had to learn to read through the press but also around it. This involved subscribing to alternative and foreign periodicals, and these are not all just liberal-radical stuff. (In fact, I have found much of what is written in the liberal or radical press as worthy of deconstruction as anything in the mainstream media.)

The Economist—a fairly conservative publication on the whole—has proved a good source of information. In its August 1986 issue, for example, I read a shocking report on lung cancer, smoking, and the media. The statistics were gruesome: 350 million premature deaths a year occurred in the United States in the early eighties, with estimated costs at $65 billion a year in medical bills and lost productivity. The human costs, of course, were incalculable. Why was there no outcry in the press? It was not hard to figure out: the tobacco industry was and remains a powerful lobby in Washington, so we can't expect politicians who depend on huge influxes of cash from tobacco companies for their war chests to do anything serious about smoking. Even Senator Bill Bradley's modest proposal to eliminate the business-expense tax deductions for tobacco promotion sent his colleagues running the other way. Before the recent grassroots attack on tobacco companies began, it was left to the press to drum up support for any measures that might be taken against the industry. One might assume it to have been the duty of the media to inform Americans that they were being seduced and poisoned by a powerful corporate league. *The Economist* reported that *Sports Illustrated, Time,* and *Newsweek* regularly suppressed articles on the dangers of smoking because of pressure from the tobacco industry, as did the leading women's magazines.

When I returned to the States in the fall of 1986, I found myself increasingly upset by the way the media went out of its way to support the Reagan obsession with the Sandinistas. More than $100 million dollars in overt tax dollars went to support the contras, and at least as much covertly—through the Israelis, for example. Nevertheless, the media stood firmly behind the president. Writing in *The Nation* at that time, Alexander Cockburn pointed out that during the first three months of 1986, the *New York Times* and *Washington Post* printed eighty-five pieces on Nicaragua between them. Of these, not one showed anything but outright hostility toward the Sandinista government, which (despite a justified sense of paranoia and a touch of the usual demagoguery) carried out a far-reaching program of social reform, improving health care and education quite dramatically since being elected to office. (Not even those "experts" who opposed the Sandinistas denied that those reforms actually took place.) What was remarkable was that those reforms were made under conditions of siege: in defiance of the World Court and U.S. law, Reagan had carried out an active military campaign against a foreign government. The CIA had been trying to undermine the Sandinistas since William Casey took over the agency. David MacMichael, who worked with the CIA in 1981 when it began plotting to overthrow the Sandinistas, later testified to the World Court, saying, "It was hoped that the Nicaraguan government would clamp down on civil liberties within Nicaragua itself, arresting its opposition, demonstrating its allegedly inherent totalitarian nature and thus increase domestic dissent within the country." Despite massive efforts to undo it, the Sandinista government remained both popular in Nicaragua and relatively open, given the wartime conditions under which it operated. Would the United States ever have permitted those who openly plotted to violently overthrow our government to travel and speak here? The Sandinistas nevertheless allowed procontra speakers such as Robert Leiken to travel widely within their borders. The United States wouldn't even let Farley Mowat, the Canadian writer, into this country because he had once been critical of our government. The list of writers banned from the United States is a long one, in fact (including Nobel laureate Gabriel Gárcia Márquez and the English novelists Graham Greene and Iris Murdoch).

One could go on and on. The media were astonishingly unskeptical of George Bush during the Gulf war, fueling a kind of rabid patriotism reflected in the yellow ribbons streaming from every car radio antenna in the country. It took the election of a moderate Democrat, Bill Clinton, to turn the media against a president. Clinton's main problem, I suspect, has been his interest in health care reform, which threatens to disturb the profitability of a vast weblike empire that includes doctors, insurance and drug companies, even hospitals. The insurance companies have spent more than $100 million dollars in anti-Clinton advertising alone, trying to sway public opinion. How does one calculate the effect of such blocks of money on the democratic system? Would it even be possible to change a system so predicated on the fact that opinion can be bought, that consent can, as Walter Lippmann once said, be manufactured?

The fact remains that we have a good deal of personal freedom in this country; we do not, however, have enough of the right kinds of freedom, such as the freedom of easy access to unbiased news. Our media are largely an extension of the entertainment industry, beholden to their audiences, whom they feel they must not disturb, and terrified of alienating their advertisers, on whom they depend. This means that we must learn to read all over again. Schools and colleges must do what they have hardly ever done: teach students to question authority and think critically. The United States has never, like France or England, had a strong tradition of public debate, and such a tradition is the ne plus ultra of a genuine democracy. I want my children to learn to interrogate the system, so that they will not, as adults, feel powerless and indeed be powerless.

As I said at the beginning of this essay, I would prefer to remain nonpolitical. It is my nature. If anything, I am by disposition a Tory socialist. I would even qualify the word *socialist* to mean social democrat. By *Tory*, I mean that I enjoy good wine, opera, and clothbound first editions of my favorite authors. I prefer large houses to small ones. I wish that everyone could live like an eighteenth-century English gentleperson, just so I could do the same without pangs of conscience. But I can't avoid what I know to be true, which is that the huge majority of human beings, whom I must consider my brothers and sisters, live in miserable poverty without hope of improving their situation. They have bad water, tyrannical governments, and no access to the benefits of civilization. My country, which is terribly wealthy and powerful, has rarely worked to help these people and often, I'm afraid, it has worked to harm them. For the most part, the media do not care. They do not even notice, and when they do—when a famine strikes in Africa or a particularly cruel and unlikely war in the Balkans—they rush to ogle, sometimes shaming rich governments to provide temporary aid. The situation is a mess, and I do not have any answers.

All I know is that I cannot remain entirely nonpolitical. I happen to fall into that rather pretentious-sounding group called *intellectuals*. Broadly defined, intellectuals are those who create and sustain ideology. They are writers and journalists, television commentators, filmmakers, and teachers. Dwight Macdonald, an important thinker in the middle years of this century, wrote some interesting essays on personal responsibility, focusing on World War II. To what extent were the German or Japanese people responsible for the atrocities committed in their name? With all good intentions, Macdonald turned the question back on his own country: To what extent were the American and British people responsible for the destruction of Hiroshima and Nagasaki? The questions could be multiplied. Who, for instance, was responsible for the millions killed by Stalin in the gulags? In every case where atrocities occur, actual people are responsible, and the foot soldiers who pull the trigger are as guilty as the dictator who issues the command to kill. (Although one is basically lucky not to be, by an accident of history, in the situation of the foot soldier with the lethal orders in hand.)

Noam Chomsky quite properly lays a good deal of responsibility at the feet of intellectuals, as do I. In *American Power and the New Mandarins* (1969), Chomsky writes,

> Intellectuals are in a position to expose the lies of governments, to analyze actions according to their causes and motives and often hidden intentions. In the Western world at least, they have the power that comes from political liberty, from access to information and freedom of expression. For a privileged minority, Western democracy provides the leisure, the facilities, and the training to seek the truth lying hidden behind the veil of distortion and misrepresentation, ideology, and class interest through which the events of current history are presented to us.

My sense of truth, as a poet and novelist, is, I suspect, different from Chomsky's in certain ways, at least on the abstract level. He is an Enlightenment rationalist wandering the post-Nietzschean landscape. Truth, for me, is rarely a thing one simply uncovers; one pulls back the veil only to find the veil itself is one's perceiving mind, and there is nothing behind it. Nevertheless, on the level of public affairs and everyday politics, there are many hard facts, and they are bluntly individual and easily perceived if one simply looks in the right places with a relatively open mind: a rat chewing off the fingers of a child in an orphanage in China, a farmer and his family dispossessed of their land in Honduras, a family sprayed with machine-gun fire in Malaysia. The catalogue of misery is overly stuffed and seemingly infinite.

Some of this misery is a direct result of American corporate and government practices and policies, but the United States is not the only demon in the world; increasingly, the transnational corporation—that terrifying entity—is the culprit, and individual governments (and therefore the people who have some influence over these governments) seem to be losing their regulatory grip on them. But, quite naturally, I tend to focus on this country and its influence, still considerable, abroad. It is not that Americans are not good people. Most people who have enough to eat and a decent place to live and some rudimentary sense of well-being are good people. The system I want to analyze and reconstruct is in the United States, in that abstract entity that Dwight Eisenhower referred to as the "military-industrial complex," which has caused so much pain to so many people in unlikely and far-flung places.

I continue to feel acutely the inadequacy of any personal response to each large-scale international crisis. One can give money to good causes, march on Washington, send flyers, write letters to members of Congress: the usual activist maneuvers. These give one a sense of belonging to a substantial group of concerned people trying to effect a change for the better. But fundamental change is always a far, impossible shore. One sails, nevertheless, in its direction, asking difficult questions all the way: Who sets policy and what interests do these people represent? Who stands to gain by pushing funds in this direction rather than that direction? Because special interests (and the sheer power of vast capital) control our government and our media, it is our duty as citizens to understand the mechanisms of control and to learn how to gain access to the right kinds of information about these interest groups, whatever their bias. It is hard work, but there is no other hope for the survival of either freedom or democracy. The spiritual and moral aspects of the human condition presuppose a degree of political awareness. Thomas Mann's nonpolitical man is, in our time or his, a costly anachronism.

2. The Poetry of Earth

BLAKE AND ROETHKE
When Everything Comes to One

Not all the dead are used: we must take what we can from them.
—THEODORE ROETHKE, NOTEBOOKS

In an essay entitled "How to Write Like Somebody Else" Theodore Roethke said that in a time when "the romantic notion of the inspired poet still has considerable credence, true 'imitation' takes a certain courage. One dares to stand up to a great style, to compete with papa." Implicit in this statement is a distinction between false imitation, which comes down to mimicry of certain stylistic effects, and true imitation, which involves a confrontation, an appropriation and *re*creation of the precursor's visionary stance. This latter kind of imitation occurs in the case of William Blake and Theodore Roethke. For Blake remains the single most important poet for Roethke, not so much on the level of style (though I shall point to similarities at this level) but at the deeper level of mythopoetic action. Both poets were intent upon making a system or a personal *mythos* (in Northrop Frye's sense of the term as a shaping principle of literary form), and this mythos moves beyond allegory to anagogy, so that the characters in the system do not simply represent another stage or level of reality but move toward embodiment. This is the stage often called *mystical*, when (as Roethke said in "In a Dark Time") "The mind enters itself, and God the mind, / And one is One, free in the tearing wind." Here Roethke seems close to the heart of Blake's visionary stance; as Frye said in *Fearful Symmetry* (1969), "The true God for such visionaries is not the orthodox Creator . . . but an unattached creative Word. . . . Unity with this God could be attained only by an effort of vision which not only rejects the duality of subject and object but attacks the far more difficult antithesis of being and non-being as well."

It is mostly in his last volume, *The Far Field* (1964), that Roethke comes to express his visionary sense of wonder, particularly in the *Sequence Sometimes Metaphysical* and the *North American Sequence*. Here Roethke approaches the apocalyptic identification of the kingdom with his own body that was Blake's culmination in *Jerusalem* (1804). When one is one, free in the tearing wind, Blake's vision has been accomplished, although his imagery is drawn from the New Testament and Roethke's is taken from the Old Testament. Blake's method, especially in the later phase, was to outleap the world, to claim the transcendental vision directly, whereas Roethke, fascinated by the spirit *as manifest* in nature, ascends the ladder of creation by gradual—indeed loving—steps. But the influence of Blake on Roethke can be detected much earlier, in *The Lost Son* (1948) sequences. In these poems, Roethke set out to create his mythos, the struggle of the lost son in his quest for identity and his efforts to overcome Papa. Blake proposed the same process in his "Orc cycle," which occupies a central position in his work as a whole. Orc represents the natural man, and his struggle to resolve the contraries of Los and overcome the opposing specters of Urizen and Urthona becomes the equivalent mythos in Blake. Orc, like the lost son, moves through various stages of maturation; he opposes the old man, Urizen, until he naturally becomes an old man himself (at which point regeneration occurs and the cycle begins again). "Implicit in the myth of Orc and Urizen," Frye comments in *Fearful Symmetry*, "is the allegory of the young striking down the old, the most obvious symbol of which is the son's revolt against a father." The Oedipal myth resides at the base of Blake's cycle, and it is this same myth that links Roethke's sequences to Blake.

Orc, says Martin Price in "The Standard of Energy" (1970), "embodies the rebellious principle of renewed and independent life." Orc is the son of Los, the redeeming power of imagination, and Enitharmon, the "first female now separate." But Orc is fallen man as well. Los and Enitharmon chain their son to a rock, and the matter of Blake's cycle involves Orc's struggle for freedom, especially against Urizen (who is a negative aspect of Los). Urizen represents pure rationality and lifeless order, a version of Roethke's Papa, who represents *Ordnung* in *The Lost Son*. Blake does not oppose intellect in its complete form, where it combines with freshness of perception and feeling, but in this fallen (Urizenic) aspect he condemns it. "Like Milton," Price says, "Blake sees all human existence as shot through with moments of fall and moments of redemption, and one fall provides an archetype for all others." Ultimately, Blake's myth, like Roethke's, looks forward to a redemptive vision, to the restoration of that primal unity lost in the fall. But Blake's protagonist, Orc, must first release himself from the treadmill of desire; as Frye puts it in "The Keys to the Gates" (1970), "The natural tendency of desire (Orc) in itself is to find its object. Hence the effect of the creative impulse on desire is bound to be restrictive unless the release of desire becomes the inevitable by-product of creation."

The body of Roethke's work focuses on the single mythos that begins in *The Lost Son,* his second book. This volume provides the key to the rest of his work, for all the essential symbols of his system are present here in one form or another. Papa, the Urizenic father, is Otto Roethke, the greenhouse owner. Otto is at times seen as God; he is terrifying and powerful. Roethke's mother, Helen, is present but in the background. Like Enitharmon, she is passive, sometimes conflated with nature itself in its passive aspect. The greenhouse is a cultured Beulah world (an earthly paradise associated with unfallen sexuality) apart from the harsher nature outside, Roethke's "symbol for the whole of life, a womb, a heaven-on-earth," writes Ralph J. Mills Jr. (1965). In his notebooks of the forties Roethke tried to understand this luminous symbol occupying the center of his work: "What was this greenhouse? It was a jungle, and it was paradise, it was order and disorder. Was it an escape? No, for it was a reality harder than the various suspensions of terror." There is also the open field, a place of illumination and, sometimes, mystical experience. "The Lost Son" itself, the title poem, contains the primary symbols; it is the text that informs the rest of his work, reiterating the elementary hero myth with its classic pattern of flight (separation from the tribe), testing in the wilderness, descent into the underworld, and return (atonement, transfiguration). This cycle, like the Orc cycle in Blake, recurs in successive volumes—though it finds fullest expression in *The Lost Son, Praise to the End!* (1951), and *The Waking* (1953), of which the initial poem, "O, Thou Opening, O" completes *The Lost Son* sequence per se.

In "The Lost Son" Roethke invokes the Blakean dialectic of innocence and experience. Scattered through his working notebooks of the period (1943–1953) is the famous proverb from Blake's *The Marriage of Heaven and Hell* (1790): "Without Contraries is no progression," which could serve as an epigraph to Roethke's *Collected Poems.* In Blake's system, the mind pulls into its orbit those forces that might exist outside its control; the dialectic absorbs all resistances; necessities become internal. Hence, the lost son journeys toward identity, self-affirmation, and, later, self-transcendence, but his path remains tortuous, marked by detours and culs-de-sac as in section 3 (of five sections in *"The Lost Son"*), which begins,

> Where do the roots go?
> Look down under the leaves.
> Who put the moss there?
> These stones have been here too long.
> Who stunned the dirt into noise?
> Ask the mole, he knows.

In the last line Roethke alludes directly to *The Book of Thel* (1789) and Blake's epigraph: "Does the Eagle know what is in the pit? / Or wilt thou go ask the Mole?" The lost son is instructed to look downward, to dig into nether regions of psychic history for answers to his questions.

The Book of Thel concerns the failure of a heroine, Thel. She fails to progress from innocence, from Beulah to Generation (fallen sexuality but a necessary condition, the phase at which Orc begins his struggle). By failing to make this fall, Thel refuses to exercise a vital power of the soul, the *will.* She is timid, afraid of incarnation and the terrors of sense experience. By staying a virgin for too long, she forfeits the opportunity for progress and final redemption. As a result, she cannot remain static—Blake does not admit of this possibility—rather, she is destined to fall back into the solipsistic state of Ulro, the lowest condition in Blake's scheme. Her fear recalls the moment in section 4 of "The Lost Son" in which the boy says, "Fear was my father, Father Fear." But unlike Thel, the lost son passes from the world of the greenhouse and his family cloister into the dangerous zone of Generation, here represented as a swampy bogland:

> Hunting along the river,
> Down among the rubbish, the bug-riddled foliage,
> By the muddy pond-edge, by the bog-holes,
> By the shrunken lake, hunting, in the heat of summer.

At this stage of his journey the boy hero enters into the cyclical process of nature; the summer (which Blake associates with Generation) gives way to late autumn or early winter in the last section of the poem, a time when

> It was beginning winter,
> An in-between time,
> The landscape still partly brown:
> The bones of weeds kept swinging in the wind,
> Above the blue snow.

"The Lost Son" cannot be said to conclude; conclusion goes against the cyclical grain. Instead, the hero reaches an "irresolute resolution," an ending that is as well a beginning. This parallels the movement of Blake's cycle, in which each poem achieves a partial conclusion, as in *The Book of Urizen* (1794):

> 8. So Fuzon call'd all together
> The remaining children of Urizen:
> and they left the pendulous earth:
> They called it Egypt, & left it.
>
> 9. And the salt ocean rolled englob'd

This ending prepares for the opening of *The Book of Ahania* (1795), in which Blake resumes the Orc cycle: "Fuzon, on a chariot iron-wing'd / On spiked flames rose."

The last section of "The Lost Son" seems a long way from the seasonless paradise of Eden, the uppermost estate in Blake's overall scheme, but a partial cleansing of the senses certainly occurs: "The mind moved, not along, / Through the clear air, in the silence." *The Book of Thel*, on the other hand, ends with an unredemptive thud as Thel is shown "the secret of the land unknown" but has not the courage to make an adequate response; indeed, "The Virgin started from her seat, & with a shriek, / Fled back unhindered till she came into the vales of Har." She will doubtless lapse into the condition of nonparticipation characteristic of Ulro, where desires go perpetually unsatisfied, having failed to make the journey *through* desire, which can lead to freedom from desire. Her destiny is the "single vision" Blake reviled, a dreadful retreat from the "threefold vision" of Beulah or the ideal "fourfold vision" enjoyed by those in Eden. Roethke's lost son, and this again has parallels in the Orc cycle, lacks none of the required courage; just as Orc has the dual aspect of Adonis, the dying and reviving god, and Prometheus, the thief of fire, the protagonist of *The Lost Son* sequence is dismembered, psychologically, in the wilderness, buried (section 2 of "The Lost Son"), and revived; like Prometheus, he accepts the responsibility of fire: "I'll take the fire." The fire, in this case, is sexual desire; the lost son sees that he must face up to his passion if he will control it.

The contraries of innocence and experience, so crucial to Blake's system, operate in the whole of Roethke's work, but they have a special place in *The Lost Son,* which concerns the hero at the point of maturation where sexuality must be repressed (Thel's choice) or accepted (the option taken by Blake's later heroine, Oothoon). The "married land" of Beulah from which Roethke's hero is "lost" appears once again in the lyric "The Waking," which precedes *The Lost Son* sequence in the 1948 volume. The poem recalls the opening of Blake's lyric from *Poetical Sketches* (1783), "How sweet I roam'd from field to field, / And tasted all the summer's pride"—although Roethke in "The Waking" avoids the harsh ironies into which Blake falls:

> I strolled across
> An open field;
> The sun was out;
> Heat was happy.
>
> This way! This way!
> The wren's throat shimmered,
> Either to other,
> The blossoms sang.
>
> The stones sang,
> The little ones did,

And flowers jumped
Like small goats.

A ragged fringe
Of daisies waved;
I wasn't alone
In a grove of apples.

Roethke's lyric invokes the world of Blake's *Songs of Innocence* (1789), a place where the glow worm gives counsel ("A Dream"), the sun "make[s] happy the skies" ("The Ecchoing Green"), and "the green woods laugh, with the voice of joy / And the dimpling stream runs laughing by" ("Laughing Song"). The last lines of Roethke's poem recreate the bliss of "Infant Joy," where Blake writes,

Pretty joy!
Sweet joy but two days old.
Sweet joy I call thee:
Thou dost smile.
I sing the while
Sweet joy befall thee.

In much the same way Roethke concludes,

My ears knew
An early joy.
And all the waters
Of all the streams
Sang in my veins
That summer day.

But neither poet has yet dramatized the separation of subject and object that follows inevitably as the realm of innocence gives way to experience. In Roethke as in Blake, the fall of man is coincident with the creation; both poets posit a condition of unity, a golden age, before the fall. And both look ahead to the restoration of that unity, a state raised above "the hateful siege of contraries" (in Milton's phrase). "Blake gives us," says Price in "Standard of Energy," "a world conceived as the manifestation of imaginative energy, hardened into opacity as energy fails, raised through intense and confident assertion to the image of One Man, containing all powers within himself and exercising them in the creation of works of art." Likewise, Roethke, in "The Far Field" envisions "the end of things, the final man" whose "spirit moves like monumental wind / That gentles on a sunny blue plateau." But this is to look well beyond Orc and the lost son.

The poems of Roethke's *Lost Son* sequence, individually and as a whole, recapitulate the journey from disorganized innocence through Generation, the crucible of summer, to organized innocence. As Harold Bloom observes in *The Visionary Company* (1971), "The only road to creativity and apocalypse lies through the realm of summer, the hard world of experience." Roethke's dialectic in "A Field of Light"—the penultimate poem in *The Lost Son*—exacts a share of pain for each portion of joy in this summery woodland where

> Small winds made
> A chilly noise;
> The softest cove
> Cried for sound.

Or where the hero

> Reached for a grape
> And the leaves changed;
> A stone's shape
> Became a clam.

Not until the end of summer, "Along the low ground dry only in August," does the hero catch a glimpse of Eden, and that only after an intimation of mortality ("Was it dust I was kissing?"):

> I could watch! I could watch!
> I saw the separateness of all things!
> My heart lifted up with the great grasses;
> The weeds believed me, and the nesting birds.
> There were clouds making a rout of shapes crossing a
>   windbreak of cedars,
> And a bee shaking drops from a rain-soaked honeysuckle.

The worms were delighted as wrens.
And I walked, I walked through the light air;
I moved with the morning.

The intensity of the lost son in his moment of ecstasy contrasts sharply with
the infantile joy of "The Waking," although the sense of oneness with the
natural world remains constant. Having come through the harsh world of
experience, which underscores the division of subject and object, the boy
hero enters this momentary flash of vision. It is the dramatic context that
provides the intensity.

One self-contained sequence of brief lyrics within *The Lost Son* has come
to be known as the Greenhouse Poems; it contains some of Roethke's most
widely anthologized pieces. These tough, sensual, and concrete poems
recreate the texture of experience in the manner of *The Songs of Experience*
(1794) and serve as a prelude to *The Lost Son* sequence in the way Blake's
Songs adumbrate the Orc cycle. Roethke's lyrics establish the mythopoetic
context necessary for *The Lost Son* sequence to work and prepare the
ground for the symbolist methods characteristic of the later poems. In
short, he invents a sequence of natural fables; his poems exploit various
mythic structures and allude to such standard hermetic symbols as the rose
and the worm. "Cuttings" is the first fable:

> Sticks-in-a-drowse droop over sugary loam,
> Their intricate stem-fur dries;
> But still the delicate slips keep coaxing up water;
> The small cells bulge;
>
> One nub of growth
> Nudges a sand-crumb loose,
> Pokes through a musty sheath
> Its pale tendrilous horn.

The human parallels (the metaphor) are submerged; the sticks are "in-a-
drowse," and the slips "coax" up water: both figures suggest a form of con-
sciousness above the level commonly associated with the plant world.
Roethke's cuttings are primordial nerve ends, low on the phylogenetic scale,
but they prefigure something higher. The poem calls up a state of begin-
nings, a condition where the life force is reduced to an urge, an importu-

nate breathing. Again, the poem derives its force from the tacit myth of awakening.

Still, it is in *The Lost Son* sequence as it stretches over three books that Roethke accrues his largest debts to Blake. The lost son gropes toward self-awareness and separate identity in the manner of Blake's "fierce child," Orc, born in *The Book of Urizen* and struggling through many of the major poems against his various opposing specters. The apocalyptic imagery and associational logic of both poets operate within a consistent, albeit difficult, symbol system. These systems are closed and full of internal references. The lost son engages in the cycles of nature, advancing slowly toward his goal of identity and self-transcendence; his way out of nature is *through* it. Blake, by contrast, does not identify with Orc or suggest that his involvement with the natural cycles is a good thing. For him, the cycles of nature were a kind of death, a grinding down. As Frye explains in *Fearful Symmetry*, "The vision of life as an Orc cycle is the pessimistic view of life." In Blake's system, Orc is equivalent to the giant Albion in his fallen aspect. At the end of the cycle, Orc comes face to face with Urizen and the specter of Urthona, who represents clock time (an aspect of the grinding down effected by the natural cycles). Orc's destiny is, of course, to become Urizen himself; then the cycle must begin again. Roethke's "lost son"—on the other hand—goes beyond these cycles, transcending the self-consciousness that leads into Ulro and the fate of Orc. Nonetheless, both Roethke and Blake were aiming toward a myth of creation and destruction, a poetics of redemption.

The Lost Son sequence resumes in *Praise to the End!* (1981) with the hero-as-infant; the language of these poems suggests the process of disintegration that accompanies the fall into creation, akin to the breakup of the giant Albion into the four Zoas in Blake's system. Both poets reformulated the myth of disintegration at several stages in their careers. Jenijoy La Belle, writing in *The Echoing Wood of Theodore Roethke* (1976), finds this myth in Blake emerging in the *Songs of Innocence* and compares the "Little Boy Lost" to Roethke's lost son: "For both poets, the physical condition of the little boy lost in the Stygian darkness and trapped in the mire is an emblem for state of psychological disorientation and for a loss of the true vision of innocence." In Blake's companion piece, "The Little Boy Found," the child is restored to innocence by God, who is "ever nigh," and who "Appear'd like his father in white." In a similar way the lost son encounters Papa, who represents *Ordnung*, or authority (in its negative Urizenic aspect, however), upon his return from "The Pit" and the terrifying journey into experience. Throughout *The Lost Son* sequence Papa reappears at crucial moments as a "beard in a cloud" to provide (or force) order.

Praise to the End! opens with a birth poem, "Where Knock Is Open Wide," in which the poet reconstitutes the dream world of infancy. The poem opens with the infant hero in some confusion over what is happening to him; he cannot distinguish cause from effect: "I know it's an owl. He's making it darker." He still thinks he is in Beulahland, the state of primal unity, in which God answers to every need within the instant: "God, give me a near. I hear flowers." This world is absolutely self-centered, and all sexual pleasure is onanistic: "Hello happy hands." But the truth of his new condition, which is postlapsarian, occurs to him rather suddenly: "I fell! I fell!" he cries, "The worm has moved away. / My tears are tired." He complains, "God's somewhere else," and darkness seems to have come for "a long long time."

"I Need, I Need" follows immediately and reviews the condition of loss. The title derives from the ninth design of Blake's series *For Children: The Gates of Paradise* (1793) with its inscription, "I want! I want!" The poem chronicles the infant's first encounters with unsatisfied desire, the terror of Blake's Orc as well. "I can't taste my mother," Roethke's infant cries. For the first time, the hero feels cut off from his source, separate. His consciousness has been divided, which leads him to wish for a prior state. And so unsatisfied desire leads necessarily to the habit of wishing:

> I wish I was a pifflebob
> I wish I was a funny
> I wish I had ten thousand hats,
> And made a lot of money.

Through this section Roethke uses the language of schoolchildren without being condescending; he enters into the child's consciousness by imitating verbal patterns that are thought to be childlike, a technique used by Blake in his *Songs of Innocence.* As S. Foster Damon writes in *William Blake: His Philosophy and Symbols* (1924), "Blake does not contemplate children, in the manner of Wordsworth, Hugo, and Longfellow; he actually enters into their souls and speaks through their own mouths." So Roethke, in the passage just quoted, uses the most basic of childhood tropes, a series of wishes. In Blake's engraving there are three figures, one of whom is a naked child poised for climbing a moonbeam and clearly destined to failure. The child here has yet to move from innocence to experience, although the picture itself contains within its perimeter both contrary states. As La Belle says in *The Echoing Wood*, "The viewpoint and the final significance of many of Blake's and Roethke's poems about childhood become very complex because the two contrary states of innocence and experience are not mutually exclusive and can exist in the same child or the same poem at once."

In Roethke's sequence, the states of innocence and experience alternate, and nature is by turns sympathetic and antagonistic. In "I Need, I Need," a poem about the fall into experience, nature appears unresponsive:

> Went down cellar,
> Talked to a faucet;
> The drippy water
> Had nothing to say.

But nature responds with robust sympathy in the next poem, "Bring the Day," which begins with a nursery-rhymelike chant:

> Bees and lilies there were,
> Bees and lilies there were,
> Either to other,—
> Which would you rather?
> Bees and lilies were there.
>
> The green grasses,—would they?
> The green grasses?—
> She asked her skin
> To let me in:
> The far leaves were for it.

Similar rhythms occur in many of Blake's *Songs,* such as "The Ecchoing Green"—though Roethke remains more tentative than Blake throughout:

> The Sun does arise,
> And make happy the skies.
> The merry bells ring
> To welcome the Spring.

The skylark and thrush,
The birds of the bush,
Sing louder around,
To the bells' cheerful sound.
While our sports shall be seen
On the Ecchoing Green.

Both poets use what Gerard Manley Hopkins called "sprung rhythm," a meter familiar to readers of Mother Goose; they use other devices common to the nursery rhyme, such as repetition, short lines, internal rhyming, and alliteration. Roethke, in his essay "Some Remarks on Rhythm," comments on Blake's "A Poison Tree": "The whole poem is a masterly example of variation in rhythm, of playing against meter. It's what Blake called 'the bounding line,' the nervousness, the tension, the energy in the whole poem. And this is a clue to everything. Rhythm gives us the very psychic energy of the speaker, in one emotional situation at least." True enough, but more than meter is involved. The underlying pattern of gradually sharpened antitheses that force the hero of Roethke's sequence into a moral choice works as a principle of organization in much the same way as it does in Blake's Orc cycles and the later prophetic books.

The progress of Roethke's infant hero in *Praise to the End!* is steady but not linear. "By snails, by leaps of frog, I came here," he says. The hero treks a landscape of few comforts, a *paysage moralisé* (moralized landscape) where "Eternity howls in the last crags. / The field is no longer simple." As he says, "It's a soul's crossing time." This setting resembles the familiar testing ground of most quest literature; Roethke's woodlands, far from being the enchanted forests one associates with childhood, come closer to Dante's *selva oscura*: "It's a dark wood, soft mocker." These dark woodlands resemble in character the Urizenic "dens / Mountain, moor, & wilderness" that trap Orc in the *Book of Urizen*. The path through these dark woods that leads to transcendental vision is beset with crossroads and detours. Sometimes the hero makes a wrong turn and finds himself in a place of total disaffection:

Touch and arouse. Suck and sob. Curse and mourn.
It's a cold scrape in a low place.
The dead crow dries on a pole.
Shapes in the shade
Watch.

Yet later the hero can say with pride, "I've crawled from the mire, alert as a saint or a dog; / I know the back-stream's joy, and the stone's eternal pulseless longing." In general, the speaker arrives at some temporary conclusion near the end of each poem, slipping back again at the start of the next one but never back quite so far. "I go back because I want to go forward," Roethke says in his notebooks. The lost son accepts his difficult quest with a certain equanimity: "What grace I have is enough."

What Roethke's lost son and Blake's hero, Orc, have in common is a belief in the powers of intuition; "Knowledge," Blake writes, "is not by deduction but Immediate by Perception or Sense at once." Conceptual discourse bears no interest. In *Jerusalem,* Blake's last prophetic book, the contraries of rational and emotional discourse find mythic equivalents:

> Rational Philosophy and Mathematic Demonstration
> Is divided in the intoxications of pleasure & affection
> Two Contraries War against each other in fury & blood,
> And Los fixes them on his Anvil, incessant his blows:
> He fixes them with strong blows. placing the stones
>   & timbers.
> To Create a World of Generation from the World of Death:
> Dividing the Masculine & Feminine: for the comingling
> Of Albions Luvahs Spectres was Hermaphroditic

Los, the terrifying artificer, creates out of these contraries a better world; however, the act of submitting to these contraries, to the sublunary world of Generation, requires genuine courage. Those without this courage, like Thel, must slip back inexorably into the sleep of Ulro.

The naive romantic sides with feeling against reason in a simpleminded way. Blake does not do this; for his ultimate goal, Jerusalem, is a vision of the giant Albion restored. Head (Urizen), body (Tharmas), loins (Orc), and legs (Urthona) come together in the end. The imagination subsumes both feeling and thought. "The act of creation," says Frye in "Keys to the Gates," "is not producing something out of nothing, but the act of setting free what we already possess." Nevertheless, Blake, with some justice, attacks the "single vision" of John Locke, Isaac Newton, and other rationalist thinkers of his time:

> I turn my eyes to the Schools & Universities of Europe
> And there behold the Loom of Locke whose Woof rages dire

Wash'd by the Water-wheels of Newton. black the cloth
In heavy wreathes folds over every Nation; cruel Works
Of many Wheels I view, wheel without wheel, with cogs
    tyrannic
Moving by compulsion each other: not as those in Eden:
    which
Wheel within Wheel in freedom revolve in harmony &
    peace.

Roethke says the same thing in a much less complex way in the last poem of *Praise to the End!* entitled "I Cry, Love! Love!" (itself a quotation from Blake):

Reason? That dreary shed, that hutch for grubby school
    boys!
The hedgewren's song says something else.
I care for a cat's cry and the hugs, live as water.

The lost son is learning to begin, as Blake suggests, with perception and sense.

The title "I Cry, Love! Love!" comes from the *Visions of the Daughters of Albion* (1793) in which the character of Oothoon answers to the feckless virgin Thel. Oothoon attempts to move beyond innocence into experience, from Beulah into Generation; she is "a virgin fill'd with virgin fancies / Open to joy and to delight where ever beauty appears." Her failure to do as she wishes comes as no fault of her own; rather, the object of her desire, Theotormon, is utterly self-enthralled, sitting "Upon the margin'd ocean conversing with shadows dire." The central passage in *Visions* gave Roethke his theme:

I cry, Love! Love! Love! happy happy Love! free as the moun-
    tain wind!
Can that be Love, that drinks another as a sponge drinks
    water?
That clouds with jealousy his nights, with weepings all the
    day: To spin a web of age around him. grey and hoary! dark!
Till his eyes sicken at the fruit that hangs before his sight.
Such is self-love that envies all! a creeping skeleton
With lamplike eyes watching around the frozen marriage
    bed.

Oothoon makes the crucial distinction between narcissism and "that generous love" that attaches itself to another person; the first is nugatory, even destructive, denying the reality of anything beyond the self. It brings on the dread sleep of Ulro. But this "happy happy love" does not drink another "as a sponge drinks water," merely feeding on the other person's energies. It exults in the other, celebrating itself in the process; it knows how "everything that lives is holy"—a phrase that Roethke liked to quote.

The hero in "I Cry Love! Love!" says, "Delight me otherly, white spirit," playing on *utterly* to gain a double sense. The maturing speaker now sees that he can discover his own identity only through another. "Bless me and the maze I'm in!" he says, accepting the siege of contraries and the world of objects: "Hello, thingy spirit." He has now fully accepted the fall into creation and will try to use this misfortune to his best advantage. He accepts Blake's sacramental view of nature, that everything alive is holy: "Behold, in the lout's eye, / Love." The last stanza of the poem brings this realization to its conclusion:

> Who untied the tree? I remember now.
> We met in a nest. Before I lived.
> The dark hair sighed.
> We never enter
> Alone.

The question "Who untied the tree?" shows how mature the boy has become; it is equivalent to "Who made me and turned me loose in this fallen world?" He recollects a spirit that was present with him in the womb, the nest. And he takes great comfort merely in the fact that someone other than him exists. The narrow self-consciousness of Ulro is denied, and the possibility of self-transcendence through love seems within the hero's reach.

But such optimism proves short-lived. As Roethke later notes, "From me to Thee's a long and terrible way." His last three books, from *The Waking* (which brings *The Lost Son* cycle to a close) to *Words for the Wind* (1958) and the posthumous *The Far Field* (1964), record the steady movement toward self-transcendence on "the long journey out of the self." The myth of the lost son, with its attendant symbols, remains at the center of his work, but the myth widens. A similar pattern occurs in Blake as he recapitulates his personal myth in *Milton* and *Jerusalem* (both written and etched between 1804 and 1820). As Frye says in *Fearful Symmetry*, "*Milton* describes the attainment by the poet of the vision that *Jerusalem* expounds in terms of all humanity." It is the same myth, the story of the fall of man, his struggle through the cycles of nature, and his redemption, which occupies him almost from the beginning. Similarly, *Words for the Wind* describes the transcendence of the self through love of another, the major theme of Roethke in his middle years (1953–1959). *The Far Field* represents his *Jerusalem* or *Paradiso;* it recounts his hero's attainment of "the imperishable quiet at the heart of form."

North American Sequence, in particular, moves toward a fullness of vision characteristic of *Jerusalem.* Blake's identification of the New Golgotha with the body and his daring to look directly into the fierce light of the godhead find an analogue in Roethke's last meditations. In "The Longing," for instance, he writes,

> I would be a stream, winding between great striated
> rocks in late summer;
> A leaf, I would love the leaves, delighting in the
> redolent disorder of this mortal life.

The meditations all contain passages in which the poet wishes to identify with the world outside himself, to enter the body of nature and move with his "body thinking," thereby extending human consciousness, perhaps indefinitely. The mortal self, as in *Jerusalem,* is destined for extinction: "Annihilate the Selfhood in me." Nothing will come of retaining the old self but the dreaded sleep of Ulro. Los, the heroic figure in Blake's epic, confronts the specters that threaten him, saying,

> I know that Albion hath divided me, and that thou O my
> Spectre,
> Hast just cause to be irritated: but look stedfastly upon me:
> Comfort thyself in my strength the time will arrive
> When all Albions injuries shall cease, and when we shall
> Embrace him tenfold bright, rising from his tomb in
> immortality.

The great themes of *Jerusalem*—the restoration of the God in man and the triumph of imagination and fourfold vision—occupy Roethke as well in his last poems. In a moment of summary vision he declares,

My eyes extend beyond the farthest bloom of the waves;
I lose and find myself in the long water;
I am gathered together once more;
I embrace the world.

Roethke, unlike Blake in method, embraces the world to find redemptive vision; yet both poets find themselves transfigured, sloughing off the old self for the new one, the Self, to be born.

But the quest, even in this last book, remains antithetical. The hero often lapses into self-doubt as he proceeds. He reenters the jungle world of "The Lost Son" in "The Long Waters," which begins the *North American Sequence:*

I return where fire has been,
To the charred edge of the sea
Where the yellowish prongs of grass poke through the
     blackened ash,
And the bunched logs peel in the afternoon sunlight

In these "unsinging fields where no lungs breathe," the old fear returns, and the poet cries out for help to Blake's nurse, Mnetha, the guardian of Beulah: "Mnetha, Mother of Har, protect me / From the worm's advance." As in *Jerusalem,* the poet in *The Far Field* sharpens the antitheses, moving gradually toward illumination, restoration. In these last poems, Roethke is working out an *analogia visionis* not unlike Blake's; he reads the world as "A steady storm of correspondences!" and approaches that apocalypse where "one is One, free in the tearing wind." This comes close to Blake's "mysticism," which "is to be conceived neither as a human attempt to reach God nor a divine attempt to reach man, but as the realization in total experience of the identity of God and Man in which both the human creature and the superhuman Creator disappear," as Frye writes in *Fearful Symmetry.* Roethke puts it this way in "A Walk in Late Summer":

It lies upon us to undo the lie
Of living merely in the realm of time.
Existence moves toward a certain end—
A thing all earthly lovers understand.

92

This end toward which all existence moves is the restoration of that primal unity of perception sought by Blake; it also involves a resolution of contraries and a rejection of temporal or clock time (the specter of Urthona) in favor of an eternal present. For Blake, this condition is represented, finally, by Golgonooza, the city of art. For Roethke, in his final mystical sequences, the rose becomes his symbol of eternity (as it had for Dante, Rilke, Eliot, and Yeats before him): "this rose, this rose in the sea-wind, / Rooted in stone, keeping the whole of light."

The Far Field gives final evidence of Roethke's continuing dialogue with Blake; the *North American Sequence* with its search for "imperishable quiet at the heart of form" parallels Blake's "fearful symmetry." For it is in the city of art that fallen man is restored in the New Golgotha (Golgonooza). As God and man come together in the figure of the visionary poet, the apocalypse occurs, and the mythopoetic action moves from allegory to anagogy: the level where spiritual truth is embodied. It is, at last, at the level of mythic structure that Blake affected Roethke most significantly. This structure, according to Frye in *Fearful Symmetry*, has its most fitting analogy in music: "The beauty of *Jerusalem* is the beauty of intense concentration, the beauty of the Sutra, of the aphorisms which are the form of so much of the greatest vision, of a figured bass indicating the harmonic progression of ideas too tremendous to be expressed by a single melody" (p. 359). It is this same "harmonic progression of ideas" that underlies Roethke's mystical sequence too. Commenting on "The Longing," which opens the *North American Sequence,* Hugh B. Staples writes in "The Rose in the Sea-Wind" (1964),

> In a manner that suggests counterpoint in music, the principle of alternation controls the elaborate pattern of contrasting elements in the poem: body and soul, the sense of self and the release from subjectivity, earth and water, past and present, motion and stasis. . . . The sequence, then, can be regarded as a tone poem consisting of an overture ("The Longing"), in which the major themes appear, followed by four movements in which the tensions and oppositions of the whole sequence are summarized and move toward a resolution.

Roethke's sequence, then, moves in the manner of *Jerusalem*—via a series of gradually heightened antitheses—toward its resolution, the resurrection of Roethke's "final man" or Albion restored.

The last poem in Roethke's last book is "Once More, the Round," and here the poet provides more than could be wished for, a final summary of his complex relationship to Blake couched in Blakean terms, a poem in celebration of the cosmic dance and visionary mode:

> What's greater, Pebble or Pond?
> What can be known? The Unknown.
> My true self runs toward a Hill
> More! O More! visible.
>
> Now I adore my life
> With the Bird, the abiding Leaf,
> With the Fish, the questing Snail,
> And the Eye altering all;
> And I dance with William Blake
> For love, for Love's sake;
>
> And everything comes to One,
> As we dance on, dance on, dance on.

ROBERT FROST

Robert Frost was a canny poet, given to sly self-parody and ironic implication, full of contempt for most of his contemporaries, and quite willing to mislead sentimental readers into thinking that they understood his poems. Perhaps because he received so little in the way of public attention until his late thirties, when his first two volumes of poetry (*A Boy's Will* [1913] and *North of Boston* [1914]) were finally published, he craved the spotlight ever after. This mania for attention undid him—as a poet—in the end. As William H. Pritchard notes in *Frost: A Literary Life Reconsidered* (1984), "The final two decades of his life were those of a man whose productions as a poet, for the first time in his career, took a position secondary to his life as a public figure, a pundit, an institution, a cultural emissary." Frost's late posturings—in the late poems as well as in his life—were detrimental to his reputation among academic critics, who preferred the more abstruse work of T. S. Eliot, Ezra Pound, and Wallace Stevens to Frost's apparently straightforward pastoral verse, which did not cry out for exegesis on the same scale.

Yet even when Frost's public and critical reputations were most desperately at odds, the most perceptive readers (many of whom were poets themselves), such as Randall Jarrell, Robert Penn Warren, Lionel Trilling, and W. H. Auden, wrote important essays that, in essence, suggested that the "real" Robert Frost—as opposed to the grandfatherly figure who read simple moralistic poems to enthusiastic audiences across the country—was a complex, even difficult, poet of extraordinary power and lasting importance. In recent years, full-length studies by Reuben Brower, Richard Poirier, and Pritchard have permanently settled the question of whether Frost was a "major" poet in the sense that we apply that label to, say, Eliot or Yeats. Frost was. In more than half a century of active composition, he lodged dozens of poems in the collective literary memory of this country: poems that, like all worthy poems, constitute a palimpsest of meanings, admitting a number of plausible readings. Perhaps more essentially, Frost's poetry stays in the mind, providing comfort and consolation as well as a coherent sense of the world. As Randall Jarrell puts it in "To the Laodiceans," his famous essay on Frost, "When you know Frost's poems you know surprisingly well how the world seemed to one man." This, of course, is no small thing.

A Boy's Will, like so much of Frost, owes a great deal to the Wordsworthian tradition. Wordsworth insisted that a poet was no more (or less) than "a man speaking to men." With Samuel Taylor Coleridge and the other romantics, he urged poets to use the idioms of spoken English and, when possible, to rely on commonplace, even rustic, imagery. The romantics wanted to reconnect poetry to the folk tradition, to what Yeats referred to as "ballad, rann, and song." In basing his language on the speech of New England farmers, with its idiosyncratic diction and syntax, Frost was participating in one of the main trends in poetry since Wordsworth and Coleridge published *Lyrical Ballads* in 1798.

The emphasis on poetry as spoken language had been diminished by the Victorians and Edwardians, who preferred a more inflated, even rhetorical, type of poetry that depended for effects on such techniques as syntactical inversion, pleonasms (as when Tennyson called grass "the herb"), and Latinate diction. Among the most popular poets in the first decade of this century, when Frost began to write, were G. K. Chesterton and Alfred

Noyes, poets whose loose rattling meters and superficially poetical diction (as in "Lo! the wind doth strip the harried trees!") owed little to the rhythms and textures of ordinary speech. The Georgian poets (Edward Marsh, W. H. Davies, Edward Thomas, Edmund Blunden, and others), who came of age in the second decade of this century, made a radical break with their immediate predecessors, favoring realistic rural subjects and a direct idiomatic language. Frost was in England when Edward Marsh's famous *Georgian Anthology* (published in five editions between 1912 and 1922) achieved popularity, and his closest friend at the time was one of that anthology's exemplary poets, Edward Thomas. Somehow, Frost was able to adopt the virtues of Georgian poetry without succumbing to the shallowness of feeling, the slightness of intellectual content, and the false simplicity associated with the Georgian school.

Frost certainly did not see himself as belonging to a school. Indeed, he enjoyed bragging about his originality. "I dropped to an everyday level of diction that even Wordsworth kept above," he boasted to a friend in a letter. In letters, essays, and public lectures, he explained his self-conscious poetics, referring constantly to what he called "the sound of sense," a phrase that, as William Pritchard observes, can be read two ways, laying stress either on the word *sound* or the word *sense*. The phrase sets up two poles between which meaning shuttles to highlight the poem-as-music or the poem-as-meaning. Frost believed that a good poem "says" something before the reader understands it (Eliot said much the same thing), writing to his friend John Bartlett that the best way to hear "the abstract sound of sense is from voices behind a door that cuts off the words." A poet, according to Frost in *Selected Letters* (1964), must learn to "get cadences by skillfully breaking the sounds of sense with all their irregularity of accent across the regular beat of the metre." This was nothing new, of course: poets have always understood that meter is an abstraction and that one superimposes the rhythms of normal speech across the theoretical beat of the metrical pattern. Take, for instance, a passage from Milton's *Paradise Lost*:

> Hail, holy Light, offspring of Heav'n first-born,
> Or of the Eternal coeternal beam.
> May I express thee unblamed? since God is light,
> And never but in unapproached light
> Dwelt from eternity, dwelt then in thee,
> Bright effluence of bright essence increate.

If one were to scan this passage in strictly iambic terms, the first word, *hail,* would not be emphasized. Nor would *dwelt* in the fifth line. One would have to distort the word *offspring* to favor the first, not the second, syllable. The word *of* would outflank *Or* in the second line. The word *thee* in the third line would be absorbed, unaccented. In fact, the abstract meter bears little relation to the spoken language. The poetry is, instead, a function of the difference between the abstract and the actual performance of the lines. Gerard Manley Hopkins labeled this common poetic ploy "sprung rhythm," as if he had discovered it. Frost invented "the sound of sense" to explain something he found himself doing that poets had always done: playing the acoustic baseline of the metrical line off the irregular melodies of idiomatic speech. Frost's real originality lay in the actual practice of verse writing, where he could accommodate the sound of sense to New England's rural speech, a dialect that had not previously been exploited in poetry.

One can find Frost's theories in action in even the earliest of his poems, such as "Storm Fear":

> When the wind works against us in the dark,
> And pelts with snow
> The lower-chamber window on the east,
> And whispers with a sort of stifled bark,
> The beast,
> "Come out! Come out!"—
> It costs no inward struggle not to go,
> Ah, no!

That lovely first line owes its force to Frost's colloquial rhythms' working against the grain of the blank iambic line (in which stresses fall on *the* and *in,* whereas *When* and *wind* remain unstressed). It is the blunt spondaic quality of "When the wind works," with its heavy alliteration, that attracts our ear. The line is also subtly mimetic, the rhythms and sounds suggesting the pull of the wind and the way the speaker would feel about going outside in such weather. In the seventh line, which is quintessential Frost, the colloquial use of *costs* (with its oddly and abstractly negative direct object, "no inward struggle") enchants the ear: "It costs no inward struggle not to go." There was nothing quite like this in English or American poetry before Robert Frost.

The poems of *A Boy's Will* and *North of Boston,* two of Frost's strongest books, together define his pastoral world. It was not for nothing that Robert Frost was once a high school Latin teacher: his poetry shows intimate familiarity with the pastoral tradition embodied in the poems of Theocritus, Virgil, and others. John F. Lynen defines the pastoral mode in relation to Frost in an incisive book-length essay on this subject called *The Pastoral Art of Robert Frost* (1960). He writes, "The pastoral genre can best be defined as a particular synthesis of attitudes toward the rural world. . . . Pastoral comes to life whenever the poet is able to adopt its special point of view—whenever he casts himself in the role of the country dweller and writes about life in terms of the contrast between the rural world, with its rustic scenery and naive, humble folk, and the great outer world of the powerful, the wealthy, and the sophisticated." That is, the pastoral poet is *not* himself a rustic who writes simple poems for his country neighbors. He is a sophisticate who looks to the rural world for emblems, symbols, instances. He believes that the rural world is representative of human society in general, and he chooses to limit his poetic world to a specific place with a discrete number of objects for contemplation. Symbols taken from the pastoral landscape that implicitly refer to the great world beyond the rustic scene appear powerfully (and paradoxically) amplified by self-conscious limitation.

Among the subtlest poems in *A Boy's Will* is "Mowing," in every way a typical Frost pastoral:

> There was never a sound beside the wood but one,
> And that was my long scythe whispering to the ground.
> What was it it whispered? I knew not well myself;
> Perhaps it was something about the heat of the sun,
> Something, perhaps, about the lack of sound—
> And that was why it whispered and did not speak.
> It was no dream of the gift of idle hours,
> Or easy gold at the hand of fay or elf:
> Anything more than the truth would have seemed too weak
> To the earnest love that laid the swale in rows,
> Not without feeble-pointed spikes of flowers
> (Pale orchises), and scared a bright green snake.
> The fact is the sweetest dream that labor knows.
> My long scythe whispered and left the hay to make.

The poem's narrator is a farmer at work with a scythe, which makes the only sound the speaker can hear, even though (as Poirier points out) there surely must have been other sounds about: the rustle of wind in the grass, birdsong, perhaps even a tractor in the distance. But Frost is a thoroughly humanistic farmer, insisting that his own agency is crucial to the process of signification, to *making meaning*. The narrator, no ordinary farmer, meditates on the sound of his mowing, wondering if the point about the sound is the absence implied by the presence of the sound itself: "Something, perhaps, about the lack of sound." He resorts, finally, to a mundane (that is, earthly) resolution that doesn't answer the question but puts the questioner at his ease: "Anything more than the truth would have seemed too weak / To the earnest love that laid the swale in rows." So far so good. The fact of mowing (writing/speaking/thinking) needs no embellishment; its actuality is not in question. The work is its own pleasure and reward, its own meaning. Fine. But in that penultimate summary line of almost infinite suggestiveness, Frost insists, "The fact is the sweetest dream that labor knows." A fact is, indeed, not something tangible after all, as in the stone that Dr. Johnson kicked to demonstrate to his friend Boswell that matter existed. Facts are dreams, what Shakespeare called "airy nothings." Frost has pulled the rug out from under us once again.

As with so many Frost poems, one thinks one "has it" but one doesn't. In "Mowing," as in so many of these early pastoral poems, Frost invites the reader into his world, saying, "I shan't be gone long.—You come too." Once into this world, however, we realize that the way out is not so simple. The poet can only lead one to the complex image: the woodpile (in "The Wood-Pile"), the man in the field with a pitchfork ("Putting in the Seed"), the old man in his cottage who can no longer "keep" a house ("An Old Man's Winter Night"), the edge of a dark forest ("Stopping by Woods on a Snowy Evening"). The act of interpreting this experience is left to the reader; the poet, much as the farmer in "Mowing," is content to walk away from his work and let it "make." The poet's job is not one of interpretation. He presents the image, which is drawn from a "truth" that is, of course, no more than "a dream," albeit a sweet one. Idealists such as Plato, Thomas Aquinas, and Bishop Berkeley would all, in their different ways, have applauded Frost for not allowing the concrete fact too much sway.

Despite this incipient idealism, Frost thought of himself as a celebrant of earth, of fact. Like the Georgians, he considered himself a realist, emphasizing the down to earth, the rueful laugh, a Yankee stoicism. *North of*

Boston and *Mountain Interval* (1916) exude a philosophy of limitation, of groundedness. "Love has earth to which she clings / With hills and circling arms about," he writes in "Bond and Free." "Earth's the right place for love," he says in "Birches," adding, "I don't know where it's likely to go better." Unlike his spiritual forebear, Ralph Waldo Emerson, Frost does not feel constrained to spiral off into some outer region. This does not mean that he rejects heavenly things, the realm of spirit; rather, his poems, as James M. Cox says in "Robert Frost and the End of the New England Line" (1974), "become strongholds where imaginative leverage can powerfully be exerted—where, in other words, the earth itself seems sufficient ground on which to stand and does not have to be transformed into symbolic nature."

Frost's sense of limitations is nowhere more apparent than in the fierce little dramas of New England farm life he presented in the early collections, such as "The Death of the Hired Man," "Home Burial," "The Hill Wife," and "Out, Out—." In "Home Burial," for instance, we encounter a tense family scene as a husband and wife are locked in silent battle after the death of an infant. Like black smoke, the question of who is to blame hangs in the air they breathe. The distraught wife pauses on the staircase, looking out to her baby's grave, which her husband digs too vigorously for her grief to bear. He works methodically, "Making the gravel leap and leap in air." In Frost's harsh rural world, man and nature seem inextricably bound to work out whatever fate has ordained. In this, Frost exhibits an innate conservatism: reason is never exalted (indeed, it is ridiculed in poems like "The Bear"); people have only minimal control over what happens. Acceptance is all. "Three foggy mornings and one rainy day / Will rot the best birch fence a man can build," says the father of the dead infant, much as the narrator at the end of "Out, Out—," having witnessed the unimaginable death of a young man in a chainsaw accident, says quite plainly, "No more to build on there." The response of his family is equally stoic but not unfeeling: "And they, since they / Were not the one dead, turned to their affairs."

The pastoral aspect of Frost is implicit in these poems too. "Out, Out—," for instance, with its specific allusion to Shakespeare, is not the work of a ploughman-poet. The title directs the reader back to Macbeth's famous soliloquy that follows upon his wife's suicide. Life for the tragic hero of Shakespeare's play comes down to nothing but "a tale / Told by an idiot, full of sound and fury, / Signifying nothing." Macbeth has not understood the meaning of death nor that he is responsible for his wife's demise. The boy in Frost's poem, on the other hand, "sees all." He understands that in his agrarian world a boy without a hand would be dependent for his livelihood on others. He sees that his life has been radically, if accidentally, changed by the loss of a hand. Frost, like Virgil and Theocritus before him, comments on the larger world from a rural "unsophisticated" viewpoint. But his emblems, his rural myths and dramas, radiate meaning, turning the limitations of the poem to his advantage in commenting on the human condition generally. One cannot help but think that Frost actually believes that the rural world is coherent, if not superior to the urban world. He appears, at least, to celebrate the doggedness of his country people, even if—as with the mad wives of "The Hill Wife" or "Home Burial"—the rural life exacts its pound of flesh.

Unlike Eliot, Pound, Yeats, or Stevens—his fellow modernist poets—Frost did not "develop" from book to book. That is, one can place a good early poem, such as "Mowing," next to a good late poem, such as "The Most of It," without finding obvious differences in approach, style, or even subject matter. It is true, overall, that Frost's work decreases in quality as the career lengthens and the poet becomes more of a public figure; one has increasingly to rummage among inferior poems to find poems of depth and power after the publication of *West-Running Brook* in 1928. Nevertheless, Frost continued to produce poems equal to his best early work almost to the end. An argument could be made that several of his later poems—"The Most of It," "The Subverted Flower," "Design" (a late revision of an early poem called "In White"), "Directive," "The Silken Tent," and "Take Something Like a Star"—show, if anything, an increase in power and subtlety as Frost began to reckon the price he had paid for his art.

Lionel Trilling first emphasized the dark side of Robert Frost at a party in New York on the occasion of the poet's eighty-fifth birthday. As reprinted in *Robert Frost* (1962, edited by James M. Cox), Trilling said,

> I have to say that my Frost is not the Frost I seem to perceive existing in the minds of so many of his admirers. He is not the Frost who confounds the characteristically modern practice of poetry by his notable democratic simplicity of utterance: on the contrary. He is not the Frost who controverts the bitter modern astonishment of human life: the opposite is so. He is not the Frost who reassures us by his affirmation of old virtues, simplicities, pieties, and ways of feeling: anything but.

Trilling went on to compare Frost to Sophocles, "the poet people loved most . . . because he made plain to them the terrible things of human life."

Trilling drew attention to some of Frost's best work, such as "Design," "Acquainted with the Night," and "Desert Places," poems as chilling, as redolent of evil, as anything Franz Kafka ever wrote. Indeed, "Design" takes the old argument—that the sheer existence of design in the universe argues for the existence of God—and turns it on its head, showing us a ghastly scene: a blighted spider killing a white moth on a bleached-out flower. "What but design of darkness to appall?" he asks, the word *appall* echoing through its Latin root, meaning to 'make white.' It would be nothing less than foolish to read Frost as a simple purveyor of homely truths and Yankee wisdom.

It would also be a mistake to imagine that Frost is easy to understand because he is easy to read. Even poems that focus on casual country scenes, such as "Spring Pools" or "The Road Not Taken," can be maddeningly difficult. They are certainly deceptive. The latter, one of Frost's most popular poems, is worth examining in detail:

> Two roads diverged in a yellow wood,
> And sorry I could not travel both
> And be one traveler, long I stood
> And looked down one as far as I could
> To where it bent in the undergrowth;
>
> Then took the other, as just as fair,
> And having perhaps the better claim,
> Because it was grassy and wanted wear;
> Though as for that, the passing there
> Had worn them really about the same,
>
> And both that morning equally lay
> In leaves no step had trodden black.
> Oh, I kept the first for another day!
> Yet knowing how way leads on to way,
> I doubted if I should ever come back.
>
> I shall be telling this with a sigh
> Somewhere ages and ages hence:

Two roads diverged in a wood, and I—
I took the one less traveled by,
And that has made all the difference.

Usually quoted out of context, the last three lines are among the best known in modern poetry. They are commonly paraphrased as follows: "Life often presents two choices: the well-trodden path and the more rugged, unworn path, the path of individualism. Frost advises the reader to follow him, to take the unconventional route, because that—for him—made all the difference; that is, the poet's nonconformity accounts for his happiness and success." This is a crude but not uncommon summary of how many, perhaps most, readers have interpreted these lines. In public performances and interviews, Frost himself encouraged this kind of misreading. Nonetheless, one must listen to the advice of D. H. Lawrence and trust the tale, not the teller. A close look at the poem reveals that Frost's walker encounters two nearly identical paths: so he insists, repeatedly. The walker looks down first one, then the other, *"as just as fair."* Indeed, "the passing there / Had worn them really about the same." As if the reader hasn't gotten the message, Frost says for a third time: "And both that morning equally lay / In leaves no step had trodden black." What, then, can we make of the final stanza? My guess is that Frost, the wily ironist, is saying something like this: "When I am old, like all old men, I shall make a myth of my life. I shall pretend, as we all do, that I took the less traveled road. But I shall be lying." Frost signals the mockingly self-inflated tone of the last stanza by repeating the word *I*, which rhymes—several times—with the inflated word *sigh*. Frost *wants* the reader to know that what he will be saying, that he took the road less traveled, is a fraudulent position.

"The Road Not Taken," like so much in Frost, resists easy interpretation. The poet presents contradictory readings within the same poem, tempting the reader this way, then that. "Mowing," "Putting in the Seed," "Birches," "Two Look at Two," "Mending Wall," "The Grindstone," "Gathering Leaves"—each is, in its way, a poem about the process of discovery, what Poirier calls "the work of knowing." The road to knowledge, in Frost's shifty poetics, is tortuous, and the outcome is never guaranteed, especially because Frost is the reader's guide and one "Who only has at heart your getting lost." That last line is from "Directive," a late poem that can be read as a road map to Frost's imaginary country:

Back out of all this now too much for us,
Back in a time made simple by the loss
Of detail, burned, dissolved, and broken off
Like graveyard marble sculpture in the weather,
There is a house that is no more a house
Upon a farm that is no more a farm
And in a town that is no more a town.

It seems one could never in reality approach this sacred place, lost in time, buried in language. The poet is our archaeologist and guide, unearthing the Holy Grail (the poem?), which is really nothing more than a goblet taken from a children's playhouse. Ever *homo ludens,* man-the-player, Frost plays with the rapt seriousness of a child. As with the ancient Hippocrene, the spring on Mount Helicon that fed the muses, there is a brook on this imaginary property:

Your destination and your destiny's
A brook that was the water of the house,
Cold as a spring as yet so near its source,
Too lofty and original to rage.

One cannot help but hear in these beautiful lines Frost's churlish commentary on the poetry of his age, which he apparently took to be low and unoriginal and raging, unlike the high original calm of his verse. Ever the didact, he is offering the world a "Directive." The poem, for him, is a means of controlling the chaos of ordinary life; it offers "a momentary stay against confusion," as he liked to say. In a time of increasing cacophony, when even the static begins to sound good, Frost's antidote is as powerful as ever. This is the essential Frost, the notoriously unreliable guide of "Directive" who—by his wit and guile—entices his reader to the secret playhouse by the brook, where he takes that unsuspecting follower by the collar and says, "Drink and be whole again beyond confusion."

EMERSON AND FROST
The Present Act of Vision

The etymologist finds the deadest word to have once been a bril-
liant picture. Language is fossil poetry.
—RALPH WALDO EMERSON

When Wordsworth said, "Write with your eye upon object" . . .
he really meant something more. That something carries out
what I mean by writing with your ear to the voice.
—ROBERT FROST

La poète est celui qui regarde.
—ANDRÉ GIDE, *LE TRAITÉ DU NARCISSE*

I

Only in recent years has the centrality of romanticism for
any serious reappraisal of modern poetry become clear.
Modernist leaders such as Ezra Pound, T. E. Hulme, and
T. S. Eliot should be blamed for this lapse, of course; they
wanted their "revolutionary" poetics to occupy a position
similar to that of their romantic counterparts who, a cen-
tury earlier, overthrew a century of neoclassical decorum.
But modernism was not a reversal of romanticism; it was
an extension of it, a modification. The connections
between Yeats and the romantics, especially Blake and
Shelley, have been pointed out, as have the major links
between Wallace Stevens, Wordsworth, and the French

symbolists. Even Eliot himself has been exposed for romantic "tendencies." Of the major modern poets Frost alone has remained untied to any specific romantic ancestors; indeed, he is on his own in this century, a dominant yet perpetually enigmatic figure, and it would be a mistake to force unnatural ties.

Granted Frost's rugged singularity, it remains true that his most fundamental notions about poetry, its nature and function, come out of the romantic mainstream. He is especially an American romantic—one whose primary source can be traced to Emerson, himself the watershed for American poetry, which divides from his high peak into innumerable streams: Whitman, Ginsberg, and Pound forming one major valley, Thoreau, Robinson, and Frost another. Anomalous figures like Emily Dickinson and Theodore Roethke both, in different ways, owe a great deal to Emerson too. The mind in fact boggles in the face of Emerson's generative powers, and his influence on American poetry has yet to be thoroughly examined, though Hyatt Waggoner maps the terrain in *American Poets: From the Puritans to the Present* (1968). And his chapter on Frost is the starting point for any consideration of Frost and Emersonian thinking.

What Emerson does in essence is to give European romanticism a local habitation, a vernacular. One fact that in part accounts for the survival of romanticism on such a broad scale has been its ability to find native expression in starkly different cultures. The English, apart from the Americans, were among the last to join the revolution. As could be expected, the shape that romanticism assumed in England was distinct from that in France or Germany. Yet certain basic principles give European and, later, Anglo-American romanticism just enough coherence to make any discussion of an international "movement" credible. In a sense Emerson's *Nature* (1836) can be thought of as a summary document, a recapitulation of key romantic ideas in the American vernacular.

"To speak truly," Emerson writes, "few adult persons can *see* nature" (italics mine); this is the premise of *Nature,* the point of departure. Modern secular man, cut off from traditional sources of revelation (God, sacred texts, the pulpit), finds himself alone in the world, a prisoner of self-consciousness. The sense of being severed from the external world is the primary source of all truly romantic writing. Given this separation, the poet's job becomes to restore what Yeats called Unity of Being, which involves a recovery of true vision. According to romantic writers from Jean Jacques Rousseau to Wordsworth and Emerson, the child—possessed of a naturally innocent eye—enjoys a special relation to nature. The child's vision has not yet been occluded; as Wordsworth says in his famous "Ode" (1807),

> There was a time when meadow, grove and stream,
> The earth, and every common sight,
> To me did seem
> Apparelled in celestial light,
> The glory and the freshness of a dream.
> It is not now as it hath been of yore;—
> Turn wheresoe'er I may,
> By night or day,
> The things which I have seen I now can see no more.

Or, as Emerson writes in this vein (in *Nature* [1836]), "The lover of nature is he whose inward and outward senses are still truly adjusted to each other; who has retained the spirit of infancy even into the era of manhood." He speaks of an "occult relationship" between mind and the natural world and in this special context vision has a superior role: "I become a transparent eyeball; I am nothing; I see all." Thus runs the well-known formulation.

Emersonian vision, then, involves an alignment of natural objects with the inward eye, a condition of "radical correspondence between visible things and human thought." To an "aroused intellect," he says, "facts, dull . . . despised things," become "an Epiphany of God." Emphasis therefore devolves upon the moment of alignment, the present act of vision. One finds endless versions of this idea, from Wordsworth's "spots of time" to Proust's *moments privilégiés* or Joyce's "epiphanies." The romantic moment of vision, in which *chronos* becomes *kairos*—in Frank Kermode's phrase—survives into modern poetry intact. The idea that a deep image underlies every good poem is indeed the unspoken assumption of Frost's classic essay, "The Figure a Poem Makes." A poem begins, he observes, with an initial image, then "runs a course of lucky events, and ends in a clarification of life . . . a momentary stay against confusion." The initial image is not discarded, for the poem "has an outcome that though unforeseen was predestined from the first image of the original mood."

The whole notion of poetry as *clarification,* of course, presupposes the primacy of vision; the poet, seeing with the inner eye, grasps the object, contemplates it, transforms it into a symbol. The artist's mind flares outward like a lamp to illumine the object, which becomes something more than itself in the process, a representative object, the center of a widening context of vision. As Frost wrote to a friend, "Imagery and after-imagery are about all there is to poetry. Synecdoche and synecdoche." The poet allows the part to stand for the whole, thus endowing natural facts with greater meanings than they normally would carry. Again, in *Nature,* Emerson makes a similar point: "The world is a temple whose walls are covered with emblems, pictures and commandments of the Deity—in this, there is no fact in nature which does not carry the whole sense of nature." Likewise, in his essay on Plato, he reformulates the synecdochal function, saying that metaphysical truths can be apprehended through objects in nature: Truths "are knowable, because being from one, things correspond. There is a scale; and the correspondence of heaven to earth, of matter to mind, of the part to the whole, is our guide." Here Emerson writes directly in the visionary mode; his doctrine of correspondence provides a way for the "true love of nature" to bridge the gap between self and other, mind and nature. The symbolic image itself, the illumined object, assumes a central role in the quest for unity. Frost, in his 1930 essay "Education by Poetry," takes his place beside Emerson, saying, "Greatest of all attempts to say one thing in terms of another is the philosophical attempt to say matter in terms of spirit, or spirit in terms of matter, to make the final unity." This final unity becomes, as it were, the ultimate clarification.

Like Wordsworth before him, Emerson in *Nature* argues for the equality of natural objects: "The distinctions which we make . . . of low and high, honest and base, disappear when nature is used as a symbol." Because the most commonplace or trivial thing in nature, seen properly, is a symbol *in potentia,* there can be no arbitrary banishment of certain "base" or "low" phenomena from the poetic field of vision. Although Emerson's poetry is disappointing in this respect, Whitman and Frost fill their poems with objects base and low. The "dull . . . despised fact" becomes a chink in eternity, a symbol, when studied by the aroused intellect, as in so many of Frost's best lyrics, such as "The Wood-pile" or "Design" or "Mowing," in which he claims "the fact is the sweetest dream that labor knows." Whereas the philosopher is free to abstract (*abtractare,* pull away from) reality, the poet is bound to move closer, to return to things as they are. "Say it!" William Carlos Williams writes in book 1 of *Paterson* (1946). "No ideas but in things." An idea cannot become a symbol: only an object can. Perhaps of all modern poets Stevens has explained this best in "An Ordinary Evening in New Haven" (1950):

We keep coming back and coming back
To the real: to the hotel instead of the hymns
That fall upon it out of the wind. We seek

The poem of pure reality, untouched
By trope or deviation, straight to the word,
Straight to the transfixing object, to the object

At the exactest point at which it is itself,
Transfixing by being purely what it is,
A view of New Haven, say, through the uncertain eye,

The eye made clear of uncertainty, with the sight
Of simple seeing, without reflection. We seek
Nothing beyond reality. Within it,

Everything.

Stevens locates the origin of the lyric in vision: beholding the object. In the greater romantic lyric (as defined by M. H. Abrams) description gives way to evaluation and finally to revelation. Art becomes what D. H. Lawrence in *Etruscan Places* (1927) calls an "act of attention," a sustained vision. The eye, the *inner* eye, in recollection lights upon and illumines a significant object or experience, which is in turn contemplated until its symbolic aspect is revealed, leading to a resolution. The classic example is Wordsworth's "Tintern Abbey," though Matthew Arnold's "Dover Beach" and Whitman's "Crossing Brooklyn Ferry" fit the pattern. Among modern examples Frost's "Directive" may well be the finest example of the genre, founded as it is upon a single image, "a house that is no more a house." Ingenious description gives way to brilliancies of evaluation:

This was no playhouse but a house in earnest.
Your destination and your destiny's
A brook that was the water of the house,
Cold as a spring as yet so near its source,
Too lofty and original to rage.

The initial image has become symbolic, and the brook signals a widening context of meaning as the poem hurtles toward its resolution: "Here are your waters and your watering place. / Drink and be whole again beyond confusion."

In "Directive," as in most lyrics of its kind, the landscape or setting of the poem is at once its occasion and center of gravity. The speaker is a persona, a mind in action; this is a defining characteristic, the psychic dramatization, the present act of vision. In *The Poetry of Experience* (1957) Robert Langbaum points to similarities between the romantic lyric and the dramatic monologue. Both forms share the presence of mental drama and often the presence of an auditor. A line could be traced from early romantic "dramatic lyrics" or monodramas through Browning and Tennyson down to Eliot and Frost. But the dramatic monologue usually lacks the visionary destruction, with its implicit metaphor of descent (into memory, reverie), the inward journey, and the progress from the literal to the imaginative (description to revelation). Frost was a master of both the monologue ("Home Burial," "The Death of the Hired Man," "A Hundred Collars," "The Hill Wife") and the romantic lyric ("The Wood-Pile," "Desert Places," "Design"), but what lifts a poem like "Directive" into the category of greatness is the joining of both forms. It is at the same time a narrative and visionary performance.

Frost counted himself among the "new" poets, those who attempted a break with late Victorian verse. His alliance with Pound should point this out. And part of this break involved the rejection of romanticism as a category, one equated with dreaminess and illusion, Gothic nostalgia, poetical diction, and the substitution of magic for plain sense. Nonetheless, as the true debt of modernism to romanticism becomes known, it seems clear that Frost's most fundamental notions about poetry—*and* his practice of the art—owe a great deal to what Abrams calls "the poetics of expression." More specifically, Frost is an American romantic, one whose poetic field of vision is best defined in terms of its special relation to Emerson's.

II

Frost's typical response to Emerson, particularly in later years, is one of acceptance with major reservations. "I have friends it bothers when I am accused of being Emersonian," he writes in his important essay "On Emerson" (1956), "that is, a cheerful Monist, for whom evil does not exist, or if it does exist, needn't last forever." He goes on: "A melancholy dualism is the only soundness."

Indeed, Frost's universe admits a great deal more of evil than Emerson's from the start. The end of *Nature* typifies the latter's optimism; his eyes tend perpetually upward: "Every spirit builds itself a house, and beyond its house a world, and beyond its world a heaven." Conversely, Frost's eyes move earthward; he regards the immediate world and frames one question repeatedly: "What to make of a diminished thing?" Here Frost's modernism obtains, for any poet writing in the period after the Great War—to be treated seriously—must accept a diminished world. If, as Emerson speculated, a man is a god in ruins, the emphasis falls upon the ruins, although a number of modern poets, including Frost, have discovered a divine aspect of man that persists despite diminished expectations. Humans' recalcitrance, their capacity to endure and finally to celebrate *within* the conditions of ruin, is what attracts Frost. The point is better put by the poet himself in "Lost in Heaven," one of his least read poems; the speaker, out walking, sees a brief opening in the clouds while searching for "old sky-marks in the blue."

> But stars were scarce in that part of the sky,
> And no two were of the same constellation—
> No one was bright enough to identify;
> So 'twas with not ungrateful consternation,
>
> Seeing myself well lost once more, I sighed,
> "Where, where in Heaven am I? But don't tell me!
> Oh, opening clouds, by opening on me wide.
> Let's let my heavenly lostness overwhelm me."

The poet does not give in to fear or despair; he allows he admits the Emersonian possibility of "heavenly lostness," suspending his disbelief momentarily. Diminishment is not enough.

When Frost refers directly to Emerson, it is usually to praise him—then qualify or contradict him in almost the same breath, as in *A Masque of Reason* (1945), when Job says,

> Yet I suppose what seems to us confusion
> Is not confusion, but the form of forms,

The serpent's tail stuck down the serpent's throat,
Which is the symbol of eternity
And also of the way all things come round,
Or of how rays return upon themselves,
To quote the greatest Western poem yet.
Though I hold rays deteriorate to nothing:
First white, then red, then ultrared, then out.

"The greatest Western poem yet" is Emerson's "Uriel," in which the archangel of the sun declares,

"Line in nature is not found;
Unit and universe are round;
In vain produced, all rays return;
Evil will bless, and ice will burn."

In "On Emerson" Frost quotes "Unit and universe are round" and says, "Another poem could be made from that, to the effect that ideally in thought only is a circle round. In practice, in nature, the circle becomes an oval. As a circle it has one center—Good. As an oval it has two centers—Good and Evil." The metaphor could be taken further: Frost is always turning Emerson's circles into ovals; he usually refuses to contradict his master; he modifies by extension.

The dialogue with Emerson carries through Frost's career; as Waggoner says, Frost's world is defined by "its special closeness to and distance from Emerson's world." In many of Frost's poems one encounters a worldview grounded in Emersonian presuppositions. The certainty is missing, of course, replaced by a rueful skepticism; the assumed benevolence of the Creator seems missing too—that dogged faith of Emerson's in a mysterious "unity" underlying nature. Yet certain key Emersonian notions persist in Frost: the concentration on the individual quest for selfhood, the belief in a occult relationship between man and nature, and the reliance on the natural world for sustenance. Another profound similarity, perhaps the central one, is the insistence upon sense experience, and vision in particular, as the way toward final truth. This approach to knowledge has roots deep in Lockian epistemology. Seeing is believing. The bedrock of both poets is the raw data of experience: "I thank the Lord for crudity which is rawness, which is raw material, which is the part of life not yet worked up into form, or at least not worked all the way up," Frost says in a letter to R. P. T. Coffin (March 7, 1938).

On this latter point Frost and Emerson make their critical contact. Both believed that "the whole of nature is a metaphor of the human mind" (*Nature*), though Frost was often called, to his annoyance, a "materialist." In "Education by Poetry" Frost speaks plainly: "It is wrong to call anybody a materialist simply because he tries to say spirit in terms of matter, as if that were a sin. . . . The only materialist . . . is the man who gets lost in his material without a gathering metaphor to throw it into shape and order. He is the lost soul." Whereas Emerson, in his poetry, makes no effort to disguise his spiritual motives, Frost takes great pains to avoid the appearance of writing "metaphysical poetry." Although many of his best lyrics, such as "Mowing," must certainly be read as elaborate conceits, the first impulse of the reader is to eschew all secondary meanings. As in symbolist verse, the image is left on its own: the tenor is stripped of its vehicle: the metaphor remains austerely implicit. The greatness of such poetry derives from the subtle resonance of its symbolism: given that nature is the symbol of the spirit, the poet need do no more than *see* nature properly. Description becomes revelation. One knows the whole by the part. Frost's virtue is in seeing "the thought upon the object" (in Emerson's great phrase): he observes nature with the intensity of a visionary, perpetually aware of the larger realms underlying the concrete image.

The ideal romantic lyric, then, is *reflection* in the radical sense: the illumined representation of a true image. And the image, as Pound says, is not merely visual; it represents an emotional complex as well. The image must shine inwardly as well as outwardly, the fact observed, the fact observed from within. So Frost notes in "Mowing": "The fact is the sweetest dream that labor knows," alluding to the final spirituality or insubstantial quality of all facts perceived as emblematic. The transmutation of substance into spirit is the poet's goal as *seer*. Writing in "Robert Frost and the End of the New England Line" (1974), James M. Cox says that "Emerson's primordial act is Man *seeing* Nature. If he truly sees nature, then he becomes a transparent eyeball, and if he becomes that, he can truly see nature. That is the first and last metaphor for Emerson." Cox explains how the "I" is constantly becoming the "Eye," the *self,* in process, becoming the *soul,* the *personality,* likewise, becoming *character,* an inward quality of being that precedes behavior. These are the transformations witnessed in the poems of both poets—as the image gathers to itself the luminous significance of the fact truly seen, the I in process becoming the Eye, the present act of vision. It is the process that determines, finally, the shape of so many romantic and postromantic lyrics, including those of Emerson and Frost.

III

The progress from description to revelation, from the literal to the imaginative, can be charted in both poets. Emerson's best lyrics, like Frost's, have at their center an image or at least a metaphor. Emerson is less of a poet, of course. Many of his poems lack cohesion: they get caught in the updraft of abstraction—and meaning is lost to the heavens like wood ash. He is best in the shortest poems, his epigrams—many of which sound distinctly Frost-like. "Suum Cuique" (To each his own) would not surprise anyone if it were printed in Frost's *Collected Poems* (1949):

> The rain has spoiled the farmer's day:
> Shall sorrow put my books away?
> Thereby two days are lost:
> Nature shall mind her own affairs;
> I will attend my proper cares,
> In rain, or sun, or frost.

The poem arises out of a direct factual observation—a commonplace; it rapidly moves toward contrast—the intrusion of a speaker whose productive day is also threatened. Then Nature arrives, a neutral third, a moral neutralizer. The implication here, of course, is that every man is alone with Nature, free to work his own relation with this great and threatening force. The puritan notion of every man alone with his God no doubt underlies this idea. Emerson's speaker is thus relieved of one kind of responsibility toward the farmer, but he confronts a more powerful demand, that he attend to the minute fluctuations of his spirit, "in rain, or sun, or frost."

Emerson's model leads directly to a poem such as Frost's "A Mood Apart." The speaker is digging in his garden, when

> becoming aware of some boys from school
> Who had stopped outside the fence to spy,
> I stopped my song and almost heart,

For any eye is an evil eye
That looks in onto a mood apart.

Frost's point complements Emerson's, emphasizing the uniqueness of every person's angle of vision, as well as the responsibility of each to a personal perspective. Any eye that interferes is an "evil eye," for the present act of vision demands solitude, the silence of complete attention, submission of all senses to the inner eye. Both poets concern themselves with the problem of sustaining the image and the conflict of reality and the imagination, what Stevens calls "a war between the mind and sky," a chief subject of romantic poetry.

Emerson's typical persona, again like Frost's, is the Solitary, a familiar character in Wordsworth and Shelley—the man who lives outside civilization (with the demands of *civitas*) or one who, at least, breaks out occasionally for solace in nature, a refreshment of the senses, especially the visual. Emerson's "The Apology" comes to mind:

Think me not unkind and rude
That I walk alone in grove and glen;
I go to the god of the wood
To fetch his word to men.

The prophet comes in from the wilderness bearing Truth; but that truth can only be found in nature: "To go into solitude, a man needs to retire as much from his chamber as from society. . . . But if a man would be alone, let him look at the stars." So the pattern of self-imposed isolation and discovery occurs in Frost from beginning to end (as it does in Emerson), in poems like "A Late Walk," "Waiting," "The Vantage Point," or "Reluctance" from the early work or later poems like "Come In," "The Most of It," "Directive," or "The Quest of the Purple-Fringed." These poems all, in their ways, recapitulate the theme of separation and illumination.

Frost, I should add, was more an ironist than Emerson ever could be. What poet writing in this century is not? The revelations Frost attains are always more tentative, exploiting the evasive ambiguities of language wherever possible. As he wrote to a close friend in 1932, "I have written to keep the over curious out of the secret places of my mind both in my verse and in my letters to such as you." Frost, then, *appears* to be a wry skeptical materialist—and a pessimist to boot—the antithesis of Emerson, but the truth lies elsewhere. He stands directly behind Emerson, a unique modern visionary; as Cox observes, "Indeed Frost's skepticism and relativism, though they have deeply qualified the transcendental realm of Emerson and Thoreau, have if anything merely made his eye for nature more acute." Frost in fact fulfills the Emersonian goals in ways Emerson himself, being less of a poet, never could. The true goal of vision, in which the I becomes the Eye, the Self becomes Soul, is not easily attained, though a false version, an illusion, is easily come by. As the poet answers in Emerson's "The Sphinx":

> "The Lethe of Nature
> Can't trance him again,
> Whose soul sees the perfect,
> Which his eyes seek in vain.
>
> "To vision profounder,
> Man's spirit must dive;
> His aye-rolling orb
> At no goal will arrive."

The physical eye, the outer eye, must give way to the inner; the "Lethe of Nature" must be avoided, for nature can be deceptive. The Sea, personified in Emerson's "Seashore," says, "I too have arts and sorceries; / Illusion dwells forever with the wave." The sea can deal with the "credulous" species of man, it claims. Less overtly, Frost makes the same point in "Neither Out Far Nor In Deep," one of his most haunting poems. The poet-speaker watches some people standing by the sea, backs to the land, staring out across the waters. They ignore, in their outward gazing, the mirrorlike surf right under them:

> They cannot look out far.
> They cannot look in deep.
> But when was that ever a bar
> To any watch they keep?

Real scorn comes through as the lyric snaps its tail, the poet disassociating himself from the impersonal "they" who keep watch. *Keep*, as it were, is a key Frostian term, and one rich in ambiguity. As a verb, the *Oxford English*

Dictionary lists fifty-eight separate entries for it, though its original (Old English) meaning is 'to seize, lay hold of; to snatch, take.' The visual element attaches itself around the year 1000, when keep becomes a common translation of the Latin *observare*. Frost takes the act of "keeping," *seeing*, as the poet's main job, but he derides those false visionaries (the watchers in "Neither Far Out") who search the horizon for truth without really knowing where or how to look. They should begin looking, of course, where they stand, at the margin, the "wetter ground like glass," the mirror of nature that reflects them. The sea perhaps represents the mysterious realm of the ineffable, the *beyond;* the land, on which Frost's searchers after truth turn their backs, is the material world. Frost seems to have disliked almost anyone who was an extremist, one who (as he says in "The Bear")

> sits back on his fundamental butt
> With lifted snout and eyes (if any) shut,
> (He almost looks religious but he's not),
> And back and forth he sways from cheek to cheek,
> At one extreme agreeing with one Greek,
> At the other agreeing with another Greek—
> Which may be thought, but only so to speak.

Here, as elsewhere, Frost derides the falsely pious, the poseur who looks to heaven with eyes shut.

The seer, one who sees with the soul, has the patience to wait, to *attend* nature inwardly as well as outwardly, to find the thought upon the object. Emerson writes in *Nature,* "If a man would be alone, let him look at the stars. . . . If the stars should appear one night in a thousand years, how would men believe and adore; and preserve for many generations the remembrance of the city of God which had been shown!" With characteristic irony, deflating the Emersonian balloon but not relinquishing its string, Frost says in "On Looking Up by Chance at the Constellations,"

> You'll wait a long, long time for anything much
> To happen in heaven beyond the floats of cloud
> And the Northern Lights that run like tingling nerves.

He acknowledges that "the longest drouth will end in rain," but he cautions the overexpectant stargazer against believing anything will happen "on his particular time and personal sight." He goes further along this route in "Skeptic":

> Far star that tickles for me my sensitive plate
> And fries a couple of ebon atoms white,
> I don't believe I believe a thing you state.
> I put no faith in the seeming facts of light.

The universe, he declares, may or may not be immense. Indeed, it closes in at times "like a caul in which I was born and still am wrapped." But, again, this is all by way of keeping the "over cautious" out of his secret places, and the question of the universe's spatial dimensions is a red herring.

A major writer rarely gets to his truth in letters: he sees the immense leap from literal to imaginative truth and shudders, leaving the difficult act of truth finding to fictive thought. I think we come closest to Frost's true relation to the universe in "Desert Places," one of his major lyrics:

> They cannot scare me with their empty spaces
> Between stars—on stars where no human race is.
> I have it in me so much nearer home
> To scare myself with my own desert places.

The infinite silent spaces between the stars that terrified Pascal are cast aside as trifling when compared to the poet's inward profundity, the vastness of his soul, the great silences that exist between words themselves. The emptiness seen in night skies is finally a mere reflection of an inward blankness: "The ruin or the blank that we see when we look at nature, is in our own eye," writes Emerson in *Nature,* going further in "Self-Reliance" (1839): "A man should learn to detect and watch that gleam of light which flashes across his mind from within, more than the lustre of the firmament of bards and sages." This inner light is what Frost, like Emerson, attends. To see nature truly, the I' must dissolve; the inner Eye seeking what Emerson calls *correspondence,* a condition wherein the inner and outer senses are "adjusted," where there is "intercourse with heaven and earth."

The special "occult" relation between heaven and earth comes out least mysteriously in one of Frost's best later poems, "Take Something Like a Star," a poem whose stately rhythms and immense compression at the end earn it the permanence of great art. Again the poet looks up at the firmament, this time choosing a special star and addressing it:

> O star (the fairest one in sight),
> We grant your loftiness the right
> To some obscurity of cloud—
> It will not do to say of night,
> Since dark is what brings out your light.
> Some mystery becomes the proud.

It is possible, I hope, to read this poem without distortion as an address to the muse; the poet perhaps refers to his need for impersonality when he grants his star "some obscurity of cloud." Access to a seer's angle of vision *must* be difficult or everyone would possess it. Truth, true vision, comes most often in the form of a glimpse, unexpectedly, like a phone call in the middle of the night that in the morning seems more like something one has dreamed. (Frost treats this point in "For Once, Then, Something.") Frost uses the traditional metaphor of light and darkness to dramatize his conflict; the night sky here perhaps alludes to his own inner darkness, a *necessary* negativity, "since dark is what brings out your light." But he allows the star only a measure of taciturnity, "to be wholly taciturn / in your reserve is not allowed." The threat of silence remains the greatest threat to poetic imagination, to the human enterprise. Man is to Aristotle a "creature of the word," a speaking animal, *zoon phonanta*. And the poet may be recognized as the ultimate embodiment of this creature, the Promethean thief of language, once the solitary province of God, the Divine *logos*. Of course, the poet must suffer the anxieties of speech all the more, especially as his speech must become more and more exacting in the face of revelation. Thus the visionary dilemma: as the poet climbs upward toward the Triune Rose of Fire (Dante's symbol for true visionary experience), speech falters. At last, language, our common speech, collapses, as in *Paradiso*, and even the memory fails with it:

> *Da quinci innanzi il mio veder fu maggio*
> *che 'l parlar mostra, ch'a tal vista cede,*
> *e cede la memoria a tanto oltraggio.*

[Thenceforward my vision was greater than speech can show, which fails at such a sight, and at such excess memory fails—Singleton translation.] So

Frost, terrified by the possibility of losing speech and memory, asks the muse for "something he can learn by heart," something to repeat at the visionary summit. This particular "something" is a language that must "burn" and keep his vision singular, "steadfast as Keats' Eremite." Of this star Frost says, talking metaphorically about the poet's responsibility as zoon phonanta,

> It asks of us a certain height,
> So when at times the mob is swayed
> To carry praise or blame too far,
> We may take something like a star
> To stay our minds on and be staid.

Again Emerson's "Self-Reliance" comes to mind: "It is easy in the world to live after the world's opinion; . . . but the great man is he who in the midst of the crowd keeps with perfect sweetness the independence of solitude." Frost, like Emerson, values *inward* character more than anything else. What nature can teach us, he argues, is self-knowledge; the man who truly sees nature sees himself most truly, sees into his soul, for "nature is the symbol of the spirit." An occult relation between self and other occurs.

A great deal has been made of the "darker" Frost since Randall Jarrell and Lionel Trilling first isolated this particular strain in the poet's work. Clearly, Frost has a fiercely chilly side, a strange weather of disaffection and aloneness. But, as Cox says, "Those who require the dark Frost in order to 'elevate' him into the realm of 'serious poetry' invariably miss the delicacy and depth of that fully conditional world where the very nature of experience is registered in language showing always a skeptical edge. That edge . . . which produces the sharp and precise image or impression." Far from contradicting Emerson, Frost performs the poet's function as Emerson himself conceived it, "to fasten words again to visible things." To read Frost properly is to read him whole, and the darker side remains only one side; the neutral or even malevolent universe presupposed in such poems as "Design," "Acquainted with the Night," or "The Most of It" is counterbalanced by poems like "Mowing," "Birches," "To Earthward," or "Two Look at Two," all of which celebrate our hold upon the earth and the triumph of "human" nature. Blake's magnificent epigram—"Without man, nature is barren"—could serve as an epigraph to many of Frost's best poems.

"The Most of It," for example, seems on the surface to turn the Emersonian universe on its head; the speaker in this lyric wants more than his "own love back in copy speech" when he calls across a lake. Echo alone is not enough. He wants "counter-love, original response." But he gets no response except from a great buck of a sudden charging out of the lake, lurching into the underbrush, a terrifying and inhuman force. But such a poem as this *must* be read against its counterpart, Frost's "Two Look at Two." In this latter poem, a couple in love climb a mountainside until a tumbled wall reminds them of approaching dark and the difficult way back. "This is all," they sigh, turning back, when suddenly a doe stands looking at them from across the wall. Amazed, "*This,* then, is all," they conclude, again. But once more something proves them wrong: a snort urges them to wait, and a buck comes around as well, antlered and lusty of nostril. They are stunned:

> "This *must* be all." It was all. Still they stood,
> A great wave from it going over them,
> As if the earth in one unlooked-for favor
> Had made them certain earth returned their love.

The situation here differs sharply from that in "The Most of It," in which the speaker was alone and in his condition of extreme solitude calls up a response equal to his inward vehemence. A condition of correspondence has in fact been established; the poem rings true because the vision, the central image of the violent buck, is adequate in this instance to the experience being rendered into verse. Yet again, writes Cox, "Frost's skepticism is a means of doubting unity enough to need another voice both to corroborate and express his own existence." So in "Two Look at Two" the speaker obtains corroboration; the "he" becomes "they" (still in the third person to emphasize the poem's dramatic form) and the double vision is itself doubled. Nature answers back, not exactly as "counter-love, original response" but as a simple reinforcement of what has already been given: the love of one human being for another.

IV

The importance of Emerson to Frost can hardly be overstated; the latter's poetry represents a continuing dialogue with his great predecessor. The echoes abound from early to late Frost, but where he quotes Emerson, Frost usually qualifies by addition, not contradiction. He adds a skeptical note usually, although Emerson was himself more of a skeptic than most critics realize, especially in the later years, in view of the summary expression in his essay on Montaigne (1845). "The ground occupied by the skeptic," he writes, "is the vestibule of the temple. Society does not like to have any breath of question blown on the existing order. But the interrogation of custom at all points is an inevitable stage in the growth of every superior mind, and is the evidence of its perception of the flowing power which remains itself in all changes." The skeptic perceives with a steady eye—an energetic eye that fastens upon the object and holds it firmly in the mind. This is the "act of attention" that Lawrence says is characteristic of all great art. Emerson's is a mind in constant motion, Man Thinking (in his own phrase), but his eye is fixed austerely on the image. Frost too regards vision as his primary duty, adding to Emerson that quality of ironic humor that allowed him to maintain the vision long enough for description to give way to revelation. In this he is writing directly in the line of visionary romanticism that reaches back to Wordsworth on one side, but most important to Emerson, his most direct ancestor. For both Frost and Emerson the present act of vision remains central to their respective arts, as Frost eloquently affirms in his little-read poem "All Revelation" (1938):

Eyes seeking the response of eyes
Bring out the stars, bring out the flowers,
Thus concentrating earth and skies
So none need be afraid of size.
All revelation has been ours.

SEAMUS HEANEY
The Ground Possessed

In "Ocean's Love to Ireland," from Seamus Heaney's 1975 volume, *North,* the poet likens Ireland to a ruined maid undone by Ocean, who has "scattered her dream of fleets." The Spanish prince "has spilled his gold / And failed her." Now "iambic drums / Of English beat the woods," and her poets sink like Onan. From all sides, the island is under seige, her dainty fartheringale lifted by Ocean's lecherous fingers "like a scarf of weed lifting / In the front of a wave." As always, she heels under pressure, tugs her forelock, and speaks with pure English vowels. But she remains inviolable from within, her "ground possessed and repossessed."

North is a major accomplishment, a book-length sequence of lyrics that exploits the metaphor of possession more fully than any other Irish poet has done. The poems are richly autobiographical, yet the poet consistently weaves the particulars of his life into a mythic frame; he has evolved a unique species of political poetry that refers at once to the current Irish "troubles" and to the human situation generally. One would have to invoke Pablo Neruda's *Heights of Macchu Picchu* (1948) for a parallel. His poetry has evolved with remarkable integrity from the beginning. He has drawn ever-widening concentric rings around the first few themes he circled; his language has grown steadily more dense, more resonant, more singularly his own with each successive volume. And now, at the height of his powers, one awaits each new book with the same expectancy afforded Yeats and Eliot in their middle years.

Heaney comes from the north, from Derry, and his first book conjured the pastoral topography of his childhood on the farm. One should remember, of course, that even Theocritus and Virgil did not write for country folk, to put it mildly; rather, they evinced the atmosphere of rural life for the benefit of cultivated city dwellers who would appreciate the subtle texture of meaning embedded in their eclogues. This is the pastoral tradition, and Heaney's *Death of a Naturalist* (1966) fits into it. He was in fact a farm boy, and he writes from immediate experience, but he learned his craft in the city, at Queens University, Belfast, where he enjoyed the tutelage of Philip Hobsbaum, the poet-critic, among others. Hobsbaum's bias toward lean physical language wedded to intellectual toughness shows up in Heaney's early work, as in the first lines of "Digging":

> Between my finger and my thumb
> The squat pen rests: snug as a gun.
>
> Under my window, a clear rasping sound
> When the spade sinks into gravelly ground:
> My father, digging. I look down
>
> Till his straining rump among the flowerbeds
> Bends low, comes up twenty years away
> Stooping in rhythm through potato drills
> Where he was digging.

Heaney furls us into his vision with lines admitting no abstraction; his experience thrusts itself upon us directly, and we cannot doubt "the cold smell of potato mould, the squelch and slap / Of soggy peat, the curt cuts of an edge." The violence of Heaney's sight, which holds each image firmly in the mind as a butterfly in pincers, looks forward to the line from Wallace Stevens quoted in *North:* "Description is revelation." Like Wordsworth, who says in *The Prelude* (1850) that he was "fostered alike by beauty and by fear," this poet lays claim to a similar parentage.

The title poem, "Death of a Naturalist," recollects a frightening instance when the poet as a boy was confronted by a horde of frogs attending their spawn, which he used to steal every spring in his role of amateur naturalist:

> I would fill jampotfuls of the jellied
> Specks to range on window-sills at home,
> On shelves at school, and wait and watch until
> The fattening dots burst into nimble-
> Swimming tadpoles.

This (of course) angered the frogs, so they invaded the flax-dam to avenge the youthful offender:

> The air was thick with a brass chorus.
> Right down the dam gross-bellied frogs were cocked
> On sods; their loose necks pulsed like sails. Some hopped:
> The slap and plop were obscene threats. Some sat
> Poised like mud grenades, their blunt heads farting.

Heaney's shocking phrases, like "their blunt heads farting," avoid being gratuitous because of the charged atmosphere present from the outset: "All year the flax-dam festered in the heart / Of the townland." *Festered* prepares us for a strong succession of verbs: *sweltered, gargled, croaked, pulsed,* and so on. The reader's eye tends obsessively to the verbs, which claw and pick at the attention and funnel us through each poem. The accuracy of every natural detail lends an authority to Heaney's voice; when he explains, "You could tell the weather by frogs too / For they were yellow in the sun and brown / In rain," we believe him implicitly.

Death of a Naturalist is an apprentice volume, one in which a young poet tests the limits of his abilities, tries out various verse forms and metrical patterns. But if there are echoes in these poems, they are well assimilated. A major poet often steps into his own clearing from the start, and Heaney does this here. The controlled irony of "The Early Purges," with its adumbration of things to come in later volumes, shows this young writer possessed of a maturity beyond his years. The poem recounts another childhood instance, a time when Dan Taggart drowned some kittens, "'the scaggy wee shits,'" in a bucket of stinging cold water:

> "Sure isn't it better for them now?"
> Like wet gloves they bobbed and shone till he sluiced
> Them out on the dunghill, glossy and dead.
> Suddenly frightened, for days I sadly hung
> Round the yard, watching the three sogged remains
> Turn mealy and crisp as old summer dung
> Until I forgot them.

Yet the fear returns when Dan pursues a mean vendetta against living creatures: rats and rabbits, crows and hens. The poet, half-believing himself, asserts that "living displaces false sentiments"; nonetheless, a heavy irony in the last line fumes like invisible sharply scented smoke: "But on well-run farms pests have to be kept down." None of the sentimental flurries characteristic of Yeats as a novice can be found in Heaney; he writes with a stern grip on reality.

The boyhood evoked in these poems is tinged with violence, as we have seen, but not blotted out by it. "Follower," for example, investigates a complicated father-son relationship:

> My father worked with a horse-plough,
> His shoulders globed like a full sail strung
> Between shafts and the furrow.
> The horses strained at his clicking tongue.

Heaney follows through with the sailing analogy:

> His eye
> Narrowed and angled at the ground
> Mapping the furrow exactly.

Then he brings himself into the picture:

> I stumbled in his hob-nailed wake,
> Fell sometimes on the polished sod;

Sometimes he rode me on his back
Dipping and rising to his plod.

The poem ends with a swift reversal, for the follower is not merely the son tripping and falling behind the father:

> But today
> It is my father who keeps stumbling
> Behind me, and will not go away.

The poet, having forsaken an ancient call to the soil, cannot exorcise the father, nor will he ever.

Family deaths, the persistence of old ghosts, hunting expeditions, potato diggings, and the normal preoccupations of a life in County Derry provide material for *Death of a Naturalist*, yet the loveliest poems in the book are those addressed to Marie Heaney, the poet's wife. "Valediction" sets the standard:

> Lady with the frilled blouse
> And simple tartan skirt,
> Since you have left the house
> Its emptiness has hurt
> All thought. In your presence
> Time rode easy, anchored
> On a smile; but absence
> Rocked love's balance, unmoored
> The days. They buck and bound
> Across the calendar
> Pitched from the quiet sound
> Of your flower-tender
> Voice. Need breaks on my strand;
> You've gone, I am at sea.
> Until you resume command
> Self is in mutiny.

The naval conceit is drawn up tight with the final, consummate phrase. The alternate rhymes lend polish to the otherwise roughly finished trimeter in which the rhythm mimics the theme: the unsettling effect of the beloved's absence. Not an ounce of fat detracts from the poem's swift statement and hard clear edges.

A full rhetorical flourish adorns "Poem: For Marie":

> Love, I shall perfect for you the child
> Who diligently potters in my brain
> Digging with heavy spade till sods were piled
> Or puddling through muck in a deep drain.

The poem is about fathering; the lovers come together "within one golden ring" to perfect their dreams, to flesh out their imaginings with the particulars of experience, arranging the world "within new limits." The metaphor shifts slightly in "Scaffolding," an elaborately metaphysical conceit that compares the scaffoldings erected against a wall to hold up masons at work to the emotional ramparts sustained by lovers.

When the masons finish, the scaffolding naturally disappears; the poet says,

> So if, my dear, there sometimes be
> Old bridges breaking between you and me
>
> Never fear. We may let the scaffolds fall
> Confident that we have built our wall.

"Personal Helicon" concludes the book, and it might be taken as Heaney's *ars poetica*. It pulls into a single locus the varied themes of *Death of a Naturalist*, and it may be thought of as a poetic credo, a guide to this poet's personal iconography. Heaney's version of Helicon, the stream that ran from Parnassus and the source of inspiration to ancient poets, is the well on his farm:

> As a child, they could not keep me from wells
> And old pumps with buckets and windlasses.
> I loved the dark drop, the trapped sky, the smells
> Of waterweed, fungus and dank moss.

The well of memory, with its slippery sides and musky odors, goes down "so deep you saw no reflection in it." Like a poem, it "gave back your own call / With a clean new music in it." This world of dangling roots and slime, of soft mulch and scary ferns, recalls the greenhouse poems of Theodore Roethke, with whom Heaney had much in common at this stage in his development. Here is concrete poetry with a vengeance, what Roethke called "that anguish of concreteness." Heaney mocks his own adult pretensions, the priggish refusals (which he never makes) to delve into this subterranean source:

> Now, to pry into roots, to finger slime,
> To stare big-eyed Narcissus, into some spring
> Is beneath all adult dignity. I rhyme
> To see myself, to set the darkness singing.

With *Door into the Dark* (1969), Heaney opens a new vein of subject matter and works his way slowly, at times painfully, toward the mature style fully realized in *North*. There is the expected carryover from *Death of a Naturalist;* anything that good deserves carrying over. The folksy pastoral side begins to dwindle, although poems like "The Outlaw" (about an old man named Kelly who keeps an illegal stud bull), "The Thatcher," and "The Wife's Tale" are a fine addition to earlier poems like "Churning Day" and "The Diviner." Heaney's geniality, compassion, and impish wit run through these poems like a watermark. There is great precedence in British poetry for this kind of poem, of course, and this poet adds a few fresh lyrics to this tradition (which reaches back well beyond Wordsworth, who comes to mind as a master of this genre). What interests me especially about *Door into the Dark* is Heaney's discovery of natural symbols in rural life—which gives his work a new resonance; also, I am intrigued by the sudden compression of style, the tough intellectual sinew flexed in phrase after phrase, and the laser focus of his vision: the image is seared indelibly on the reader's mind, while the style itself shifts without extinguishing the voice raised in the previous book.

Heaney pushes his style toward a spareness, an absence of rhetoric and normal syntactical connective tissue, which culminates in the granite style of *Wintering Out* (1972). "Dream," for instance, establishes this new style early in the book:

> With a billhook
> Whose head was hand-forged and heavy

I was hacking a stalk
Thick as a telegraph pole.
My sleeves were rolled
And the air fanned cool past my arms
As I swung and buried the blade,
Then laboured to work it unstuck.

The next stroke
Found a man's head under the hook.
Before I woke
I heard the steel stop
In the bone of the brow.

The style recalls Hopkins, one of Heaney's dominant ancestors, with its heavy alliteration, sprung rhythm, and tightly packed imagery. A tendency toward symbolism is also in evidence: we are given nothing but one side of most analogues, tenor without vehicle, the same technique used by Blake in early lyrics such as "The Sick Rose" (1794). Heaney supplies us with the barest image in "Dream," but the context is sufficient; the poem gathers to itself the luminosity of a natural symbol caught in the poet's energetic eye.

"The Forge," a poem similar to "Dream" and one of the best in the collection, illustrates my point about symbolism further. As a metaphor, "the crucible of art" has a long past. One thinks of Hephaestus, who crafted the shield of Achilles, or, more recently, of Joyce's Stephen Dedalus and his wish "to forge in the smithy of [his] soul the uncreated conscience of [his] race." The poem begins with a line from which the book takes its title: "All I know is a door into the dark." The suggestiveness of this line, which takes us from the literal to a metaphoric level instantly, signals that Heaney has more in mind than simple description of a forge. This becomes clearer when he describes the anvil in religious (almost sacrificial) terms:

Horned as a unicorn, at one end square,
Set there immoveable: an altar
Where he expends himself in shape and music.

The blacksmith, a modern anachronism, reminds us of the poet in today's world:

He leans out on the jamb, recalls a clatter
Of hoofs where traffic is flashing in rows;
Then grunts and goes in, with a slam and flick
To beat real iron out, to work the bellows.

So the poet withdraws into the dark room of his imagining, beats out the "real iron" of language into significant form. Heaney is himself a maker in the old sense. Like Yeats, he wants only to "hammer his thoughts into unity."

"Description is revelation"—the great phrase from Stevens—illumines the technique behind many poems in *Door into the Dark*, where each act of description becomes a repossession of experience. Often Heaney's tone, as in "Girls Bathing, Galway 1965," is whimsical, using bathos as a common trope, but one finds a seriousness underlying even this light poem. It begins,

The swell foams where they float and crawl,
A catherine wheel of arm and hand;
Each head bobs curtly as a football.
The yelps are faint here on the strand.

Yet "the breakers pour / Themselves into themselves, the years / Shuttle through space invisibly." Generations labor "in fear of flesh and sin / For the time has been accomplished." These pronouncements would weigh too heavily on us were the bathers not "bare-legged, smooth-shouldered and long-backed." Their immediate attractiveness and their ignorance of the fact that "the time has been accomplished" work against all pretentious efforts to interpret their meaning sub specie aeternitatis. "So Venus comes, matter-of-fact," we are told, not like Botticelli's classic maiden with her arms full of flowers, wafting in on a shell. Revelation is matter of fact, almost accidental. The poet's job is simply *to see exactly* what is in front of him. And he must keep one foot firmly planted on the ground, like Antaeus, the giant who is the subject of two poems in *North*.

The remaining poems of *Door into the Dark* are closely autobiographical and anecdotal. "The Wife's Tale" and "Mother" recall the looser colloquial style of *Death of a Naturalist*, although much of the earlier sentiment is stripped away. "Elegy for a Stillborn Child" stands out among these more personal poems for its startling analogies; it begins with the poet speaking to the dead child:

Your mother walks light as an empty creel
Unlearning the intimate nudge and pull

Your trussed up weight of seed-flesh and bone-curd
Had insisted on.

The creel simile arrests us with the image of a woman moving along, her ribs like the creel's wooden bars, all air and light; the metaphorical compounds, *seed-flesh* and *bone-curd,* have a skaldic ring, a new aspect of Heaney's work that looks forward to *North.* "Elegy" charts the progress from husband to father and then the disappointment of bewildered parents. The final section is a meditation on emptiness in which the poet refrains from all assertions of either despair or false hope:

On lonely journeys I think of it all,
Birth of death, exhumation for burial,

A wreath of small clothes, a memorial pram,
And parents reaching for a phantom limb.

I drive by remote control in this bare road
Under a drizzling sky, a circling rook,

Past mountain fields, full to the brim with cloud,
White waves riding home on a wintry lough.

One has the sense of powerful emotion held tightly in check by the formal control of Heaney's sprung pentameter and slant-rhymed couplets.

"Bogland" concludes *Door into the Dark* and lends additional meaning to the title, for the Irish bogs (which preserve generations of Irish civilization intact) may be thought of as openings into the dark of history. The theme of this poem is the literal repossession of the ground, a theme that becomes central in Heaney's next two books. The poet observes that because Ireland has no prairies "to slice a big sun at evening" the horizon encroaches from all directions. "Our unfenced country," says Heaney, "is bog that keeps crusting / Between the sights of the sun." An amateur archaeologist, he tells of recent exhumations from bogs:

They've taken the skeleton
Of the Great Irish Elk
Out of the peat, set it up
An astounding crate full of air.
Butter sunk under
More than a hundred years
Was recovered salty and white.
The ground itself is kind, black butter

Melting and opening underfoot.

The suggestive possibilities of bog land seem unbounded, and Heaney knows this, but he refuses to go much beyond a literal representation until the last line: "The wet centre is bottomless." As a symbol of the unconscious past that must be unfolded, layer by layer, the bog image will prove indispensable. For this reason, "Bogland" is a watershed poem in the Heaney corpus. After it, one rereads with a new lens all the poems coming before it, realizing that this poet's vision of historical sequence reaches beyond the pastoral folk tradition. The theme of digging, registered twice in *Death of a Naturalist* (potato digging, then), moves into a rich light now, acquiring new potency from the symbolic force of the bog land metaphor.

In *Wintering Out* (1972) Heaney is quick to pick up the end note of *Door into the Dark,* to mine the ore still locked inside this vein. Ireland's archaeological sites yield poems like "Bog Oak," "Anahorish," and "Toome," and Heaney's research into Danish excavations results in "The Tollund Man" and "Nerthus." These poems tenaciously exploit the metaphoric plunge backward through time. As one delves in bog land, history peels away like the layers of an onion; one falls through shelves of civilizations often represented by odds and ends such as the oak beam that was once "a carter's trophy" in "Bog Oak." "Anahorish"—the term means 'place of clear water'—is an ancient site where the mound dwellers lived, a place "where springs washed into / the shiny grass / and darkened cobbles in the lane." Heaney evokes the pristine quality—a translucent crispness—of neolithic life:

With pails and barrows

those mound-dwellers

go waist-deep in mist
to break the light ice
at wells and dunghills.

The poems in part 1 of this collection all reconstruct historical instances or offer a meditation on some fact of the lost past. "Servant Boy," for example, draws a simple portrait of a lower-class child who

comes first-footing
the back doors of the little
barons: resentful
and impenitent.

The poet clearly identifies with this "jobber among shadows." Placed where it is, in the sequence of bog poems, "Servant Boy" stands out as a reminder of Heaney's breadth of vision, his empathetic range. The poem recollects the old feud between invading noblemen and the indigenous servant classes; it helps to explain the present Irish conflict by pointing to centuries of accrued resentment. Nothing about "Servant Boy" is overtly political, of course. Heaney stays rather far from engagement of this sort until *North*, but one senses the gathering storm.

The theme of "the ground possessed and repossessed" finds only oblique expression in these poems, insofar as the theme is political. But in "Land," the repossession is personal and literal as the poet confronts the ground like a lover:

If I lie with my ear
in this loop of silence

long enough, thigh-bone
and shoulder against the ground,

I expect to pick up
a small drumming

and must not be surprised
in bursting air

to find myself snared, swinging
an ear-ring of sharp wire.

One "picks up a drumming" from the land, he says: the poet's alliterative drumming perhaps or the pulse of history muffled in the loam. The poet, with his earring, is marked by his curious affectation, his art, which pierces his ear uncomfortably and snares him. In "Gifts of Rain," which follows "Land," he says,

> I cock my ear
> at an absence—
> in the shared calling of blood
>
> arrives my need
> for antediluvian lore.
> Soft voices of the dead
> are whispering by the shore.

The desire for "antediluvian lore" drives Heaney, in "Toome," back into the trench:

> I push into a souterrain
> prospecting what new
> in a hundred centuries'
>
> loam, flints, musket-balls,
> fragmented ware,
> torcs and fish-bones
> till I'm sleeved in
> alluvial mud that shelves
> suddenly under
> bogwater and tributaries,
> and elvers tail my hair.

One finds not the slightest excess in any of these poems; Heaney's rhetoric errs, if at all, on the side of spareness. His diction, sprung from a serious philological delving, reminds one of Emerson's speculations in "The Poet":

The poets made all the words, and therefore language is the
archives of history . . . a sort of tomb of the muses. For
though the origin of most of our words is forgotten, each
word was at first a stroke of genius, and obtained currency
because for the moment it symbolized the world to the first
speaker and to the hearer. The etymologist finds the deadest
word to have been once a brilliant picture. Language is fos-
sil poetry.

The poet's job, then, is to restore language to its meaning, its pictorial
essence. Thus Heaney examines each word carefully: *Toome, Broagh,* or
Anahorish, that "place of clear water." He is the poet-as-archaeologist, reviv-
ing a lost past and using the past to inform a cloudy present as "we hug our
little destiny again."

In "Tradition," he complains, "Our gutteral muse / was bulled long ago
/ by the alliterative tradition" and makes fun of such English words as *var-
sity* and *deem.* England, John Bull, has long since replaced the Celtic tradi-
tion with the one in which Heaney now writes; Irish poetry is now a sub-
division of English poetry. This displacement of traditions is one aspect of
the "the ground possessed," and Heaney's repossession involves remaking
the language, grafting into it words that have been bulled under. This also
involves a willful distortion of the mellifluous English iamb. The poems in
Wintering Out are made of gristle and bone, rock and water; they are redo-
lent of Irish soil and what Gerard Manley Hopkins called "the taste of self."
Hopkins's own efforts to revive the rhythms of Anglo-Saxon verse resemble
Heaney's experiments with "the gutteral muse."

Part 2 of *Wintering Out* moves away from the wide historical rummage
of part 1 into the private arena of one man's life; I prefer the poems in this
section on the whole, no doubt because they are less dense, less tortuously
argued. "Wedding Day" sets the new tone:

> I am afraid.
> Sound has stopped in the day
> And the images reel over
> And over. Why all those tears,
>
> The wild grief on his face
> Outside the taxi? The sap

Of mourning rises
In our waving guests.

The terrified groom sees his new wife behind the tall cake "like a deserted bride" who would still go on with the ritual despite her husband's departure. He runs into the "gents" to find on the walls "a skewered heart / And a legend of love." This ancient image brings him to his senses, and he says to his bride, "Let me sleep on your breast to the airport," subsuming like a child to a power greater than himself; whether it be the feminine principle or simply the inevitability of experience, we cannot say. What matters is the gentle submission tendered by the groom's request.

"Summer Home" is a major sequence and the emotional center of part 2; in it, Heaney explores the vicissitudes of love and its attendant permutations and distortions. The poet begins by recollecting a scene in a foreign country, a time when everything was out of joint:

> Was it wind off the dump
> or something in heat
> dogging us, the summer gone soon, a foul nest incubating
> somewhere?

Something larval, alive, is discovered under the doormat and has to be scalded dead. This emblematic gesture proffers the possibility of cure, of reconciliation between man and climate, between man and woman. The second section images the husband "bushing the door" with an armload of wild cherries and rhododendron. His wife sobs inside the house, and he blames himself, crying, "Attend. Anoint the wound." And he resumes the theme in the third section:

> O we tented our wound all night
> under the homely sheet
>
> and lay as if the cold flat of a blade
> had winded us.
>
> More and more I postulate
> thick healing, like now.

as you bend in the shower
water lives down the tilting stoups of your breasts.

The poem moves from desolation to near consolation. Even in the final section, there are children who "weep out the hot foreign night"; the protagonist's "foul mouth takes it out" on his wife, and they lie "stiff till dawn / attends the pillow." But memory preserves deep within the soft unmistakable note of love that will save them:

Yesterday rocks sang when we tapped
Stalactites in the cave's old, dripping dark—
Our love calls tiny as a tuning fork.

The slant rhyme brings the sequence to a close; although the baleful atmosphere present from the beginning never quite clears, the lovers seem to have moved closer to affection. One wishes the poem were longer, something that can be wished for very few poems, indeed.

A number of poems in the pastoral folk mode reminiscent of Heaney's earliest work follow "Summer Home." "A Winter's Tale" concerns a mad daughter who likes to prance naked among cattle and bare her breasts to sympathetic neighbors, "Shore Woman" is an energetic monologue full of concrete natural description, and "Maighdean Mara" (Gaelic for mermaid) conjures an eerie scene that is equal to anything else Heaney has written, for it is full of arresting phrases and lines that fit W. H. Auden's definition of poetry as "memorable language," as in the first stanza:

She sleeps now, her cold breasts
Dandled by undertow,
Her hair lifted and laid.
Undulant slow seawrecks
Cast about skin and thigh,
Bangles of wort, drifting
Liens catch, dislodge gently.

One might argue that the diction here is slightly affected, but I find this side of Heaney attractive. He is a word hoarder, piling his phrases like stones on his bare hill, and his poems are cairns.

The last few poems of *Wintering Out* fan out like the tail of a comet into a less dense language, a looser syntax, a widening of subject matter. "Limbo" and "Bye-child" chill with their stories of mothers who drown or cage their children in henhouses; these are some of the bizarre perversions of love, of "illegitimate spawning." "First Calf" takes up the same theme in the animal kingdom:

> It's a long time since I saw
> The afterbirth on the hedge
> As if the wind smarted
> And streamed bloodshot tears.

So, the "semaphores of hurt / Swaddle and flap on a bush." The compensations of childbirth are celebrated often enough by Heaney, and beautifully, but here there is only confusion and pain. Yet the endnote remains one of restoration. "May" is a paean to Ireland:

> My toecaps sparkle now
> Over the soft fontanel
> Of Ireland.

The poem "Dawn," one of his very best, breathes beginnings, tells of the poet escaping from a scholarly conference, slipping away to the shore, where, he says,

> I got away out by myself
>
> On a scurf of winkles and cockels
> And found myself suddenly
> Unable to move without crunching
> Acres of their crisp delicate turrets.

"Westering" draws the book to a close with characteristic brilliance, entwining in one poem the biographical strand of part 2 with the vision of history witnessed in part 1. The poet sits in California now, pulled up from his native soil like a mandrake but still "Recalling the last night / In Donegal." Starting out on Good Friday, he saw a "congregation bent / To the studded crucifix." Now, he says,

Under the moon's stigmata

Six thousand miles away,
I imagine untroubled dust,
A loosening gravity,
Christ weighing by his hands.

The pocked moon skin, seen as stigmata, is a luminous emblem, an aegis under which Irish history is enacted, the small and bitter destiny mourned in the book's epigraph, a poem from which the graffito "Is there life before death?" blazes as from a city wall. In a country preoccupied with violence, Christianity seems pagan, and Christ looks more like the tiger than the lamb. To "imagine untroubled dust" is about all a poet can do in these circumstances, and Heaney does it.

North represents one of this poet's most vivid repossessions of history, of his tongue, of himself. There is a new directness here, flagged by the title, but Heaney loses none of the suggestive power of controlled ambiguity seen in earlier volumes. His "north" is not just Northern Ireland. The tone of the book rings like a struck anvil; it is stark, cold, brisk as the northerly themes and diction that suffuse these poems. The poet-as-*scop* (Old English minstrel) entertains us with our foibles, with the past (we identify with *his* past) reenacting itself on the native ground. The setting is specifically Irish, of course, but the subject matter obtains for all of us, in any country of the present. His theme, that love is what redeems the past and makes living possible in today's violent world, is set out in the two dedicatory poems, "Sunlight" and "The Seed Cutters," both of which evoke the idyll of remembrance.

Once again, Heaney uses a two-part division, working in the same overall pattern he used so effectively in *Wintering Out*. In the first part, beginning and ending with poems referring to Antaeus, the mythical giant whose strength derived from contact with the ground, Heaney investigates the burden of Irish history once more: the history of possession and repossession of the island by various tribes. The magnificent "Belderg" begins with another of the poet's bog poems. Here, "the soft-piled centuries / Fell open like a glib" to reveal "the stone-age fields, the tomb / Corbelled, turfed and chambered / Floored with dry turf-coomb." This fossilized landscape refers to an Old Norse settlement in County Mayo. The grinding stone of this community, the quern, pulls the tangled feelings of the poet into its vortex:

"But the Norse ring on your tree?"
I passed through the eye of your quern,

Grist to an ancient mill,
And in my mind's eye saw

A world-tree of balanced stones,
Querns piled like vertebrae,
The marrow crushed to grounds.

I find these bog poems much more easily comprehensible, but not less dense or complex, than similar poems in *Wintering Out.*

The linguistic exhumation continues, and Heaney uncovers words like *crannog,* an ancient lake; *pampooties,* cow-skin sandals; *pash,* head; *obols,* silver coins; and *graip,* a dung fork. I could extend the list for another full page. Instead, I will send the interested reader to the *Oxford English Dictionary,* which contains most of these words.

The majestic title poem "North" itself focuses on Viking invasions; in it, the poet returns to a "long strand, / the hammered shod of a bay." Here, the "ocean-deafened voices" of the past speak to him, explaining how "Thor's hammer swung / to geography and trade, / thick-witted couplings and revenges." The violence foisted upon man by man is rooted in economic necessity and irrational desires. The "longship's swimming tongue" says, "Lie down / in the word-hoard . . . compose in darkness." This Heaney does, consummately.

He lies down in the word hoard and whole poems sprout from single word kernels, such as *ban-hus,* meaning bonehouse:

I push back
through dictions,
Elizabethan canopies,
Norman devices,

the erotic mayflowers
of Provence
and the ivied latins
of churchmen

> to the scop's
> twang, the iron
> flash of consonants
> cleaving the line.

The abrupt alliterative rhythms, the strong caesurae and metaphorical compounds, and the eschewal of Latinate diction—all contribute to the northern quality of these poems, which occasionally sound like translations from the Old Norse.

Sadism concerns Heaney in "Punishment," another bog poem but one extending the genre into the political realm. The poet meditates on the execution of some "little adultress." He says, "I could almost love you / but would have cast, I know, / the stones of silence." He continues:

> I am the artful voyeur
>
> of your brain's exposed
> and darkened combs,
> your muscles' webbing
> and all your numbered bones:
>
> I who have stood dumb
> when your betraying sisters,
> cauled in tar,
> wept by the railings,
>
> who would connive
> in civilized outrage
> yet understand the exact
> and tribal, intimate revenge.

This poem could not be better with its simplicity and fluent movement, its concentration of thought and feeling in a single image, or its wider application to the contemporary Irish situation, and indeed to the present estate of womanhood. The "stones of silence" theme prefigures the harrowing later poem "Whatever You Say Say Nothing," in which Heaney examines the "famous / Northern reticence, the tight gag of place / And times."

"Strange Fruit" happens to be my favorite among these bog poems, another classic in its way. The archaeological diggers uncover a "girl's head like an exhumed gourd." The following description, dense and physical, is Heaney at his best:

> Oval-faced, prune-skinned, prune-stones for teeth.
> They unswaddled the wet fern of her hair
> And made an exhibition of its coil,
> Let the air at her leathery beauty.

The "Alas, poor Yorick" theme takes on new resonance; for this "murdered, forgotten, nameless, terrible / Beheaded girl" outstares "axe and beautification," outstares "what had begun to feel like reverence."

Heaney, in his artful meditation, moves beyond pathos into an eerie objectivity while he retains compassion. The ancient girl, in her deathless stare, is a poet of sorts, the voyeur of her own demise, the endlessly patient collector of evidence. This is the ideal model for a poet writing of Irish history, the persona of voyeur-accuser.

"Ocean's Love to Ireland" shifts to the Elizabethan colonial possession of Heaney's island, and its theme is summed up in the last line—my principal theme in this essay—"The ground possessed and repossessed." Heaney envisions the English-Irish relation in explicit sexual terms, making literal the metaphor of possession. "Act of Union," which follows shortly, pursues the analogy further, making the poet's beloved into "the heaving province where our past has grown." He wrings the conceit mercilessly:

> I am the tall kingdom over your shoulder
> That you would neither cajole nor ignore.
> Conquest is a lie. I grow older
> Conceding your half-independent shore
> Within whose borders now my legacy
> Culminates inexorably.

The second half of "Act of Union" concerns itself with fathering, and the inevitable Freudian duel for the possession of the mother:

> His parasitical
> And ignorant little fists already

> Beat at your borders and I know they're cocked
> At me across the water.

A deeply plunging terror underlies this poem, one of Heaney's memorable achievements. The political implications suggest that no treaty will salve the wound inflicted by England on this "ruined maid" of Ireland. To quote William Empson, "It is the pain, it is the pain endures."

Pain, in all its sinister permutations, obsesses Heaney in part 2 of *North*. The ironic "Unacknowledged Legislator's Dream" provides a glimpse of the troubles, as they are called, from the inside. The poet persona winds up in jail here: "'I am honored to add a poet to our list,'" says the commandant in charge:

> In the cell, I wedge myself with outstretched arms
> in the corner and heave, I jump on the concrete
> flags to test them. Were those your eyes just now
> at the hatch?

This reaction, one of mingled fear and detachment, characterizes these political poems; I should add that they are poems first and must be read as poems, not political tracts. They register one sensitive man's response to an impossible historical situation, a country "where bad news is no longer news." That line occurs in "Whatever You Say Say Nothing," a four-part sequence in a colloquial style harking back to a number of poems in *Death of a Naturalist*, though there is a fresh edge now: "Men die at hand. In blasted street and home / The gelignite's a common sound effect." The pastoral element has disappeared; the pastoral whimsicality of some of the earlier work fades as the poet offers a stinging new version of reality, almost without comment save in the implicit irony of such lines as "Whatever you say, say nothing."

The last sequence of seven poems is called "Singing School," a title summoning the ghost of Yeats; its theme may be called the growth of the poet, "fostered alike by beauty and by fear." "The Ministry of Fear" begins the sequence; it is a personal history of alienation, starting at school where, Heaney says, "I was so homesick I couldn't eat / the biscuits left to sweeten my exile." The poet feels dispossessed already, uprooted from his country, South Derry, a physical and spiritual exile in his own land. The poem ends with a sinister account of police surrounding Heaney's car when he was out with a girlfriend on a summer night. They jump when he repeats his name: *"Seamus?"* A sense of the suppressed and evil power represented by the authorities pervades these poems. "A Constable Calls" recollects a time when the RUC (Royal Ulster Constabulary) man came to register the family's crops; the poem displays Heaney's powers of controlled observation and understatement:

> His bicycle stood at the window-sill,
> The rubber cowl of a mud-splasher
> Skirting the front mudguard,
> Its fat black handlegrips
>
> Heating in sunlight, the "spud"
> Of the dynamo gleaming and cocked back,
> The pedal treads hanging relieved
> Of the boot of the law.

Heaney's father must account for himself, "making tillage returns / In acres, roods, and perches." We read about "arithmetic and fear," and a boy who "assumed / Small guilts." Relief overwhelms the ending, as the official departs:

> He was snapping the carrier spring
> Over the ledger. His boot pushed off
> And the bicycle ticked, ticked, ticked.

The effect is stunning.

"Orange Drums, Tyrone, 1966" reconstructs the icy spectacle of an Orange parade in stanzas that are harshly sprung, formal, and mimetic of the drums:

> And though the drummers
> Are granted passage through the nodding crowd
> It is the drums preside, like giant tumours.

The poem bites a chunk of reality from the vague air of memory, ending with a vivid line: "The air is pounding like a stethoscope." This ferocity of vision modulates into the gentler meditation "Summer 1969," which finds the poet in Madrid reading a life of James Joyce while back in Ulster the violence continues. A natural guilt of escapism wells in the speaker, though he suffers in Spain too from the oppressive authorities:

> We talked our way home over starlit plains
> Where patent leather of the Guardia Civil
> Gleamed like fish-bellies in flax-poisoned waters.

The poem ends with a retreat into the cool of the Prado, where Goya's famous *Shootings of the Third of May* presents an analogue to Heaney's role as artist: "He painted with his fists and elbows, flourished / The stained cape of his heart as history charged."

"Fosterage," the penultimate poem of this final sequence, pictures Heaney "with words / Imposing on my tongue like obols" (silver coins). Its grand first line, "Description is revelation," a quotation, could easily serve as an epigraph to Heaney's oeuvre. In his poems, description gives way continually to evaluation, to revelation. The poet becomes seer, "a transparent eyeball" in Emerson's great phrase. He becomes everything and nothing, fixing his eye on the object, transforming it. "Fosterage" ends with a tribute to Hopkins, who sought the *inscape* of each object, who "discerned / The lineaments of patience everywhere." Hopkins, of course, continues as the dominant ancestor for Heaney, the source, the starting point of Heaney's angle of vision. But "Fosterage" remains a preface to poetry, not the thing itself, a prelude to "Exposure," the last poem of "Singing School" and *North* as a whole.

"Exposure" is, again, a meditation of the poet's responsibility in a desperate historical moment. It is a poem about withdrawal, deeply autobiographical; for Heaney has in a sense withdrawn into Eire, the south. He lives now, with Marie and their children in a stone house in Dublin, looking out to Joyce's fabled Martello tower from *Ulysses*. Heaney is in his own tower of imagining there. "Exposure," as the last poem in a sequence tracing the growth of a poet, should be triumphal. That it lacks this note, for the most part, points not to the poet's failure but to a particular kind of success. Heaney's tower is not Yeats's. His escape is not into the artifice of eternity but into the recesses of his solitude; "I walk through damp leaves," he says,

> Imagining a hero
> On some muddy compound,

> His gift like a slingstone
> Whirled for the desperate.

"How did I end up like this?" he wonders, thinking of "the anvil brains of some who hate me / As I sit weighing and weighing / My responsible *tristia*." A wonderful self-irony permeates *responsible* here as Heaney acknowledges the need for detachment and engagement at the same time. Yeats could manage this combination, of course: indeed, the cutting edge of his best poems can be described as the point where these seemingly incompatible realms touch. And Heaney's greatness in "Exposure" derives from a similar balance of conflicting needs:

> I am neither internee nor informer;
> An inner émigré, grown long-haired
> And thoughtful; a wood-kerne
> Escaped from the massacre,
> Taking protective colouring
> From bole and bark, feeling
> Every wind that blows.

Heaney's memorable "wood-kerne" (foot soldier) on the run, blending with the landscape, feeling every wind that blows (including the wind of guilt), is an emblem for the modern Irish poet. Without independence and withdrawal, a poet's work becomes infected with the language of propaganda, but this independence depends, paradoxically, on an intimacy with his environment that has made Heaney Ireland's successor to Yeats.

"Ulster was British," Heaney writes in "Singing School," "but with no rights on / The English lyric." He claims for himself now the rights denied to his countrymen at an earlier date. He has turned aggressor, repossessing the ancient role of scop, and his poems have become progressively a private *reclamatio*—a protest—and a personal reclamation of a heritage buried under layers of earth and language. Heaney digs with his pen, exhuming a past that informs and enriches the present and that has designs upon the future. His delving in the philological soil has yielded a poetry of the first order.

ALASTAIR REID

Alastair Reid is one of Scotland's finest poets, and yet his work has remained relatively unknown in Scotland (or in the United States, where an ample selection of his work in poetry and prose—*An Alastair Reid Reader*—was published by the University Press of New England in 1994). Like many writers in this century, he inhabits a cosmopolitan world, refusing national ties. Indeed, he has lived in many countries, including the States, Chile, Spain, France, and Morocco, earning his living from both university teaching and writing. And he is widely considered one of the best living translators of Spanish poetry into English, with renderings of Neruda and Borges that may well become classics. The point is, however, that this poet's interests are so radically outside the bounds of his native province that it is critically useless to call him a Scottish poet. He remains difficult, even impossible, to pigeon-hole—which makes critics uneasy.

Another, more subtle, reason for Reid's obscurity lies in the nature of the poetry. Unlike much contemporary verse, it is unassertive, a poetry of restraint and uncertainty. The poet does not care to set up as another prophet. Rather, he assumes the role of sensitive observer, stranded in a foreign world, always amazed by what he sees. He is the patient investigator, the mental traveler, the perpetual beginner. He predicts nothing but the impossibility of prediction. He leaves all doors open, saying only that

> No season
> brings conclusion.
>
> Each year,
> through heart-ache, nightmare,
>
> true loves alter,
> marriages falter,
>
> and lovers illumine
> the antique design.
>
> apart, together,
> foolish as weather,
>
> right as rain,
> sure as ruin.

("Outlook Uncertain")

The emerging voice is hesitant, worldly wise, cautionary.

In this shaky world a poem is nothing more than a happy accident. The poet meditates on serendipity in "An Instance":

> Perhaps the accident of a bird
> crossing the green window, a simultaneous phrase
> of far singing, and a steeplejack
> poised on the church spire, changing the gold clock,
> set the moment alight. At any rate, a word

in that instance of realizing catches fire,
ignites another, and soon, the page is ablaze
with a wildfire of writing. The clock chimes in the square.

One can feel the excitement of the creative process as Reid presents it to us. The idea of the poem-as-inspiration is utterly romantic, of course, but Reid has given an old theme new life.

Language, obviously, is the medium of poetry, but the individual poet may assume a variety of attitudes toward this medium. On the one hand, the language itself can be of lesser importance to a poet primarily concerned with images or argument per se. The reality they seek may be somehow "outside" the words used. No one can doubt that degrees exist to which "the medium is the message." A writer may well try to create a wholly verbal world, as in *Finnegans Wake,* where language becomes the very texture of life itself, a substitute for experience. For a translator, like Reid, these issues stand out boldly as one learns to appreciate the real differences between language and life, and their mutual dependence. In a witty poem on this subject, written bilingually, Reid explains that

> *Traductores, somos fantasmas que viven*
> *entre aquel mundo y el nuestro*
> translators are ghosts who live
> in a limbo between two worlds
> *pero poco a poco me ocurre*
> *que el problema no es questión*
> *deelo que se pierde en tradución*
> I realize the problem
> is not simply a question
> of what gets lost in translation
> *sino* but rather *lo que se pierde*
> *entre la ocurrencia—sea de amor o de agonia*
> between the happenings of love or pain
> *y el hecho de que llega*
> *a existir en palabras*
> and their coming into words.
>
> ("*Lo Que Se Pierde*/ What Gets Lost")

That language is at once indispensable *and* inadequate is a constant theme in Reid's best poems. In "That Dying," for example, he says that

> As often as not, on fair days, there is time
> for words to flex their muscles, to strut like peacocks,
> discovering what to say in the act of saying—
> the music of meaning emerging from the sound
> of the words playing.

But sometimes the enchantment is broken:

> It is then that words jump to their feet and rush,
> like white-lipped stretcher-bearers,
> tight-lipped, tense, to the unspeakable scene.
> They grab at air, water, syllables, anything handy.
> There is blood. No nonsense. No adjectives. No time.

Words, it seems, can be painfully useless when most urgently required. In "Visiting Lecturer" Reid considers the problem:

> In the lull between seeing and saying,
> I wonder at the way words have
> of hardening and betraying;
> but sense and sound assert themselves
> beyond conclusion and become
> a temporary, articulated home,
> a resting place
> aloof from time and space.
>
> but only for a time.

One must not place too much faith in words, he concludes, for "Home / is where new words are still to some."

Reid's sense of poetic rhythm cannot be faulted. He has deeply understood what all poets must know from the start, that no free verse is really free. Any good line of poetry has its own perfect shape; it must open out like a leaf into its full form, its one organically possible shape. And here, for the most part, good and bad poets divide. Reid nearly always finds the necessary shape of a line and the poem as a whole, calling upon a wide range of musical effects. In the beautiful "To a Child Playing a Piano" he explains that music—like poetry, one assumes—cannot be forced. It must be allowed to develop from within. So he tells the struggling child,

> Play the tune again; but this time
> with more regard for the movement at the source of it
> and less attention to time. Time falls
> curiously in the course of it.

Meditation permits the form of the thing to leak into existence naturally:

> Play the tune again: not watching
> your fingering but forgetting, letting flow
> the sound till it surrounds you. Do not count
> or even think. Let go.

So poetry becomes an arrangement of silence. Words form a kind of grid through which reality, as silently as light, passes. A poem is something like a photographic negative, suggestive and haunting. And the print can never be made.

Nonetheless, one should not assume that Reid inhabits a completely imaginary landscape where words take the place of stones, rivers, trees, animals, and people. On the contrary, he remains firmly attached to the earth and often to a specific environment. Given his predilection for the Romance languages, it is not surprising that many of his poems occur in sun-struck seaside Latin places. His titles reflect this preference: "Galilea," "Isla Negra, Chile," "The Rain in Spain," "Mediterranean." The importance of having a home, a specific geographical square of land to relate to, comes out in "Galilea," which is the village in Mallorca where Reid owns a house on a hilltop:

> Bleached white, bedazzled
> by the bright light falling,
> the hilltop holds me up.
> Below the coastline bares its teeth.
> Winded, burned to the bones, between

the stony green of the olive,
the grey grimace of stone,
I look dazedly down.

The poet has composed a vivid scene. Now he asks himself,

How to come to rest
in this raw, whittled landscape
where earth, air, fire and water
bluntly demand obeisance?

The problem is specific. How does one relate to this landscape? Is identification necessary for stability? Is the sense of place related to the sense of self? He considers:

Perhaps to fix one place
in a shifting world where time
talks and where too many selves
criss-cross and demand
enactment and re-enactment,

somewhere decent to die in,
somewhere which could become
landscape and vocabulary,
equilibrium, home.

Reid once looked to Scotland, albeit from across the Atlantic, for "landscape and vocabulary." He came to the United States after the war and university, and his first volume, *To Lighten My House,* was published here in 1953. Many of those early poems look back to the world recently discarded with a certain wistfulness. They vary in quality, as might be expected in a first volume, and many are derivative. But the best summon a world enchanted and immediate. "The Village" begins,

This village, like a child's deliberate vision,
shimmers in sunshine. Cottages bloom like flowers
and blink across the gardens thick with silence.
No one moves here but children and ancient women,

and bees haunting the hedges. The village hangs
with more intensity than a heavy dream.

"The Waterglass," his finest early poem, evokes a small Scottish coastal town:

A church tower crowned the town,
double in air and water, and over anchored houses
the round bells rolled at noon.
Bubbles rolled to the surface.
The drowning bells swirled down.

The poem soon moves from this high level of imaginative description into
the realm of clairvoyance as the poet gazes into the sea and discovers him-
self, ominously:

Mirrored, I saw my death
in the underworld in the water,
and saw my drowned face sway in
the glass day underneath—
till I spoke to my speaking likeness,
and the moment broke with my breath.

The world of Alastair Reid is abundant with omens and supernatural
signs. The poet investigates the world with an eye to all things pointing
beyond the normally rational, his poems repeating the process of
enchantment and disenchantment; though love is important, even neces-
sary, for survival, he sees it as fickle and unpredictable. For instance, in
"March," that "ill-starred month," a vase is found on the floor in shards,
an omen:

The weather spelt disquiet—
changeable, indecisive.
We did not sleep but dozed
on the edge of bad dreams.
Nothing was what it seemed.

Words came in fits and starts.
The animals were jumpy.

We moved uneasily about the room.
A distant uncle died, in gloom.

In "The Rain in Spain" we learn that

Lovers in their houses
quarrel and make promises
or, restless, dream of cities.

Ghosts in the rafters mutter.
Goats grunt and clatter.
Birds auger water.

The Swiss poet is sick.
The postman kicks his dog.
Death overtakes a pig.

And so on. But no reasons are forthcoming. Instead, the question arises:

For who is weather-wise
enough to recognize
which ills are the day's, which his?

Most of Reid's poems on love fall into two mutually exclusive categories
that again may be termed *enchantment* and *disenchantment*. And generally,
the latter poems far outshine the former. The theme of these finds summa-
tion in the final question of "In Such a Poise Is Love":

Who has not, in love's fever,
insisted on one simple vow, "for ever,"
and felt, before the words are gone,
the doom in them dawn?

More disturbing is "Figures on the Frieze," which describes a couple locked
mercilessly in a relationship of desperation:

Darkness wears off and, dawning into light,

they find themselves unmagically together.
He sees the stains of morning in her face.
She shivers, distant in his bitter weather.

The poem follows the lovers through a nightmarish day as "Wild with their misery, they entangle now / in baffling agonies of why and how." It ends, as one might expect, inconclusively:

When night falls, out of a despair of daylight,
they strike the lying attitudes of love,
and through the perturbations of their bodies,
each feels the amazing, murderous legends move.

The play on *lying* and *perturbations* only increases the calculated ambiguities that reverberate through this poem from the opening quibble on *frieze*.

To me, yet more terrifying are Reid's seemingly benign poems like "Curiosity" and "Propinquity." In these poems people divide into cat people and dog people, and the poet clearly sides with the cats, who are unpredictable, adventurous, fickle. For them, love means nearness. But alas,

A cat minority of one
is all that can be counted on
to tell the truth. And what he has to tell
on each return from hell
is this: that dying is what the living do,
that dying is what the loving do,
and that dead dogs are those who do not know
that dying is what, to live, each has to do.

("Curiosity")

Again, ambiguity gives the poem its resonance, here with the familiar Elizabethan quibble on *dying*.

More cheerfully, the poem "Growing, Flying, Happening" treats the amazement of loving:

Eyes open on growing, flying, happening,

and go on opening. Manifold, the world
dawns on unrecognizing, realizing eyes.
Amazement is the thing.
Not love, but the astonishment of loving.

Amazement, astonishment, wonder. These words recur in Reid's verse over and
again. It is a commonplace of romanticism that the child sees with a fresh-
ness of vision unavailable to adults. So poets emerge as those who have made
the child's special way of seeing their own. But this innocence of vision is not
mere naïveté; rather, it is an *achieved* innocence, what William Butler Yeats
called "radical innocence." This is what Reid at least attempts in much of the
volume *Oddments, Inklings, Omens, Moments* (1959). In the title poem, for
example, he considers the childlike spontaneity of moments when

the air's awareness
makes guesses true,
when a hand's touch
speaks past speech
or when, in poise,
two sympathies
lighten each other,
and love occurs
like song, like weather.

In Reid's later poems, a bold new theme reveals itself as the poet reflects
on his role as father. "The Fall" pictures a boy walking along a garden wall,
calling

Look up,
papa, look up! I'm flying . . .

But he falls, as he must. And the poet-as-father thinks how

Terrible
when fear cries to the senses, when the whirl
of the possible drowns in the real.

He reaches up to catch the boy's "small, sweat-beaded body":

"I flew, papa, I flew!"
"I know, boy. I know."

Reid offers his readers an experience so direct that it stuns with its clarity. Another poem on fatherhood (and much more) is "Daedalus." It has a subtle and persuasive music of its own, unfolding from within into many unexpected layers. It begins,

> My son has birds in his head.
> I know them. I catch
> the pitch of their calls, their shrill
> cacophonies, their chitterings, their coos.
> They hover behind his eyes and come to rest
> on a branch, on a book, grow still,
> claws curled, wings furled.
> His is a bird world.

The conceit develops in many directions. The birds are selves, personae, that the boy will in turn try on. Variously, he will succeed and fail. The poet comes to learn

> the flutter of his moods,
> his moments of sweep and soar.

In the evening, at the child's bedside, the poet watches "the hooding over of eyes." And at morning attends the "twitterings, / the *croomb* of his becoming." The boy tries to be wren, hawk, swallow, owl; he explores "the trees and rooftops of his heady wishing." The poet asks,

> Am I to call him down, to give him
> a grounding, teach him gravity?
> "Gently, gently," he cautions.
> Time tells us what we weigh and soon enough
> his feet will reach the ground.
> Age, like a cage, will enclose him.
> So the wise men said.
>
> My son has birds in his head.

Again, there is no certainty. A parent can command a child for only so long, even then imperfectly. The title, alluding to the myth of Daedalus and Icarus, adds a dimension of timelessness to the poem that is portentous and suggestive.

The voice coming through in this poetry is clear, original, and deeply moving. Like all good poets, Alastair Reid can teach us something about ourselves. He shows us a new way of seeing. He takes us with him from enchantment, through disenchantment and fear, back to enchantment. And we can never be the same for having traveled with him. "The Spiral" represents something of a summary of all that is best in his poetry. Here is the whole of it:

> The seasons of this year are in my luggage.
> Now, lifting the last picture from the wall,
> I close my eyes of the room. Each footfall
> clatters on the bareness of the stair.
> The family ghosts fade in the hanging air.
> Mirrors reflect the silence. There is no message.
> I wait in the still hall for a car to come.
> Behind, the house will dwindle to a name.
>
> Places, addresses, faces left behind.
> The present is a devious wind
> obliterating days and promises.
> Tomorrow is a tinker's guess.
> Marooned in cities, dreaming of greenness,
> or dazed by journeys, dreading to arrive—
> change, change is where I live.
>
> For possibility,
> I choose to leave behind
> each language, each country.
> Will this place be an end,
> or will there be one other,
> truer, rarer?
>
> Often now, in dream,
> abandoned landscapes come,

figuring a constant theme:

Have you left us behind?
What have you still to find?

Across the spiral distance,
through time and turbulence,
the rooted self in me
maps out its true country.

And, as my father found
his own small weathered island,
so will I come to ground

where that small man, my son,
can put his years on.

For him, too, time will turn.

THE LATER POETRY
OF ROBERT PENN WARREN

I

In *Democracy and Poetry* (1975), Robert Penn Warren writes, "Poetry, especially strong poetry, is not . . . more than superficially concerned with the celebration of objective victories. Greek tragedy, though it sprang from the energy and will that made Marathon and Samothrace possible, does not celebrate those victories any more than Hamlet and Lear celebrate the defeat of the Spanish Armada. What poetry most significantly celebrates is the capacity of man to face the deep, dark inwardness of his nature and his fate." It would be foolish to posit any correlation between Warren's late-blossoming status as a major poet and any peculiar national virtues; the United States, in this late stage of its infancy, inspires little in the way of great tragic or heroic literature. Yet, as a large and various nation famous for its energy and will, we were bound—sooner or later—to hurl up a poet such as Warren, one able to confront the deep dark inwardness of his, and our own, nature and fate with the sustained vision of major poetry.

Warren's case as a poet is unique. He has been part of our national wealth since the twenties, when he first attracted the admiration of John Crowe Ransom, who in 1939 called Warren "one of the really superlative poets of our time" on the strength of his first book, *Thirty-Six Poems* (1935). Warren's early association with the Fugitives (Ransom, Allen Tate, Donald Davidson, and others) was fortunate; his work benefited from the audience of sophisticated readers generated by that movement and was propelled into a certain prominence by it. Yet already in Warren's career attention to his poetry was diluted by the attention given to his other work; his controversial essay on segregation, "The Briar Patch" (1930), initiated Warren's career as a social critic and intellectual historian; the publication of his novelette *Prime Leaf* in 1931 precipitated his wholly other career as novelist, of which *All the King's Men* (1946) remains the centerpiece. One could add to this his fine critical writings, culminating in the *Selected Essays* of 1958, and his monographs on Drieser or Melville. The point is, Warren's "other" careers had a doubly negative effect on his poetic prominence; on the one hand, critics lost sight of his continuously developing poetic oeuvre; also, the other writings—especially in the forties when he was writing *All the King's Men, World Enough and Time* (1950), and most of the short stories—absorbed his energies. What other poet has had to deal with such divergent, perhaps contradictory, writing impulses? Warren came through a thick wood of ambition and creative conflict, finding along the way those temporary points of stasis that are called *art*. He sometimes resolved philosophical crises in his essays and partially satisfied the compulsion toward narrative in his novels and stories, but he most successfully wedded the philosophical and narrative drives in his poetry, using his lyric power to unite these often antithetical impulses.

The later work of any good poet should, if the poet retains his gift, grow out of and confirm what has gone before. There is sometimes a falling off, as with Frost, who gave in too easily to his public persona in the end. Eliot simply quit writing at a certain point, having said all he wanted to say. Roethke died too early for us to know what he would have done. Lowell went to pieces, and Auden drowned in his own facility. Only Yeats and

Stevens were able to find a language adequate to a stark autumnal vision; they did so, not by forcing a violent break with their past selves but by hauling up from the same wells a chilly water. They drank deeply, becoming (as Frost said in "Directive"), "whole beyond confusion." Warren, for his part, went back to go forward, recovering early visions, revising both his past and himself in relation to that past. He attempted a dramatic confrontation with his own nature and fate, making a myth of himself in the process that entails a mixture of fiction and fact.

For the purposes of this essay, I am calling "the later poems" those that Warren published after 1975, when a fresh *Selected Poems* appeared, featuring ten new poems called *Can I See Arcturus from Where I Stand?* and known as the Arcturus sequence. The new poems had about them the compulsive, exuberant urgency of coming to some final reconciliation with fate that marks his two later, magnificently accomplished, volumes: *Now and Then* (1978) and *Being Here* (1980).

Warren's later poetry went to new imaginative lengths, testing against the fullness of a long life all the great abstractions: Time, Self, Truth, and Eternity. As he concludes in *Being Here's* "Afterthought": "Indeed, it may be said that our lives are our own supreme fiction."

II

The *Selected Poems* of 1975 opens with the Arcturus sequence. These were some of the poems that signaled that Warren was caught in a fresh spasm of thought, that he was crackling with new life. The themes that find ultimate expression in *Now and Then* and *Being Here* begin to obsess the poet here. The terrible force of time with its human and inhuman wrenchings recurs from "A Way to Love God" to the tenth poem, "Old Nigger on One-Mule Cart Encountered Late at Night When Driving Home from Party in the Back Country."

"Fix your eyes on any chance object," he says in "Brotherhood of Pain," and you will find some example of decay, some promise of doom. Nature in these poems seems to threaten the poet's very existence, as if his ego were perpetually at stake; his rather solipsistic conclusion here is that man exists only in the "delirious illusion of language." "Trying to Tell You Something" has a powerful sense of nature's various parts acting in collusion: "All things lean at you, and some are / Trying to tell you something." This mysterious something is not necessarily bad, for sometimes "They sing / Of truth, and its beauty." Indeed, nature often prepares us for its revelations.

Being prepared for revelations is a theme of this sequence as a whole. In the astonishing "Old Nigger on One-Mule Cart" the poet swings radically back to a youthful encounter after a party; as often happens in the case of revelation, the least expected encounter may lead to something extraordinary. In this poem, the central image is an accidental confrontation between the old Negro and the speaker that is nearly disastrous for both; in memory, the encounter takes on greater meaning, the old Negro becoming a type familiar in most of Warren's poetry from the twenties on: the stranger who turns out to be a spiritual guide. Repeatedly, the persona will encounter a hag or dangerous character who will provide the basis for some future revelation. Warren's point, perhaps, is that the universe is full of explanations and that the poet's job is to listen, to observe closely, allowing meaning to take hold and establish its presence.

Warren's lesser poems spend perhaps too much time waiting for revelation to occur; his best work simply embodies the vision as it was revealed. "Evening Hawk" stands out as the finest example of genuine revelation in the Arcturus poems:

> From plane of light to plane, wings dipping through
> Geometries and orchids that the sunset builds,
> Out of the peak's black angularity of shadow, riding
> The last tumultuous avalanche of
> Light above pines and the guttural gorge,
> The hawk comes.

Warren manages to hold meaning in abeyance until the final line, "The hawk comes." In this old but ageless technique, one used by Milton at the start of *Paradise Lost,* the poet piles anticipatory clauses like bricks that collapse into meaning with the final verb. As the hawk, "Who knows neither Time nor error," swings through the sky, unforgiving of the earth and unforgiven himself, one cannot help but recall Ted Hughes and his crow or Hopkins with his windhover. A hawk, crow, or kestrel in flight forces a human to confront something—however frightening—that the person is not. As always, Warren assumes that a human's purpose in this fallen world, "heavy with the gold of our error," is to discern the bat's "sharp hieroglyphics," to observe the lone star over the mountain, "steady, like Plato." He concludes,

If there were no wind we might, we think, hear
The earth grind on its axis, or history
Drip in darkness like a leaking pipe in the cellar.

III

Now and Then: Poems, 1976–1978 fulfills the promise of Warren's Arcturus sequence in the *Selected Poems,* not by breaking with anything that preceded it but by consolidating and extending well-established themes and techniques. The title reflects the typical dialectic of a Warren poem, which proceeds by antithetical maneuvers; Warren opposes past and present in two sequences entitled *Nostalgic* and *Speculative,* both of which explore the burden of time—humans' lapse into "knowledge," as it were. Recognition and acceptance of mortality become, in Warren's aesthetic, the artist's primary responsibility. As the persona of Thomas Jefferson concludes in *Brother to Dragons* (1953): "Nothing we were, / Is lost. All is redeemed, / In knowledge." Jefferson had explained to his sister that "without the fact of the past we cannot dream the future."

In a specific sense, the *Nostalgic* poems reconstitute the facts of the poet's past. Warren explores "the growth of the poet's mind" in true romantic fashion, digging into memory for relics, emblems, and events to which meaning may attach itself; the poet-as-archaeologist reconstructs his time from these loose shards of experience.

"American Portrait: Old Style" presents the boy persona of Warren "on the verge of discovering the source and character of all artistic power, the transfiguring imagination," as Strandberg has said. The poem is a tour de force of Warren's style, beginning with a rich evocation of place, that dark and blood ground beyond "the last house, where home was, / Past the marsh we found the old skull in." A huge oak marks the place, a familiar image in Warren: "the single great oak that, in leaf-season, hung like / A thunderhead black against whatever blue the sky had." As ever, Warren's eye and ear work together in the quirky rhythms and syntax characteristic of his lines, which writhe here like a young garter in the spring grass. In this place without history, where "no Harrod or Finley or Boone" stalked the wilderness, "we had to invent it all." Warren's subject is invention, "what imagination is." As he says, it is only the "lie we must learn to live by."

The poet remembers his boyhood friend, K, who "seemed never to walk, but float / With a singlar joy and silence." K makes it to the big leagues as a pitcher, although "no batter / Could do what booze finally did: Just blow him off the mound." With great wisdom, Warren observes how he went his own way too, winning and losing, and—alas—was sometimes unable to tell the "one thing from the other." He writes, "How the teeth in Time's jaw all snag backward / And whatever enters therein / Has less hope of remission than shark-meat." Late in life, the poet revisits his old friend, who refuses to acknowledge Time's jaw:

> Like a young David at brookside, he swooped down,
> Snatched a stone, wound up, and let fly,
> And high on a pole over yonder the big brown insulator
> Simply exploded. "See—I still got control! " he said.

The poet, "late, toward sunset"—his life's sunset as well as the literal going down of the sun—revisits the marsh by the single great oak, "now nothing / But a ditch full of late-season weed-growth." He lies down in the ditch and looks up at the sky, imagining "what it would be like to die." But, reversing this somewhat indulgent fantasy in the final stanzas, Warren concludes,

> But why should I lie here longer?
> I am not dead yet, though in years,
> And the world's way is yet long to go,
> And I love the world even in my anger,
> And love is a hard thing to outgrow.

The cumulative action of this last invigorating motion is typical of Warren's impressibility. His motto might well be St. Augustine's famous line: "Love calls us to the things of this world." Despite his anger against Time's rapacious jaws, Warren refuses not to love the world, not to swim out far in life's cold river.

Wordsworth's phrase, "the growth of the poet's mind," would seem appropriate to describe what Warren is getting at in "Amazing Grace in the Back Country," a vivid recreation of a night in August when, as a boy, he refused to go with the tide of fundamentalist emotion at a tent meeting; he breaks away, vomits outside the tent, then stumbles to an old hickory tree, where he looks back at the "muted gold glow" of the canvas. He hears the haunting chorus of the hymn "Amazing Grace" in the distance, but it does not cause the boy to repent. Instead, the boy collapses beside a stream, dipping his hand into the cold black water, which reflects a single star—an emblem of the poet's isolation, the magnificent withdrawal and independence of the imaginative mind. Here again, Warren declares his allegiance to the primary romantic mode.

But grace he does find, not the comfortable unfallen paradise of Eden; rather, he discovers the "paradise within you, happier far" that was promised to Adam and Eve by the archangel Michael at the end of Milton's epic. The poet finds grace through knowledge, knowledge intensified by the moral imagination. He learns of fidelity and devotion in "Boy Wandering Simms' Valley," a strange and forceful poem about a dirt farmer who nurses his sick wife until she dies, then lies down on his shotgun, having fulfilled his duty in marriage. The boy revisits the house where this happened, seeing the "old enameled bedpan" on a high shelf—"And stood wondering what life is, and love, and what they might be."

In "Old Flame" he recalls the inflammatory power of beauty first encountered, but "Red-Tail Hawk and Pyre of Youth" celebrates the possibility of recovering something of the initial flame through art, in this case taxidermy. The poet once shot the bird but preserved it: "Year after year, in my room, on the tallest of bookshelves, / It was regal, perched on its bough-crotch." In a similar way the poet shoots his image; the image falls from reality into the artificial preserve of poetry, where it takes on a special radiance, enhanced beyond all expectation. So the red-tailed hawk, in memory, serves "to bind us in air-blood and earth-blood together / In our commensurate fate, / Whose name is a name beyond joy."

Another romantic theme, the awakening of the artist to the private subliminal language of nature, finds expression in other poems of the *Nostalgic* group, such as "Evening Hour" and "Mountain Plateau." The last two poems in the sequence, though seen from the perspective of an adult persona, depend on recollection. "Star-Fall" is among the most beautiful of Warren's later lyrics; its language is rich, musical, concrete:

> We lay on the dry grass of August, high
> On our cliff, and the odor we caught was of bruised
> Rosemary at pathside, not garbage, and sometimes
> The salt air of the sea, and the only sound to our ears

Was the slap and hiss far below, for the sea has never
forgiven
The nature of stone.

Watching a sudden starfall, the poet says, "We found nothing to say, for what can a voice say when / The world is a voice, no ear needing?" The poet achieves, however briefly, a moment of identity, of Emersonian correspondence. But the final poem of the section, "Youth Stares at Minoan Sunset," recalls the fallen condition of human beings: in this spectacular poem, a boy stares across a fiery sea into a Cretan sunset, "Molten and massy, of its own weight flattened." We see a man against the sky in all his pathos: "The frail human figure thereon minted black." The figure is fixed on a Minoan coin, emblematic of the artist's artificial world, wherein the paradox of art is registered and—perhaps—overcome. The flickering moment is sometimes caught forever, frozen, yet continually reborn, redeemed by memory and imagination.

This remarkable sequence gives way to the less consistent but no less interesting sequence called *Speculative*. In his novel *Flood* (1964), Warren writes, "There is no you except in relation to all that unthinkableness that the world is." What the lyric persona does in these poems is to construct an *I* in contrast to "all that unthinkableness"—nature (in its destructive aspects), pain, evanescence. The self (as Warren and his wife, novelist Eleanor Clark, have repeatedly said) is not something you take time off to "discover." You must create your self, and poetry becomes a primary agent of this self-inventing process. The twenty-seven *Speculative* poems (*speculate* in the root sense) envision the future of not only Warren's self but the reader's as well, the poet making an effort toward self-knowledge and responsible identity amid the flux of experience.

A fair number of the poems in this sequence deal with Time, one of Warren's favorite great abstractions; time, of course, remains inscrutable, the present crumbling instantaneously into the past after hanging a perilous moment on the lip of the future. So, in "Dream," Warren begins *Speculative* with two questions:

What can you dream to make Time real again?
I have read in a book that dream is the mother of memory,
And if there's no memory where—oh, what—is Time?

Through the poems of *Speculative,* Warren wrestles like Jacob with his angel, hoping to wring a blessing from the elusive spirit.

These poems differ in tone and intention, more so than the poems of *Nostalgic,* but what makes them of a piece is Warren's ceaseless questioning. In "Dream of a Dream," he asks, "From what dream to what dream do we / Awake when the first bird stirs to declare / Its glimmering dream of the golden air, / Of green and of dapple?" In "Ah, Anima!" he asks, "Can you locate yourself / On the great chart of history?" From the first volume of his published poetry through the novels and critical essays to the later poems, Warren characteristically began by asking, What does it all mean? In "Not Quite Like a Top," a grand poem, he frames his work at either end with a question. The initial whimsicality of tone belies a profound seriousness toward which the poem builds: "Did you know that the earth, not like a top on its point, / Spins on an axis that sways, and swings, from its middle?" The question is in essence rhetorical, because Warren doesn't care if "you" know or don't. The point is that he didn't but now does: experience is not redeemed by knowledge so much as made more real. He goes on:

> It is like
> So many things they say are true, but you
> Can't always be sure you feel them,
>
> Even in the dark, in bed, head north.
> I have, in shameless dark, sometimes
>
> Wept because
> I couldn't be sure something precious was true,
>
> Like they say.

As an example, he recalls lying once in a Pullman berth, desperately praying to God to exist so that he might have "the exalted horror of denying / Him." But nothing came of the project, he says in a mingled tone of whimsy and despair, concluding,

> And maybe the axis of the earth
> Does not really sway from its center, even if

Ancient Egyptian and modern astronomers say so,
And what good would it do one to have firsthand evidence,

When there's so much that I, lying in darkness, don't know?

Thus Eliot asked, "After such knowledge, what forgiveness?" Great poets must step into a clearing and ask great questions, risk being struck by God's thunderbolts or, worse, risk hearing their own voice come back like the cry that echoes across the lake in Frost's "The Most of It." Warren's poem, like most of his, offers no resolution. It is enough to ask the right questions, he says in "Waiting," "Until it grows on you that, at least, God / Has allowed man the grandeur of certain utterance / True or not. But sometimes true."

Self-creation hinges directly on self-assertion, utterance. The movement to utter something that might be true preoccupies Warren in the final *Speculative* poems, wherein he tests, as Brooks has said, the truths of abstract utterance against what, in "When the Tooth Cracks—Zing!" he calls "For lack of a better word, / Reality." Reading experience for signs, he remembers that Jacob Boehme, the mystic, saw a splash of sunlight on a pewter platter and found his life totally changed. Thus the poet questions, tests, observes, meditates on small changes, exploring not memory now but "Memory Forgotten," the title of an oddly wonderful poem about the unconscious zone that may well be tied into memories but that persists as unnamed feelings:

Afar,
In a thicket, it sings like
Some unidentified warbler. No, don't move.

If you break a twig, it may stop. But now!—
Oh, light, elate, more liquid than thrush,

It sings.

To get to this "liquid note," the unnamed foundation of reality, one has to begin by forgetting: "Forget it to know it." One forgets in order to sidestep rational faculties that may block the way to deep intuitive knowledge, that tacit ground that a poet must recover, repossess, name. Selfhood, as before, begins with utterance, which is the primary existential act.

In *Democracy and Poetry,* Warren defines *self* as "the felt principle of significant unity." He means two things by *significant:* continuity—"the self as a development in time, with a past and future" and responsibility—"the self as a moral identity, recognizing itself as capable of action worthy of praise or blame." The poet turns these aspects of self like a diamond in the sun in "Identity and Argument for Prayer," reflecting on the evolution of the self in time and the need to be wholly present in the now. To confirm this present, the reality that may be a dream, one has to apprehend the physical universe literally; one has to kick the stone to refute Bishop Berkeley: "As I stand in the spruce-deep where stars never come," he says in "Rather Like a Dream,"

> I stand, hands at sides, and wonder,
> Wonder if I should put a hand to touch
>
> Trees or stone—just to know.

Knowledge of this sort confirms not only the exterior but its analogue, the interior world. Poets scan the physical world for objects to which they may attach their feelings. Warren confirms himself and verifies his life among others, for the basis of any moral judgment resides in this confirmation. One begins from first principles.

The most typical poem in *Now and Then,* and perhaps the best example of Warren's later work in general, is "Heart of Autumn." The poem starts in a present autumn that quickly becomes a metaphorical autumn. Wild geese flying south become a symbol of the poet's youthful instincts, many of which are blown out of the sky by hunters. The geese follow the season's logic, which—the poet observes—is more than he can do. The typical question occurs: "Do I know my own story?" In a sense, he does. For as the geese rise toward 'imperial utterance," so does the poet, who likewise "cries out for distance." With magisterial simplicity of diction and clarity of feeling, Warren concludes,

> Path of logic, path of folly, all
> The same—and I stand, my face lifted now skyward,
> Hearing the high beat, my arms outstretched in the tingling
> Process of transformation, and soon tough legs,
> With folded feet, trail in the sounding vacuum of passage,

And my heart is impacted with a fierce impulse
To unwordable utterance—
Toward sunset, at a great height.

IV

Age seems to have wrung from Warren's imagination an astonishingly fresh vision—or re-vision—of the world. And whereas Frost, say, in old age settled into complacent repetition of earlier discoveries, Warren—so often compared to Frost as a "regionalist" poet—discovered a whole new subject in reviewing his past from the vantage point of age.

Being Here: Poetry, 1977–1980 is a diverse book—a "shadow autobiography," as he calls it—representing a "fusion of fiction and fact." This is the necessary fusion of great art; the job of poets is to turn the floodlamp of their imagination on reality, casting shadows, pouring their peculiar brilliance on the object under view. *Being Here,* taken with the *Nostalgic* sequence of *Now and Then,* represents something of a *Prelude* for Warren as he traces paths backward into what Wordsworth called those "hiding places" of a poet's power:

> The hiding places of my power
> Seem open; I approach, and then they close;
> I see by glimpses now; when age comes on,
> May scarcely see at all, and I would give,
> While yet we may, as far as words can give,
> A substance and a life to what I feel.

This substance and life accrue as the poems of *Being Here* unfold.

Two poems frame this collection, one in the nostalgic vein, "October Picnic Long Ago," the other a simple, vaguely philosophical lyric called "Passers-by on Snowy Night." These poems form the base of the arc of *Being Here,* an arc parallel in its rough contour to that of *Now and Then,* moving from the nostalgic to speculative modes. Yet *Being Here* is something of a tangle between the framing poems, as Warren acknowledges in his "Afterthought." "Speleology" sets the book in motion, establishing the poet's central direction here: inward, backward, down. On the literal level, the poem recalls a time when the child-poet entered a cave, disinheriting himself of the superficial identities of light, assimilating the darkness.

"Light out, unmoving, I lay," he says, "Lulled as by a song in a dream, knowing I dared not move in a darkness so absolute." He thinks: "This is me." The poem ends with a chilling realization:

> Years later, past dreams, I have lain
> In darkness and heard the depth of that unending song,
> And hand laid to heart, have thought once again:
> > *This is me.*
> And thought: *Who am I?* And hand on heart, wondered
> What would it be like to be, in the end, part of all.
> And in darkness have asked: *Is this all? What is all?*

He relentlessly searches out those hiding places of power. A good number of these poems—such as "Boyhood in Tobacco Country"—run back to the poet's youth. Apart from the fine evocative details present in this and other poems that resuscitate the past ("an autumn sunset, / Red as a hayrick burning"), there is the recurring theme of the need to name, to attach to some external correlatives the vague, unrealized, but powerful emotions that are any artist's secret hoard: in a poet's case, to words.

A deep wisdom underlies and steadies this work, which is typically full of questions about Time and the meaning of life. What other poet these days would dare ask:

> Success or failure—what can alleviate
> The pang of unworthiness built into Time's own name?

> Why have I wandered the asphalt of midnight and not
> known why?

> What kind of world is this we walk in?

This takes courage, not because Warren thinks he has the answers but because he risks putting these stark questions so baldly. Sometimes he falls flat, I must admit. Like any poet worth talking about, Warren is capable of hideous awkwardness. He goes out on endless limbs, and they snap off once in a while. Nevertheless, the spectacle of a person asking the big questions and finding a rueful solace in small answers will suffice. The search for what Warren, self-consciously old-fashioned in his terminology, calls *Truth* motivates his work, although he knows full well that "Truth is the trick that History / Over and over again, plays on us." For the fallen person, truth adheres in the particulars of reality, preferring to dress in lowercase letters:

> Truth is what you cannot tell,
> Truth is for the grave.
> Truth is only the flowing shadow cast
> By the wind-tossed elm
> When sun is bright and grass well-groomed.

Poems of winter dominate *Being Here,* and snow functions as a healing ground cover, a prophylactic against despair. Snow covers up what must be covered. Snow offers the comforts of forgiveness and forgetting. This is one of the small truths realized over and over. "God does the best / He can, and sometimes lets snow whiten the world / As a promise," Warren writes in "Functions of Blizzard," among his finer late poems. Another truth that dominates this volume is night. These poems often open with a question like the one that begins "The Moonlight's Dream": "Why did I wake that night, all the house at rest? " Not surprisingly, the moon swims into view often enough too, "Gold like a half slice of orange / Fished from a stiff Old-Fashioned." Finally, there is a good deal of dreaming here; Warren, like all poets, knows that dreams are inchoate poems, that the dream world provides a glimpse of the afterlife and that the images that have power to become true symbols may be found more readily in sleep's kingdom than elsewhere. And typically, Warren represents sleep as a return to the womb world, the prelapsarian twilight before dawn. Dawn represents birth, the fall into existence:

> Dawn bursts like the birth pangs of your, and the world's,
> existence.
> The future creeps into the blueness of distance.
> Far back, scraps of memory hang, rag-rotten, on a rusting
> barbed-wire fence.

From these scraps of memory this poet fashions the elaborate quilt cover of his work.

The final poems of *Being Here* own a peculiar strength, having about them an elegiac cast set by "Eagle Descending," itself an elegy. Reminiscent of "Evening Hawk," the poem traces the flight of the bird, a metaphor for the lost friend's soul, as it uncoils in the wind, "Spiral on spiral, mile on mile," fulfilled. But lest no ironic distance fall between Warren and his meditations on death and the autumnal season of a person's life, he quickly follows with "Ballad of Your Puzzlement," a poem puzzle of sorts, what he calls in his "Afterthought" a kind of "backboard against which the poems of this section are bounced." It begins,

> Purge soul for the guest awaited.
> Let floor be swept, and let
> The walls be well garlanded.
>
> Put your lands and recollections
> In order, before that hour,
> For you, alas, are only
>
> Recollections, but recollections
> Like a movie film gone silent,
> With a hero strange to you
>
> And a plot you can't understand.

Shorn of sentimentality by this poem's endearing but insistent self-mockery, the poet-as-septuagenarian opens a cool space for himself, a high clearing from which he can stand to review his life.

Two poems about language, reality, and their delicate interfusion—"Aspen Leaf in Windless World" and "Acquaintance with Time in Early Autumn"—prepare the way for "Night Walking." It is in some ways the archetypal poem of *Being Here* and one that others seem to anticipate. As always in Warren's best work, his natural lyricism deepens a strong narrative line; the narrator-poet begins with waking. Interrupted sleep leads him out of doors at night under a big moon. He thinks he hears a bear; but, no, it is his son. Crouching to observe the boy's activity undetected, the poet—in love with his son—trails him for a while, then watches in amazement as the boy lifts his arms suddenly to the moon. The poet will not follow farther but returns "to bed and the proper darkness of night."

I start, but alone then in moonlight, I stop
As one paralyzed at a sudden black brink opening up,
For a recollection, as sudden, has come from long back—
Moon-walking on sea-cliffs, once I
Had dreamed to a wisdom I almost could name.
But could not. I waited.
But heard no voice in the heart.
Just the hum of the wires.
But that is my luck. Not yours.

At any rate, you must swear never,
Not even in secret, the utmost, to be ashamed
To have lifted bare arms to that icy
Blaze and redeeming white light of the world.

As with "Heart of Autumn" in *Now and Then,* Warren builds his book to a climax of emotion and understanding. The great abstractions fall away, finally, as the poet bows to the indifferent hard light of the world, praising—above all else—the mystery itself, the unutterable word.

CHARLES WRIGHT
The Remembered Earth

Good poets reinvent the language, taking the given of
ordinary speech and pushing it beyond itself, making in
effect a translation from one sense of reality to another.
But what results is not necessarily a lingua franca of the
imagination. A poet like Charles Wright, intent upon
creating a mythopoetic language every bit as inspired and
singular as William Blake's, presents a challenge to the
reader unlike that of any other poet now writing. One
has to read the whole of Wright to understand any part
of him, which means one can't understand him on first
reading except in that mysterious way in which one picks
up the so-called atmosphere of any fully imagined poem
on first encounter.

It is best to begin reading Wright with one eye closed,
forgetting about ordinary sense, listening with an inner

ear to his seductive music. The logic of his poems is similar to the logic of dreams; that is, it is alogical, not illogical; the symbols do add up, which is to say one can find a consistency of representation and similitude in the work as a whole. But one becomes aware only gradually that certain words and images are in fact symbols. Like a photograph in the developing tank, the lines of a Wright poem become firm only gradually, as the image resolves and the shadowy areas deepen. The total effect, after many rereadings, is both intellectually satisfying and emotionally rewarding. Despite his obvious difficulties, Charles Wright is what Henry James would have called The Real Distinguished Thing.

Wright's earliest model was Ezra Pound, whose *Cantos* he used "first as a guidebook, then as a reference book, finally as a copybook." During seven formative years, Wright lived in Italy; there he began to haunt the ghost of Pound, to whom he pays rueful homage in his second book, *Hard Freight* (1973):

> Today is one of those days
> One swears is a prophesy:
> The air explicit and moist,
> As though filled with unanswered prayers;
> The twilight, starting to slide
> Its sooty fingers along the trees;
> And you, Pound,
>
> Awash in the wrong life,
> Cut loose upon the lagoon (the wind
> Off shore, and gaining), the tide going out . . .
> Here is your caul and caustic,
> Here is your garment,
> Cold-blooded father of light—
> Rise and be whole again.

Given this eloquent homage, it is tempting to overplay the effects of Pound on Wright's development. Wright is, perhaps, one of the few contemporary poets to answer the modernist call to arms, writing what might be called cubist poems (in the sense that Picasso defined cubism as "a dance around the object"). His continuous flirtations with the surreal, with the symbol, with myth making of a kind Joyce and Eliot would have admired, beckon to the would-be explicator. There is also the determinably European cast of Wright's poetry, with its evocations of Dante and Rilke, Eugenio Montale (whom he has translated) and Georg Trakl, Giacomo Leopardi and Cesare Pavese. One might also point to Wright's instinctive imagism. He often constructs a poem around a single shimmering image—a deep image, if you will, letting the image ramify as it lingers.

Nevertheless, Wright is not just another neomodernist, one of the many sons of Ez who haunt contemporary poetry. It could be argued, I think, that Pound has had a largely negative influence on many American poets, such as Robert Creeley, Lawrence Ferlinghetti, and Allen Ginsberg, all of whom stalk the fabled elk of art with a sawed-off shotgun. Wright, by contrast, has understood and absorbed Pound's advice to "make it new" by reaching back through modernism to romantic autobiography. The high modernists— Eliot, Stevens, and Pound, in particular—rarely wrote about themselves without the shield of myth firmly in place (Eliot as Tiresias, Pound as Homer, Stevens in the guise of pale Ramon). Wright aligns himself with the romantic autobiographical strain while depending upon the luminous opacity learned from the modernists—an alignment much in opposition to the confessional vein of Robert Lowell, Sylvia Plath, and John Berryman.

In *Country Music* (1982) Wright brought together what he took to be the best of his first four collections. He mistakenly culled only five mediocre prose poems from his first book, *The Grave of the Right Hand* (1970), killing off a dozen poems of remarkable lyric grace, such as "Homecoming"—a poem that prefigures and in fact becomes a prototypical elegy in the work of this most elegiac of contemporary poets:

> I sit on my father's porch.
> It is late. The evening, like
> An old dog, circles the hills,
> Anxious to settle. Across
> Our road the fields and fruit trees,
> Hedgerows and, out beyond, in
> Another state, the misty
> Approaches to the mountains,
> Go quietly dark. In the
> Close corners of the yard white
> Cape jasmine blossoms begin
> To radiate light, become

Cold eyes. Into the sky the
Soft, loose Milky Way returns,
Gathering stars as it swarms
Deeper into the west. Now
Fireflies, like drops of blood, squirt
Onto the stiff leaves of the
Ivy vines, onto the bell
Lilies. Now I remember
Why I am here, and the sound
Of a breathing no longer
My own cuts through as I wait
For what must happen, for the
Flurry of wings, your dark claw.

The prototypicality of "Homecoming" has to do with structure and tone. Wright often stations a poem in time and place, usually in the past. He writes simply, accumulating details in a diachronic fashion. Landscapes quickly deepen into metaphors, growing inward: note the receding fields and fruit trees, the "out beyond" of line 6, which dissolves into "misty approaches." The landscape in the act of darkening recapitulates the death process. As ever, Wright tantalizes with details that suggest rebirth, but he postulates a curious—eerily unsatisfactory—rebirth: "Cape jasmine blossoms begin / To radiate light, become / Cold eyes." The fireflies here, squirting blood on the ivy vines, become positively ominous. At the crucial turn in the poem, the lyric *I* wakens to its presence in the landscape. On the most literal level, the poet has come home to mourn the death of a parent. But the poem is about more than an immediate death. It is about "coming home" in a broader sense. The poet is remembering, even learning, "Why I am here." The spirits rise up through him, haunt him, as he awaits his own death, "the / Flurry of wings, your dark claw." The weirdly powerful effect of the last line owes much to the word *your*. Whose? The parent's? The specter of death's? This lack of specificity captures the apprehension we all feel in the face of disintegration and death. The poem at once thrills and terrifies.

The predominance of the elegiac tone in a first book is, of itself, unusual. But Wright is a religious poet, the most aggressively so since Eliot, and an acute awareness of death often precipitates a spiritual journey. Among the most arresting poems in *The Grave of the Right Hand* (1970) is "To a Friend

Who Wished Always to Be Alone," written in memoriam for a friend who had recently died. The poem tries to imagine what dying was like for him, assuming that "Finally, it must have been / Much as you imagined / . . . As you began to recede, / And settle, with no sound, far / Backward, into yourself, like / Some fountain turned off at dusk." That final image derives much of its power from the oddity of the comparison. How is life like a fountain? The strange, though temporary, finality of a fountain's diurnal "conclusion" seems exactly right; the water, like the soul, becomes invisible, running underground now, contained. But it remains there, a pressure that could erupt again, that will erupt in the morning. Wright doesn't pursue these implications here. He probably wasn't aware of them. But his preconscious mind moved wisely toward this image as he wrote.

In "Piccola Elegia," another fine elegy for a dead friend called Nicky, the poem's addressee, Wright pictures the soul as a boat adrift:

> it is
> On fire; the flames at the gunwhales; and you
> Are smoke, Nicky, you are smoke.

Smoke, of course, is a more conventional metaphor, the image of a funeral pyre bedded somewhere in the reader's mind. Still, the drifting boat on fire retains a ghostly quality. The transmutation by fire is not a dead end, merely a passage. Wright, from the beginning, grasps every symbol of transmutation, alert for signs of transcendence, knowing—as he says in "Illumination"—that "Darkness dissembles."

Many poems in *The Grave of the Right Hand* fail as poems. Wright has always been something of a note taker, writing poems in the margins of his life. He resists the urge to make poems. His images, instead, seem to gather, like flies drawn to the flame; occasionally, they hit the flame and disintegrate. "Addendum" is one of those poems that doesn't quite come off as a poem because it is too fragmentary, but it foreshadows the mature Wright. The poem opens beautifully:

> Under the stone the lizard breathes,
> His tongue a semaphore
> In the blinding darkness.

Meaning appears everywhere, encoded. The semaphore flashing in the dark-

ness gives the poet courage to proceed, suggesting that there is a message,
however difficult to interpret. Nature, in Wright's view as in Renaissance
theology, is everywhere "signed." The conclusion of "Addendum" points
directly toward the later Wright: "The path will open, the Angel beckon, /
And we will follow. For light is all."

Hard Freight (1973) is Wright's most self-conscious book, showing off
his neomodernist aesthetic in bright colors. An early ars poetica is "The
New Poem," an eye-grabbing poem whose title insists on its contempo-
raneity, if not its avant-guardism:

> It will not resemble the sea.
> It will not have dirt on its thick hands.
> It will not be part of the weather.
>
> It will not reveal its name.
> It will not have dreams you can count on.
> It will not be photogenic.
>
> It will not attend our sorrow.
> It will not console our children.
> It will not be able to help us.

But exactly how is the new poem different from the old poem? Wright is
posing as an aesthete here, praising the poem as useless object. Poetry will
never, of course, "console our children." At least not many of them. But did
it ever speak to any but the few? Irony's sharp blade cuts several ways in
"The New Poem," as in the line about the new poem not being photogenic.
The poem is indeed beautiful, photogenic, after all. Charles Wright has a
faultless ear and can't help but write lines that sing. But he wants more in
Hard Freight than beautiful music. He wants something akin to Truth.

Truth, for Wright, is not easily accessible. It can be got at but only via
indirection. The surface imagery of his poems is designed to shut down the
logical waking side of the brain and stimulate the other side, that
Wonderland where dream logic prevails and the poet, like Alice, runs daz-
zled amid many splendid, unlikely, often frightening things. But even
dreams are rooted in the waking life, drawing their validity from "normal"
truths. Thus Wright will ground his poems in time and place, as if to say,
"See, this is *real*." Local place names are crucial to this grounding in reality;

so, in "Sex," he refers to a place called Moccasin Gap, or he titles a poem "Clinchfield Station." However, these signifiers seem to grope somewhat helplessly toward their signifieds. Reality is hard to come by. Thus a poem such as "Nocturne" dissolves into et ceteras. Or a word like *Nothing*, capitalized, positions itself in a sentence as though it had real substance. Often, the image is surreal, though infinitely suggestive, as in the last lines of "Blackwater Mountain"—

> The stars over Blackwater Mountain
> Still dangle and flash like hooks, and ducks
> Coast on the evening water;
> The foliage is like applause.
> I stand where we stood before and aim
> My flashlight down to the lake. A black duck
> Explodes to my right, hangs, and is gone.
> He shows me the way to you;
> He shows me the way to a different fire
> Where you, black moon, warm your hands.

At its best, as in these lines, the surreal imagery has its origins in and returns to the real. For all its unreality, "Blackwater Mountain" retains the sumptuous concreteness of Theodore Roethke's nature poetry. It is a poem about the strangeness of the spiritual world, how it lurks in perpetual shadow, resists knowing, tricks one into acknowledging its existence, flashes, and fades.

The poems in *Hard Freight* often refer to the poet's life, most specifically in "Firstborn," a six-part sequence in which the poet speaks, as a father, with almost painful simplicity and tenderness, to his infant son, Luke. The newborn child is jaundiced, living in a "glass box" with a tube in his throat, "The name, like a new scar," at his wrist. The poet builds to this address:

> We bring what we have to bring;
> We give what we have to give;
> Welcome, sweet Luke, to your life.

The second part juxtaposes a blooming bougainvillea with the child's body, "it's slow / Network of vines / Holding the earth together, giving it breath." Wright's focus on the substantial, the body of the earth, is important, preparing the way for the fifth part, with its luminous resolution, a consolidation of wisdom into aphorism. Part 3, however, explores the ineffability of commerce between parent and child: "What can one say to a son?" In the fourth part, the poet becomes more—a little too much more—abstract in asking the same question, searching for those "few felicitous vowels / Which expiate everything." This doesn't work, of course, because "No tricks we try to invent / No strategies, can now extract them." I quote the whole of part 5, which seems central to all of Wright's poetic project:

> What I am trying to say
> Is this—I tell you, only, the thing
> That I have come to believe:
>
> Indenture yourself to the land;
> Imagine you touch its raw edges
> In all weather, time and again;
>
> Imagine its colors; try
> To imitate, day by day,
> The morning's growth and the dusk,
>
> The movement of all their creatures;
> Surrender yourself, and be glad;
> This is the law that endures.

Wright's poetry has been the active product of his struggle to indenture himself to the land, to touch its raw edges, to adapt himself, chameleon-like, to the contours of reality's great given: the physical world. His is a poetry of self-surrender, of abnegation and survival through adaptation: "This is the law that endures." The sixth and final section extends the central insight of the fifth, naming places important to the poet: "The foothills of Tennessee, / The mountains of North Carolina, their rivers and villages." The son, the addressee of the poem, is urged to "concentrate / Upon the remembered earth." In a concluding line that echoes Pope, Wright says, "All things that are are light."

The poet's religious preoccupations begin with a vengeance in *Hard Freight*. "Northanger Ridge" is about the poet's adolescent guilt and spiritual doubts at a Protestant Bible camp in 1949. He invokes Father Dog (read God for Dog, here and everywhere in Wright—one of many similar iconographic leitmotifs that occur with some consistency in book after book): "Sunday, and Father Dog is turned loose." The poem is wryly antievangelical, picturing a prayer meeting where "The children talk to nothingness." The conventional signs and symbols of Christianity have lost their meaning; they require reinvention, a resubmersion in the physical world, its pageant of mutability, its glimmers of the eternal. "The way back is always into the earth," says Wright in "Clinchfield Station"—understanding, like Seamus Heaney, that, for salvation, the ground must be "possessed and repossessed."

Bloodlines came out in 1975, and it represents a watershed in Wright's work, a summation and reformulation of early themes, images, and symbols. The book opens with the haunting "Virgo Descending," in which Wright reconstitutes his childhood home in the underworld of the afterlife, "down, / Where the worm and the mole will not go." The conceit is brilliant: the father is trying to put together the house, a symbol of family unity and affection. He wants to expand the house, which can never be finished, being beyond consolidation. Light, representing all that cannot be contained, domesticated, irritates and challenges the father, who keeps nothing: "That light . . . that damned light."

Wright pursues the theme of redemption in "Easter 1974"—

> Against the tin roof of the back porch, the twilight
> Backdrops the climbing rose, three
> Blood stars, redemptive past pain.

The possibility of redemption exists, but its access remains obscure. The poem closes enigmatically, without much in the way of traditional Easter optimism: "What opens will close, what hungers is what goes half full." Still, a glint of hope exists here. The thirst for God, for redemption, for a sign, is the beginning of its eventual slaking. Wright has this hunger, and he knows that while he is alive it must go only partially satisfied.

Two sequences of extraordinary power form the bulk of *Bloodlines*, *Tattoos* and *Skins*. *Tattoos* is a twenty-part poem in which the poet strings moments of crisis or illumination like beads. The beads glisten and seduce the reader with their oblique yet shimmering lights. In a series of endnotes that point to the source of each poem in the sequence, Wright offers the autobiographical key to each poem. That Wright is overtly a religious poet can no longer be in question. At least half the poems in *Tattoos* refer to an explicit religious experience, as in the fifth poem:

> Hungering acolyte, pale body,
> The sunlight—through St. Paul of the 12 Sorrows—
> Falls the Damascus on me:
> I feel the gold hair of Paradise rise through my skin
> Needle and thread, needle and thread;
>
> I feel the worm in the rose root.

Once the reader identifies the specific context, *Tattoos* becomes less mind-bogglingly obscure. Wright is, almost always, a poet for whom ordinary logic does not play much of a role, because the poet likes to free associate, with images clustering around themes. As Helen Vendler memorably put it, writing in *The New Yorker* in 1979: "Because Wright's poems, on the whole, are unanchored to incident, they resist description; because they are not narrative, they defy exposition. They cluster, aggregate, radiate; they add layers, like pearls."

The best moments in *Tattoos* are deeply affecting, disconcerting, slyly comforting—as in the thirteenth poem, described in the "Notes" as follows: "The janitor; kindergarten; Corinth, Mississippi."

> What I remember is fire, orange fire,
> And his huge cock in his hand,
> Touching my tiny one; the smell
> Of coal dust, the smell of heat,
> Banked flames through the furnace door.
>
> Of him I remember little, if anything:
> Black overalls splotched with soot,
> His voice, honey, O, honey . . .
> And then he came, his left hand
> On my back, holding me close.
>
> Nothing was said, of course—one
> Terrible admonition, and that was all . . .

And if that hand, like loosed lumber, fell
From grace, and stayed there? We give,
And we take it back. We give again . . .

1940

Readers can easily reconstruct this scene, without the help of notes, from
the shards of meaning provided by the poet: a janitor sexually assaults a
young boy in the basement of his schoolhouse. Imagery of guilt soaks
through the poem ("overalls splotched with soot"). The last few lines pro-
vide the only difficulties. Wright is often fascinated by the consequences of
transgression, of "crossing the line" (literally) from grace to disgrace. He
tracks the human heart's backsliding with an almost evangelical fury: "We
give, / And we take it back." The act of forgiveness is what finally matters,
he may be suggesting. Wright gives back to the janitor the sympathy that
he was trying, in his perverted way, to give to the little boy. Human actions,
for Wright, seem intimately bound up with the nature of grace; as he says
in "Grace" (a poem from *Hard Freight*), "Its face is a long soliloquy, / A lan-
guage of numerals, / Impossible to erase."

Two hauntingly lyrical elegies—"Hardin County" and "Delta Traveller"
—resurrect the poet's dead parents in *Bloodlines*:

the dead are brought
Back to us, piece by piece—
Under the sponged log, inside the stump,
They shine with their secret lives, and grow
Big with their messages, wings
Beginning to stir, paths fixed and hearts clocked,
Rising and falling back and rising.

These elegies—impressionistic, structured by sound, by musical rather
than logical arrangement—prepare the way for *Skins*, a series of twenty
free-verse "sonnets" that trace the intricate knit-and-purl of the self in cre-
ation. The poet, the poem's "Pilgrim," says to himself in the eighteenth son-
net: "There is a shine you move toward." These poems constitute a latter-
day surrealistic counterpart to Donne's *Holy Sonnets* (1633), tracking the
soul's tortuous progress toward God:

You thought you climbed, and all the while you descended.

> Go up and go down; what other work is there
> For you to do, what other work in this world?

Wright, ever liturgical, echoes the language of the mass, explicitly and covertly. He recognizes that this life is always imperfect, that we live and breathe in "the brushstroke that holds the angel's wing / Back from perfection." We occupy the vacant point between two real worlds, "The synapse of word to word." We pursue, with little hope of success, "the one note / That would strike the inner ear / And save you." We repeat, endlessly, the painful circle (as in the fourth poem) of creation and decreation, Blake's solipsistic world of Generation, wherein fallen man begets and dies and begets again his fallen kind. Always, we return to death, "back to its dish of ash." But there is hope in the movement itself, as in the fifth poem: "Nevertheless, the wheel arcs; nevertheless, / The mud slides and the arms yearn." It is desire that both damns and saves, that creates the yearning that makes fulfillment possible. In the seventh poem, the poet asks, "Where is that grain of sand that Blake saw, / The starfish that lights the way?" Wright understands that we—as human beings—are merely in transit ("You're only passing through," he says in poem 8) and that earth is a "sure sheet for the resurrection." His sequence delves in the prima materia of memory, searching for "The thread that will lead you home" (poem 9). This is Wright's salute to the via negativa, the dark way into light, which begins with a negation of the world, a sloughing off of skins. In *Skins*, the poet attempts to wriggle out of the substantial world, to escape from the text and texture of reality. He flirts, in language that boldly dislodges words from their referents, with the ineffable. The poems of *Skins* succeed, I think, in becoming a metalanguage, more like notes of music than strings of words that may have referents. Wright plays these notes, reassembling a higher reality from the broken shards of a fallen world.

Bloodlines concludes with one of Wright's best poems, "Rural Route," a poem that opens with an image of consummate poise and originality:

> The stars come out to graze, wild-eyed in the new dark.
> The dead squeeze close together,
> Strung out like a seam of coal through the raw earth.

Wright discovers signs of transcendence everywhere in nature—which is not to say he finds nature comforting. His nature is prickly, unpredictable, even menacing: "The willows let down their hooks." The poet's book of nature, "That slow code," is a text in need of unraveling, a semiotic tangle. Through all the adult poet's baffled attempts to break the code, he recalls the twelve-year-old boy whose innocent gaze apprehended something essential in what he saw. Years later, repeatedly, "the face stays." No matter where he goes, those insights remain. Time, for Wright as for William Wordsworth, gathers in those "spots of time" that intersect linear time, moments of timelessness approaching ineffability.

Wright followed *Bloodlines* with *China Trace* (1977). The poet conceived of it as a single poem, and it is. Here, as always, the poet revisits earlier insights, resurrects familiar imagery and symbols. But there is no sense of simple repetition. Wright deepens these images and symbols by providing new contexts, new juxtapositions, as poem gives birth to poem. "Rural Route," for instance, is reenvisioned in "Childhood," the initial poem of *China Trace*—

> Shrunken and drained dry, turning transparent,
> You've followed me like a dog
> I see through at last, a window into Away-From-Here, a place
> I'm headed for, my tongue loosened, tracks
> Apparent, your beggar's-lice
> Bleaching to crystal along my britches leg:
>
> I'm going away now, goodbye.
> Goodbye to the locust husk and the chairs;
> Goodbye to the genuflections. Goodbye to the clothes
> That circle beneath the earth, the names
> Falling into the darkness, face
> After face, like beads from a broken rosary . . .

The mannerisms are familiar by now: the dog, who is less God here than before but still godly, seen through a window (a symbol of an opening from one world to another), with heaven downgraded to "Away-From-Here," a typical Wrightian ploy, turning an ordinary phrase into a self-conscious construction. The diction is familiar too: *tongue, tracks, britches*. The second stanza is among Wright's most rhythmically brilliant, with its repetitions and crescendo, its falling away—an almost cinematic dissolve into ellipses. The poem also contains many references to liturgical or sacramental things, such as genuflection and the rosary, which in this case is symbolically broken. Such references add to the sense of spiritual hunger so characteristic of Wright.

The book's title, *China Trace*, contains an element of homage to Pound, whose volume of translations called *Cathay* (1915) represents his finest work. The imagistic element one associates with Chinese poetry is much in evidence in Wright's brief lyrics. And there is also the dominant elegiac tone that, at least in Pound's (and Arthur Waley's) translations, seems typical of ancient Chinese poetry. If anything, that note in *China Trace* seems almost overplucked, dominating the book from first to last. It also adds to the single-minded aura of this book.

Wright's obsession with death—he often writes from the point of view of the deceased—is evident throughout. The poet seems willing, as he says in "April," to be "Divested of everything," to be "Released as a glint, as a flash, as a spark. . . ." Helen Vendler comments: "The hunger for the purity of the dead grows almost to a lust." This is nicely put, but Vendler seems mistaken when she adds: "The eternal and elemental world is largely unrelieved, in *China Trace* and after, by the local, the social, the temporary, the accidental, the contingent." I find the opposite true in a good many of these poems, a definite sense of "the local, the accidental, the contingent, as in "California Twilight"—

> Late evening, July, and no one at home.
> In the green lungs of the willow, fly-worms and lightning
>   bugs
> Blood-spot the whips and wings. Blue
>
> Asters become electric against the hedge.
> What was it I had in mind?
> The last whirr of a skateboard dwindles down Oak Street
>   hill.
> Slowly a leaf unlocks itself from a branch.
> Slowly the furred hands of the dead flutter up from their
>   caves.
> A little pinkish flame is snuffed in my mouth.

Here, as elsewhere, the poet reiterates place names, refers to specific occasions and dates. He relies, to some extent, on the romantic tradition of associating a particular insight or moment of illumination with a specific time and place, often alluding to it only in the title, as in Wordsworth's "Tintern Abbey" or "Upon Westminster Bridge." Vendler has perhaps been misled by the ethereal quality of the imagery, as in the following lines culled from various poems:

> The plains drift through the deep daylight.
>
> > ("Indian Summer")

> The river lies still, the jeweled drill in its teeth.
>
> > ("At Zero")

> I take you as I take the moon rising,
> Darkness, black moth the light burns up in.
>
> > ("Death")

> The mist, with its sleeves of bone, slides out of the reeds,
> Everything hushed, the emptiness everywhere.
>
> > ("12 Lines at Midnight")

Not a poem in this collection lacks some arresting image, something dazzling and hushed. Perhaps this is that trace of China to which his title alludes?

China Trace is, above all else, a prayer book, a guide to the Way (the word *trace* also refers to a path). Wright has nowhere else demonstrated more explicitly a greater hunger for God or tried harder to coax Him out of hiding. He seeks the Him of "Him," which is also a hymn to the God whose "sorrow hangs like a heart in the star-flowered boundary tree." Wright wants to find this God

> Released in his suit of lights,
> > lifted and laid clear.

The Southern Cross (1981) contains much more self-portraiture than the earlier books. Pound and Chinese poetry recede as influences, while Dante and Wallace Stevens step forward. A new ars poetica at once anticipates and embodies the new voice:

> I like it back here

Under the green swatch of the pepper tree and the aloe vera.
I like it because the wind strips down the leaves.
I like it because the wind repeats itself,
and the leaves do.

Wright is explicitly romantic, an Emersonian transparent eyeball who
wants to meld with the dead, "The voices rising from the ground." He
wants also to fit in with the cyclical patterns of nature, the difficult but irre-
sistible "lying down and the rising up" described in "Mount Caribou at
Night." As Devon Jersild says in her review of *The Southern Cross* in
Midwest Quarterly (autumn 1981), "Wright's obsession with the circular
nature of time, partially formed by his readings of eastern philosophy,
grows out of Emerson."* She refers to Emerson's "Uriel"—

> Line in nature is not found;
> Unit and universe are round;
> In vain produced, all rays return;
> Evil will bless, and ice will burn.

Emerson, as Jersild notes, embraced the paradox of these cycles. But
Wright remains rueful, as in the opening line of "Hawaii Dantesca"—
"White-sided flowers are thrusting up on the hillside, blank love letters
from the dead." Wright sees "the petals of wreckage in everything," taking
no comfort here in the remembered earth. He asks for nothing but "the
wine deep forgetfulness of death."

The Southern Cross is a tentative book, less unified than *China Trace*,
though it opens new directions for Wright's work. *China Trace* was, in its
glorious completeness, a dead end of sorts. In the next book, Wright tests
other voices, tries on new personae, as in the flawed but provocative open-
ing sequence written in homage to Paul Cézanne. Mary Kinzie, in a 1981
review in *American Poetry Review*, disparaged the Cézanne sequence, sug-
gesting that "it so abounds in misjudgments in tone and in tact that the
reader is apt to forget that the painter Cézanne is supposed to be central."
Kinzie's disappointment stems from the thinness of the mask: Wright
hardly disguises the poet of *Bloodlines* or *China Trace*, who leaks through at

---

*Jersild and I are married. Her review of *The Southern Cross* appeared in the autumn 1982 issue of
The Midwest Quarterly.

every turn. "We sit out on the earth and stretch our limbs, / Hoarding the little mounds of sorrow laid up in our hearts," Wright says in the last two lines of the poem, in effect summarizing his poem. His Cézanne is full of the world sorrows typical of early Wright, while the somewhat ragtag organization of the poem is leaning, phototopically, toward the light of the latter poems in *The Southern Cross* and beyond, to *The Other Side of the River* (1984). In many ways, *The Southern Cross* begins with its second section, which contains a number of self-portraits.

The notion of a self-portrait, of course, derives from the tradition of painting, and this painterly aspect is crucial to *The Southern Cross*. Reading the table of contents is like walking in a picture gallery, with titles like "Dead Color" and "Spring Abstract," and "Landscape with Seated Figure and Olive Trees" leaping off the page. This is all reminiscent, again, of Wallace Stevens, who made a practice of adopting painterly titles. But the parallels with painting extend to more than just the titles.

Wright transforms the act of seeing into something resembling devotional duty, as in "The Monastery at Vrsac," one of the best poems Wright has written. The poet-narrator here visits some old monastic grounds, with its "icons and carved iron stalls." He sketches in the scene with swift brush strokes as "Now we sit in the brandy-colored light of late afternoon / Under the locust trees." In one of the most crucial lines of this volume, the poet says, "Light signals of dust rise uninterpreted from the road." In Wright's world, nature offers a perpetual hieroglyph in need of explanation; the poet becomes both priest and scholar, opening the text and speculating on its meaning. Writing poetry for him becomes increasingly hermeneutical, a science of interpretation. What do these signals mean? Which, of the many signs the world presents, are to be taken as signals from beyond? Wright, the interpreter, waits in the "awful" stillness for this beckoning. He ends the poem with a request for mercy that echoes (and complicates ironically) the Christian liturgy: "Mercy upon us, / we who have learned to preach but not to pray."

Critics who avoid the specifically Christian content of Wright's work miss something essential. His poetry is explicitly sacramental, shot through with liturgical moments, echoes, parodies, and affirmations. Wright's verse fits nicely into what Louis L. Martz has called "the meditative tradition." Even the less orthodox poems, where he asks for "the wind deep forgetfulness of death," remind one of the Via Negativa of St. John of the Cross, Donne, or Gerard Manley Hopkins in the "Terrible Sonnets." Wright's goal is always the awakening of something like what

Ignatius Loyola calls "the affective will," that part of the mind that yearns to merge with the spirit, to celebrate God or whatever one thinks of as Other. In moments of heightened spirituality, as at the conclusion of "Dead Color," Wright can allow himself to cry out, "Windows, rapturous windows!"—the windows through which he catches that glimpse of the eternal. One can hardly avoid seeing the cross of Jesus in the title too. *The Southern Cross* is most literally the constellation that cannot be seen from the northern hemisphere, though it can, as in the magnificent title poem of the collection, be imagined. "All we remember is wind," he says, the life of this world being nothing else ('wind' being one translation of the Latin *spiritus*).

Wright's work increasingly tries to approximate the Zen ideal of "no-mind" or "mindlessness." As Philip Kapleau, the well-known Zen scholar, explains in *The Three Pillars of Zen* (1965), "Mindfulness is a state wherein one is totally aware in any situation and so always able to respond appropriately. Yet one is aware that he is aware. Mindlessness, on the other hand, or 'no-mindness' as it has been called, is a condition of such complete absorption that there is no vestige of self-awareness." Wright's movement is continually from mindfulness to mindlessness, to a state of egoless absorption in the moment in all its rich particularity. One sees this movement especially in *The Other Side of the River* (1984) and *Zone Journals* (1988), with their long meditative poems constructed from a disjunctive sequence of lyrics—a technique brought to perfection in *Black Zodiac* (1997), a book-length meditation on the rediscovery of self in the natural world, where the poet goes "one-on-one with the visible / And shadowy overhang" of reality.

Wright has found himself drawn increasingly toward journal poems, poetic "notebooks" in which the poet is able to lose himself in the material at hand, the physical world turned emblematic and consubstantial. "T'ang Notebook," for instance, is typical of the medium-length poems of *The Other Side of the River*, all of which exhibit a meandering drive toward a mindlessness. "T'Ang Notebook" ends like this:

A water egret planes down like a page of blank paper
Toward the edge of the noon sky.

Let me, like him, find an island
of white reeds

To settle down on, under the wind, forgetting words.

All things move, as it were, toward a condition of wordlessness, a condition
that is most easily attained at noon, the time of shadowlessness. In this ideal
state, "The body is light / and feels it too could float in the wind."

At least on the surface, the poems of *The Other Side of the River* are more
explicitly autobiographical than many of Wright's earlier poems. Poems like
"Italian Days," "Roma I," and "Roma II" use material from his years in
Italy, as do "Homage to Cesare Pavese" and "To Giacomo Leopardi in the
Sky," a loping yet fiercely integrated poem that incorporates and restates
many of the spiritual insights acquired at different points throughout this
volume, which is intensely concerned with "Silences so immense they
sound like wind." Other poems, such as "Lost Souls," resurrect the poet's
boyhood in Kentucky. (After a long catalogue of autobiographical
moments, Wright—in a slyly ironic moment—says, "And nobody needs to
remember any of that, / but I do.") Wright's adult life in California also pro-
vides a setting for a number of poems or poetic moments in poems that
include other geographical landscapes that become symbolized. Among the
finest of these is "California Dreaming," which brings this collection to a
close; it's an ecstatic if pointedly inconclusive poem:

> Today is sweet stuff on the tongue.
> The question of how we should live our lives in this
>   world
> Will find no answer from us this morning,
> Sunflick, the ocean humping its back
> Beneath us, shivering out
>   wave after wave we fall from
> And cut through in a white scar of healed water,
> Our wet suits glossed slick as seals,
>   our boards grown sharp as cries.
>
> We rise and fall like the sun.

The poems *Zone Journals* (1988) are even looser, moving in broad med-
itative cycles that strain the underlying narratives to their breaking points.
In his *Paris Review* interview (1989), Wright comments on his withdrawal
from shorter lyric forms that predominate in his earlier books: "Montale

said that all poetry rises out of prose and yearns to return to it. That sounds right to me. And the interesting place to work in is that yearning, between the two power points."

Zone Journals consists of three sections, with "A Journal of the Year of the Ox" lying sphynxlike at the quiet center of this impressive volume. This nearly book-length poem occupies more than forty pages, picking up threads from the five shorter journals of the previous section. In it, Wright moves contemplatively through a single year (1985) from January through December.

Though "Year of the Ox" might be disparaged as a random assembly of images, the poem in fact has a firm consistency of tone—self-questioning, ruminative, philosophical, as in the following entry from July:

> I find myself in my own image, and am neither and both.
> I come and go in myself
>   as though from room to room,
> As though the smooth incarnation of some medieval spirit
> Escaping my own mouth and reswallowed at leisure,
> Dissembling and at my ease.
> The dove drones on the hillside,
>   hidden inside the dead pine tree.
> The wasp drills through the air.
> I am neither, I am both.

The self as a many-chambered room is not an uncommon image in Wright's work; as always, he recycles images, metaphors, and symbols. In many poets, one could not tolerate such reshuffling, such repetition; in Wright, however, the repetitions seem almost liturgical. His work, like that of Stevens (who is probably his greatest ancestor, not Pound), is of a piece. He insists upon an informed readership, one familiar with the deeply inward landscape conjured throughout his steadily evolving corpus. The ideal reader must share Wright's conviction (restated in "Chinese Journal") that "To find one word and use it correctly, / providing it is the right word, / Is more than enough." The finding of this "right word" leads, inevitably, to silence, what he calls "the silence / of risk and splendor," in "Night Journal," the haunting poem that brings *Zone Journals* to a point in the cycle of death and regeneration where everything begins again.

3. The World and the Word

THE LESSONS OF THEORY

One does not have to look far these days to find someone bashing literary theory, and in some respects it deserves bashing. Joseph Epstein, for one, has almost never tired of picking away at the motives of those who engage in literary theory: "The major impulse of theory was suspicion," he has said. "In this regard theory gave that portion of the professoriat who came through the sixties unfulfilled, and those younger professors—women, ethnic minorities, homosexuals—who chose to squeeze all they could out of their self-created status of victimhood, a large and lovely outlet for their resentment." The irony is that one hears in this semihysterical cri de coeur the very suspicion about which the author is supposedly complaining. Epstein, neither female nor gay, apparently feels passed over. Inadvertently, he has become the victim himself.

Literary theory—or just "theory"—has frightened a whole generation of intellectuals into early mental retirement, mostly because they have not had the stamina or will to enter into appropriate conversation with their younger colleagues. Perhaps the most unfortunate aspect of the debate over theory has been this extension into the academy of what, in the sixties, used to be called the generation gap; indeed, many of the same dynamics seem to apply, with theorists pitting themselves against all forms of authority. Never trust anyone over thirty has been transmogrified into never trust anyone who doesn't appreciate Foucault.

In the seventies, theory moved toward the center of the curriculum at most American graduate schools of literature, and it has remained in place for nearly a quarter of a century. The charge is often heard, perhaps with some justice, that students now spend more time reading Foucault or Derrida than Shakespeare or Dante, and that this has created an imbalance. But even here the situation is exaggerated; graduate students do indeed get a heavy dose of theory, yet one sees few undergraduate classrooms in the United States where anything resembling literary theory has displaced the teaching of canonical texts. For the most part what has happened is that the canon has been widened to include texts by previously overlooked writers—usually texts by women or minorities. Such a development hardly threatens to erase or even partially to occlude Homer, Shakespeare, and Milton.

The charge that theory is unreadable is, for me, a more important criticism. (There's a joke I like in this regard. *Question:* What do you get when you cross a deconstructionist with a mafioso? *Answer:* An offer you can't understand.) Jargon has overwhelmed literary criticism to the point where the so-called common reader is now fiercely excluded from the conversations that take place in most professional journals and academic conferences, and the consequences of this exclusionary practice are profound. The most obvious effect is that serious literature itself, and thinking about literature and its place in the world, is removed from mainstream consumption. As a result, the general quality of our national discourse—in the arts as well as collateral areas, such as politics—is diminished.

This said, I would still argue that an intellectual revolution of sorts has indeed occurred in the last thirty years and that theory has permanently changed the ways that we—as readers and writers—go about our reading and, yes, our thinking. The peak of the battle over theory passed several years ago; in fact, we seem to have entered a "post-theoretical" moment, and so the time may have arrived for reassessing some of the lessons of theory. This revolution is pretty much a literal one: a turning of the wheel. But the wheel has been spinning for a long time. Our ways of reading have been challenged almost continuously from the beginning of this century, when the philologists dislodged the belles-lettres style of criticism popular just after the Great War, and the literary historians attacked the philologists, and the New Critics pushed the historians temporarily to one side in the late forties and early fifties. And so forth. The history of criticism is simply a history of overturnings, or absorptions (I rather prefer the more organic metaphor).

Not long before he died in 1989, I sat on the porch of my Vermont neighbor Robert Penn Warren, talking about the early days of the New Criticism. He was, of course, among the founders of that movement and coauthor of one of the most influential textbooks of the century, *Understanding Poetry* (1938), which taught several generations of students how to read a poem from a formalist point of view, examining its internal workings, inconsistencies, tensions, ironies, paradoxes, and evasions. "The older members of the profession thought of us—the New Critics—as revolutionaries," Warren said. "In a way, we were. Deconstruction is already fading fast. It will be absorbed—its insights and techniques repossessed and deployed in new ways."

One gets used to dizzying changes in critical method; in a sense, that is what poststructuralism is all about. Its definition is so broad that almost any new development can be included in its large shadow. This catchall term includes feminists, deconstructionists, reader-response critics, psychoanalytic critics, New Historicists, postcolonialists, and others. These schools of criticism or hermeneutical approaches are highly permeable, and their subject can range widely from African American poetry to the constructions of gender or class. A good feminist critic, for instance, will almost certainly share a number of assumptions about the nature of textuality, author function, and determinacy of meaning with deconstructionists. Similarly, a wide range of methods are brought to bear on the subject in postcolonial studies, where the approaches of Marxist and neo-Marxist critics ranging from Theodor Adorno and Max Horkheimer to Gayatri Chakravorty Spivak and Terry Eagleton have proved useful.

The critical mainstream eventually absorbs almost any theoretical insight worth preserving. Take, for instance, the issue of textuality. One rarely called a poem or novel a *text* before deconstruction came along, although the movement from *work* to *text* preoccupied Roland Barthes, the French structuralist-turned-poststructuralist. The New Critics—who commanded center stage in literary studies from the late forties through the mid-seventies—worshipped at the shrine of The Poem, which for them became the chief form that High Art took; it was valued precisely because of its self-referential ("organic") nature, which made it ideally susceptible to New Critical techniques of interpretation, which were largely intrinsic. Barthes wished to deemphasize the enclosed nature of the poem; indeed, he found something forced about the way the form harmonizes the ironies and dissonances within a given poem. (In a famous definition, Cleanth Brooks—the archetypal New Critic—defined the poem as "a unification of attitudes into a hierarchy subordinated to a total and governing attitude.") The move from poem to text can be seen as an attempt to crack the vase, to let language spill into the world. It also let the world filter back into the text.

Despite the well-known injunction that a poem should not mean but be, the reader's task in the heyday of New Criticism was to lay bare the work's meaning. By subjecting a text—poem or play or story—to an almost excessive scrutiny, Barthes deconstructed the world of that text, seeing instead of a discrete and hermetically sealed object an arrangement of signs and signifiers that seemed almost endlessly productive of meaning. In his *S/Z*, for example, he explored a single story by Balzac with a maniacal attention to the multiplicity of meanings constituted by the text.

In deconstructive readings of a given text one hears a lot about "indeterminacy" of meaning, and it is scary stuff, especially if you happen to have a big investment in a certain line of interpretation or feel an instinctive need (as we all do, I suspect) to keep meaning within controlled boundaries. Yet there is something liberating about the fact that no single interpretation is, or should be, allowed to stand alone. Instead, meaning must be allowed to radiate in progressively widening circles like the concentric waves emanating from a stone tossed into the center of a pond. The deconstructionists seem to ride even the most distant waves without fear of losing sight of the original splash.

The deconstructive mode was neatly pictured in the early eighties by J. Hillis Miller, an early champion of Continental theory in the United States, in a 1976 essay called "Stevens' Rock and Criticism as Cure, II":

> Deconstruction as a mode of interpretation works by a careful and circumspect entering of each textual labyrinth. . . .

The deconstructive critic seeks to find, by this process of retracing, the element in the system studied which is alogical, the thread in the text in question which will unravel it all, or the loose stone which will pull down the whole building. The deconstruction, rather, annihilates the ground on which the building stands by showing that the text has already annihilated that ground, knowingly or unknowingly. Deconstruction is not a dismantling of the structure of a text but a demonstration that it has already dismantled itself.

The critic, then, enters the labyrinth of the text and finds a glitch somewhere (in deconstructive jargon: an *aporia*); this is the place where that proverbial loose thread is found, where the text is unraveled—or shown to have already unraveled itself.

Nothing is especially new about this mode of analysis. When D. H. Lawrence suggested that the reader trust the tale, not the teller, he meant—among other things—that good writers know not only more than they say but more than they consciously are aware of knowing. A kind of wisdom inheres in simply letting a passage in a poem or story fill to its full quotient of ambiguity. Bad art, I suspect, is art that has been narrowed to a point where ambiguity pretty much dissolves. On the other hand, a controlled ambiguity may approach something like "truth" while recognizing that truth is forever just beyond reach of both writer and reader.

The poststructural aspect of deconstruction comes into play here. Structuralism was a short-lived and somewhat mechanical way of thinking about texts that was born in Russia and found its first full expression in France in the early fifties, with Claude Levi-Strauss, the anthropologist. The power of structuralism, as Roland Barthes noted, had to do with its status as "essentially an activity" whereby a text or "object" could be reconstructed "in such a way as to manifest thereby the rules of functioning." The most well-known aspect of the structuralist activity was the partitioning of any given text or object (a volleyball game, for instance, could be analyzed in structuralist terms as easily as, say, *Moby-Dick*) into terms of opposition: nature and culture, light and dark, winner and loser, male and female.

This was a rather sterile maneuver, as it turns out. One sat back and merely shrugged: So what? The deconstructionists actually did something with these contrarieties, showing how genuinely complex meanings are produced by the interplay of opposite terms in such a way that an oppositional term actually co-opts its "other." Thus woman becomes "not-man," thus a rather poor version of the original male principle—an entity defined by what she lacks (a penis, a good job, power, status). But man—the other side of this particular complement of terms—needs a woman in the same way that evil needs good to exist. There would be no such thing as man without woman. His being therefore is enhanced by the degrees of separation he can discover or invent, the multiple ways that he can exclude and subordinate what is not him. Of course, as Carl Jung and others have suggested, man contains woman, and vice versa. So what is alien is also intimate. The argument grows like ivy, spreading rapidly, poking a tendril into every crevice.

"Deconstruction," as Terry Eagleton noted in *Literary Theory* (1983), "has grasped the point that the binary oppositions with which classical structuralism tends to work represent a way of seeing typical of ideologies. Ideologies like to draw rigid boundaries between what is acceptable and what is not, between self and non-self, truth and falsity, sense and nonsense, reason and madness, central and marginal, surface and depth." By insisting on a radical (or "root") reinterpretation of competing terms, deconstruction at its best encouraged a radical interrogation of cultural norms, finding things previously thought part of nature to be, instead, a part of culture.

Deconstruction tended, especially in its American versions, to stress the unnerving "undecidability" of language; this proved a blind alley of sorts, because the deconstructed text often dissolved into an endless series of "traces"—fragments of meaning like meteors streaking through the night sky and disappearing. But the critical tacks developed by deconstruction remain valuable, and they have permanently affected the ways we read. One approaches the meaning of a given text with due regard for its inherent instabilities. Indeed, one looks for terms of opposition almost instinctively now, having become aware of how texts "deconstruct" themselves naturally as oppositional terms swallow their counterparts. The idea of *meaning* itself has evolved to a point where nobody would dare to claim a single interpretation, and this can only be a good thing for readers as well as writers. Language is alive, shifting under our very eyes as we read; meanings occur, of course, but they dissolve as well; a good text (poem, story, letter) is multilayered, suggestive, and endlessly allusive; it resists being fixed.

Another useful concept that literary theory delivered into our hands is that of "author function," a critique of literary production in which the writer is seen not as a divine creator but as the custodian of language. Michel Foucault made the essential point in "What Is an Author?" (1969). The author is not a transcendent genius; rather, "he is a certain functional principle by which, in our culture, one limits, excludes, and chooses; in short, by which one impedes the free circulation, the free manipulation, the free composition, decomposition, and recomposition of fiction."

This notion of authorship, coupled with a deconstructionist deemphasis on the idea of an author's voice and authorial presence, remains unsettling to some writers, especially in its simplified (and often caricatured) form. As a writer of poems and novels, I do not like to think of myself as a limiting principle—I want to believe that my voice is unique and that my contribution stands alone. I doubt there is a writer alive who doesn't think the same way. Nevertheless, Foucault's point is useful in modifying the naive pretensions, and occlusions, of the old genius theory of creative writing. It is Language that we all serve, some better than others. The words themselves, the tropes and figures, the syntactical moves: they were all there before us. We approach them gingerly, or should. We try to find a voice within the voice, and we do so with varying degrees of success. Foucault's notion of the author as limiting principle does not, or should not, threaten our ability to see that some writers perform this function more successful than others. I am no less in awe of Yeats or Eliot or Stevens because I understand their role in limiting, excluding, and choosing signs.

Another of the lessons of theory concerns politics, that abused and misunderstood term. *Politics* has essentially been redefined by theory to underscore the historical or contextual dimensions of all texts. To imagine that theory is promoting one ideology over another seems to me quite mistaken; in fact, theory has been largely about recognizing that one cannot, however much one tries, escape politics-as-context. That is, one speaks, as an author, from a particular moment in time and from a unique place in the world; these coordinates necessarily govern the meaning of the text, at least on some level. Despite the clamor against the so-called politicizing of literature that has come from the conservative right, theorists have made their point so firmly and persuasively that critics now routinely take into account the special conditions and interests (such as race, class, and gender) that affect its meaning. They also take ideology into account when considering the reception of a given text and the place accorded its author in the hierarchy of reputation. What has followed from this awareness is a quickened sense of the contexts in which meanings are generated and a more complex understanding of the capriciousness of canon formation and the transmission of literary reputations.

In a strange way, theory has already done its work and been absorbed. Reception theory, for instance, which is also called "reader-response criticism," arose in its recent forms from the phenomenological work of Continental philosophers like George Poulet and Hans-Georg Gademer, who posited a continuous field of consciousness that is shared by the reader as subject and the text as object. This approach focused attention on the reader as an active ingredient in the production of meaning. It harked back to ancient and medieval rhetoricians, who studied the effects of language on its audience. As Walter J. Ong notes in a pioneering essay called "The Writer's Audience Is Always a Fiction" (1967), a writer creates an imaginary reader. Less obviously, "A reader has to play the role in which the author has cast him, which seldom coincides with his role in the rest of actual life."

Later critics like Stanley Fish and Wolfgang Iser mapped out the reader's side of things, trying to isolate ways that a given text might draw forth multiple meanings and yet work simultaneously to limit those meanings. Fish, in particular, did some fascinating work on the notion of an "interpretive community," examining the ways in which communal and commonsense values operate in the clarification of meaning, in the resistance to indeterminancy that all readers feel. He observed in "Interpreting the *Variorum*" (1980) that "it is the structure of the reader's experience rather than any structures available on the page that should be the object of description."

Feminist critics—the largest and most influential group of poststructural readers—have been able to absorb and deploy the techniques from the reader-response school with dazzling results, as in Patrocinio Schweickart's essay called "Reading Ourselves: Toward a Feminist Theory of Reading" (1984), in which she examines how women have had to learn to "read as men" in order to be admitted into the company of shared experience constituted by the act of reading. Commonly, a male-centered text assumes a male reader; thus a woman has to train herself to become her opposite in order to comprehend a text on its own terms. She urges women to relearn to read, to read a text as it "was not meant to be read," to read it "against itself."

Unlike most other theories, feminist theory has reached beyond mere criticism to have an influence on everyday life. It would take more space than I have here to explain this, but what brought me to feminism (and theory in general) was the experience of marriage and fatherhood. In the early eighties, when my first son was born, I began to realize the degrees to which society is constructed to impose values on him that struck me as patriarchal, and oppressive. What became thunderingly obvious to me was that he, as well as any women he might encounter, would be oppressed by these values. Having a child also forced me to confront issues of equality in marriage, and—as I slowly learned to adjust to a new way of seeing myself in relation to my wife, Devon, and our children—I began reading feminist criticism. What I found there was nothing less than a brave new world.

As for literary studies: one can hardly begin to estimate the extent to which rethinking the canon from a feminist perspective has affected the act of reading. One cannot, for instance, read Wordsworth now without taking into account the fact that nature traditionally was considered feminine, whereas the poetic imagination—in romantic terms—was distinctly male. What effect has this male-centered aesthetics had on the creativity of women? How many women have had to read against themselves in order to pass tests in college? The questions begin to multiply and circulate like spores. A groundbreaking book on this subject was Margaret Homans's *Women Writers and Poetic Identity* (1980).

Adrienne Rich, the poet, has described nicely in *Of Woman Born* (1975) what constitutes a feminist critique: "A radical critique of literature, feminist in its impulse, would take the work first of all as a clue to how we live, how we have been living, how we have been led to imagine ourselves, how our language has trapped as well as liberated us, how the very act of naming has been till now a male prerogative, and how we can begin to see and name—and therefore live—afresh."

Another leading feminist critic, Elaine Showalter, writes in "Feminist Criticism in the Wilderness" (1981) that the task for feminist criticism "is to concentrate on women's access to language, on the available lexical range from which words can be selected, on the ideological and cultural determinants of expression."

Feminist criticism is of course unabashedly political, demanding a transformation of how we read and, by obvious extension, how we live. The New Critics—or some of them—preferred to keep life and art in separate boxes, where the effects of one on the other could be limited. In my view, the separation of art and politics is deeply perverse, and it leads directly to scenes like those in Nazi Germany, where the officers who ran the death camps could spend their evenings in concert halls and theaters, imbibing high culture.

The school of theory called the New Historicism has grown out of Foucault, deconstruction, feminism, and Marxism, and it may be seen as an attempt to determine the effect of the historical moment on the author. In a sense, the moment itself becomes the author, and what we call *history* is seen as a text itself, one determined by its immersion in time. One of the leading New Historicists, Stephen Greenblatt, has said tellingly in "Resonance and Wonder" (1990) that "history cannot be divorced from textuality, and all texts can be compelled to confront the crisis of undecidability revealed in the literary text." The old-fashioned view of written history as mimesis—as a direct representation or mirroring of life—is thus modified and complicated. As Greenblatt says, "An older historicism that proclaimed self-consciously that it had avoided all value judgments in its account of the past . . . did not thereby avoid all value judgments; it simply provided a misleading account of what it had actually done." By acknowledging partiality and political engagement, the New Historicists have opened a fresh way of thinking about literature as a contingent art, bound and embedded in the political and historical matrix that forms a precondition of its existence.

Theory, then, is nothing new. Rather, it continues in the traditions of rhetorical analysis founded in ancient Greece and Rome, forcing us, again and again, to question the authority of any text or cultural object (and that object can be defined as broadly as marriage or the operation of democracy). As such, it is inherently disruptive, even "revolutionary." And it is full of questions: Who is writing this? What is his or her perspective? What values does it, implicitly or explicitly, endorse? What assumptions has the author made that might not be readily visible? Who wins and who loses in the world evoked here? What particular angle of vision is being ratified, denounced, interrogated? Who is the intended audience, and what effects has the author sought? In what ways, good and bad, might an audience "use" this text? What would constitute use?

The diversity and range of current theory are such that it can hardly be thought of as a single discipline; theory, instead, offers a particular place to stand when viewing modern culture as a whole. It should surprise nobody, then, that a critical project focused on meaning and value in relation to language should lead naturally to broader inquiries about power, sexuality, social arrangement, and other topics one might call political. It also follows that once critics—or anybody—starts asking questions about these things, there will be trouble. The so-called culture wars of the eighties and nineties have been largely about the right to ask these questions and about the validity of the answers that have been forthcoming. In the good old days, critics knew their place, and criticism was about the greatness of literature; it was not considered polite or politic, and certainly not professional, for a critic to venture beyond the ivory tower of the text. Those days are, of course, long gone, but they are deeply missed in some quarters.

This is, in fact, a fine time to work in the academy, where questions about cultural diversity, canon formation, and politics lie nakedly on the table every day. Literary theory has been crucial in bringing these issues to the fore, and it has changed forever the ways we think about texts and "textuality," about authors and readers; it has also made intellectual work defiantly cross-cultural, interdisciplinary, and responsive to the culture at large. It points to a future in the humanities, even in the sciences, in which a thoroughly interdisciplinary field akin to ancient rhetoric takes into account a broad range of discourses and "signifying practices," from making poems or films to writing treatises on the expanding universe or framing laws. We are apes, after all, but rather lucky ones, capable of gesturing to each other in so many different ways. With theory, we have come closer to understanding what those gestures mean—and how so many of these gestures are designed to help us retain our particular perch in the treetops.

THE IMAGINATION OF POLITICS

> It is not an artifice that the mind has added to human
> nature. The mind has added nothing to human nature.
> It is a violence from within that protects us from a
> violence without. It is the imagination pressing back
> against the pressure of reality. It seems, in the last
> analysis, to have something to do with our self-
> preservation; and that, no doubt, is why the expression
> of it, the sound of its words, helps us to live our lives.
> —WALLACE STEVENS

One doesn't normally think of Wallace Stevens in politi-
cal terms, but I would suggest that the power of a writer's
imagination is intimately related to that writer's grasp of
politics and that this true of poets (like Stevens) writing
in the aesthetic tradition as well as more overtly *engagé*
writers. I would define *politics* broadly to mean more
than simply the art of government. Politics, in its root
sense, refers to a complex of relations between the indi-
vidual and society; it is deeply philosophical on the one
hand, demanding an adequate definition of self as well as
a working notion of other—by which I mean the world
at large, to which the individual relates. It is also, almost
by definition, infinitely practical, requiring that one
know exactly how the individual relates to the larger
group as well as the ideology that governs that relation

and how that ideology is created and, in due course, modified and used.

Poetry, fiction, drama, autobiography: across the generic board, imaginative writing might be seen, in Stevens's terms, as an inward pressure—a force from within—that reacts to and presses back against a pressure from without. This dialectic may be expressed in different ways: as the world of the text versus the world it represents or (as a poststructuralist might say) creates, as self against other, as the individual versus society, or as the regarding subject versus the regarded object.

I want to duck most of the thorny philosophical issues and focus on the more practical matters that come up whenever one begins to contemplate the literary imagination and its relation to the larger world. Writers, for better or worse, are—as Shelley said—akin to unacknowledged legislators. That is, they create ideology through the complex exercise of the imagination. Again, I will quote Wallace Stevens, who made his lifelong project a study of the interdependence of reality and the imagination. In "The Man with the Blue Guitar," written in the mid-1930s, he plays in poetry a kind of jazz riff on the dialectic of reality, always represented in his symbology as the color green, and the imagination, represented by the color blue. The poem opens:

> The man bent over his guitar,
> A shearsman of sorts. The day was green.
>
> They said, "You have a blue guitar,
> You do not play things as they are."
>
> The man replied, "Things as they are
> Are changed upon the blue guitar."
>
> And they said then, "But play, you must,
> A tune beyond us, yet ourselves,
>
> A tune upon the blue guitar
> Of things exactly as they are."

Stevens offers us, in miniature, a political economy of art. Journalists report the news objectively—or imagine they report the news objectively. The artist—playwright, poet, novelist—reinvents the reality at hand, refigures the pattern in the carpet, reimagines "things exactly as they are." Nadine Gordimer, the South African novelist, offers much the same view in her essay "A Writer's Freedom" (1988), in which she says, "All that the writer can do, as a writer, is to go on writing the truth as he sees it." I would argue that the more original, and perhaps even the better, the artist, the more severely—and whimsically—that artist deals with the so-called real world. The real world is dead. It is unimagined facts: the number of dead Vietcong soldiers on a given day in Vietnam in 1969, the balance of payments for international trade in 1982, the color of Bill Clinton's eyes over breakfast this morning. What can all this mean?

T. H. Huxley once wrote to his friend Charles Kingsley, "Sit down before a fact as a little child." There is something wonderfully endearing about this entreaty. We must consider reality as the sacred ground, or—to change the metaphor—what Stevens calls "the necessary angel of reality." Without it, we can have no poetry, no imagination, and no politics. "The earth is not earth but a stone," Stevens writes, but it must be a stone before it can be the earth, the humanized sphere that we call *mother,* that we love and, it would seem, wish to destroy by war, pollution, or "progress" in its Hydra-headed forms. We must learn to sit down before reality like small children, open mouthed, attentive. This is the beginning of art.

A lot happens, as it were, between this sitting down and the standing up with a poem, novel, or play in our hands. We must deal with politics—the real world of stones and bones—as well as the imagined world, where earth and idea, mud and mind, comingle. There are people out there (nation-states, corporations) who want to control the products of the imagination. It is in their interests to do so, which is why they go to such great lengths to acquire publishing companies or control newspapers or television networks. As Erica Jong recently said, "The reason people invest in publishing houses is to control the word. As long as Robert Maxwell owned the *News,* he was 'Cap'n Bob' and they were writing wonderful things about him. When he went over the edge of his ship, he was suddenly discovered to be a crook who had looted the pension fund."

Nation-states have an even better reason for wanting to control the word. Historical writing can be thought of as an attempt to form what some critics call a "national narrative." In the United States, we are fiercely attached to our national narrative. We believe that our citizens are upstanding, righteous, godly, heterosexual, and generous. We are free and we are brave, and we act selflessly in the world to ensure the freedom of others. We are a democracy: one person, one vote. We have complete freedom of expression. We have goodwill toward all and malice toward none. We trust in God. We are a melting pot. And so forth. The national narrative is complex, but it runs along certain lines that most of us will find familiar (and somewhat nauseating).

One can, I think, go too far in deconstructing this narrative. If there were not some truth in the story, it would have long ago collapsed. On the whole, most citizens of the United States (and I would say the same for most Austrian, English, Egyptian, and South African citizens) mean no harm. They rather sentimentally approve of their myth of origin and the narrative that binds them as a nation. Americans, I suspect, all vaguely hold certain principles to be unalienable, hoping (rather wistfully) that "freedom rings." In fact, if you happen to be white, middle class, and well educated in the United States, you have a range of options open to you perhaps unequaled in the history of humanity.

These freedoms begin to shrink if you happen to be black or brown, speak a language other than English, prefer to have sex with people of your own gender, or happen to be female. These freedoms shrink even more dramatically if you by chance should live in a repressive country beyond our borders. We turn a blind eye to the way people are treated in sweatshops in underdeveloped countries, so long as the products manufactured by these economic slaves remain inexpensive and plentiful. When we get into a war with pesky nations like Iraq, we do not even count the hundreds of thousands of casualties—men, women, and children—on the other side as part of our imagination of the consequences of our actions.

Let me disentangle one or two little strands in our national narrative, beginning with the important concept of democracy. We say—that is, we tell our children in school and tell ourselves, implicitly, as we fall asleep watching television—that we live in a democratic society where the individual relates to the whole by way of the polling booth. We vote together, and the majority gets its way. But what happens when we don't agree, as individuals, with the reigning ideology, with the system that is often called "late capitalism" by theorists? The United States, as Gore Vidal has often noted, has only one party, which he calls the Party of Business or the Property Party; this party has two wings, the Republicans and the Democrats. In explaining the slight difference between the parties, Vidal says, "Republicans are a bit stupider, more rigid, more doctrinaire in their laissez-faire capitalism than the Democrats, who are cuter, prettier, a bit more corrupt—until recently—and more willing than the Republicans to make small adjustments when the poor, the black, the anti-imperialists get out of hand."

Vastly powerful interest groups are able to influence public opinion through media manipulation. What we have, in fact, is a form of democracy that is weighted heavily toward those who can pay for it, and the system is arranged so that—on the whole—only those who heel to the reigning ideology have access to capital. Meanwhile, billions of dollars in taxes are extracted from a helpless populace that is denied adequate education and health. The realities of our political system are rarely acknowledged or described; they do not form a conscious part of our written history.

A second strain of the U.S. national narrative that needs deconstruction has to do with our relations in the world at large. We tell ourselves, or are told, that we are mostly stay-at-homes, sticks-in-the-mud, who venture abroad armed to the teeth only with reluctance, and then we do it purely to save people or rescue them or promote "freedom." That's the myth. The reality is at odds, though not always in total opposition to, the myth. We have occasionally worked, in Somalia and elsewhere, to help people. We fought World War II for some excellent reasons. We had perfectly good reasons to oppose statist regimes in Eastern Europe and the Soviet Union, in China, and elsewhere. But, as always, the story is more complex than it appears. We have always had imperial yearnings (and by *we* I do mean *us*—those who either have capital or work for those who do, including those who shape opinion and create ideology).

In 1754, Benjamin Franklin hailed George Washington as a man who understood the need to "remove the Natives to give his own people room." Three decades later, Thomas Jefferson described "our confederacy" as "the nest from which all America, North and South, is to be peopled." And, indeed, the continent was swept clean of indigenous tribes as the armies of the United States pushed south to Mexico and westward to the Pacific to add vast lands to our domain. From the beginning we were, as Robert Frost intoned in "The Gift Outright," which he recited at the inauguration of John F. Kennedy, "a nation gradually realizing westward." Finally, the Pacific was no barrier, and after the Spanish-American War even the Philippines became American soil. But really, the myth declares, our aim was never—as in previous empires—to gain land or seek dominion. We wanted markets for our goods and raw materials for our factories. Woodrow Wilson explained all this in a rarely quoted speech:

Since trade ignores national boundaries and the manufacturer insists on having the world as a market, the flag of his nation must follow him, and the doors of the nations which are closed against him must be battered down. Concessions obtained by financiers must be safeguarded by ministers of state, even if the sovereignty of unwilling nations be outraged in the process. Colonies must be obtained or planted, in order that no useful corner of the world may be overlooked or left unused.

After World War II, the United States was in a unique position of power relative to other nations. George Kennan, perhaps the leading architect of the cold war, understood our situation and expressed it with icy plainness in Policy Planning Study #23, released to other members of the State Department in February 1948:

We have about 50% of the world's wealth, but only 6.3% of its population. . . . In this situation, we cannot fail to be the object of envy and resentment. Our real task in the coming period is to devise a pattern of relationships which will permit us to maintain this position of disparity without positive detriment to our national security. To do so, we will have to dispense with all sentimentality and day-dreaming; and our attention will have to be concentrated everywhere on our immediate national objectives. We need not deceive ourselves that we can afford today the luxury of altruism and benefaction. . . . The day is not far off when we are going to have to deal in straight power concepts. The less we are then hampered by idealistic slogans, the better.

This document, as one might imagine, was top secret for nearly four decades. The government, or those who function within the propaganda system, would never say such things out loud. The language issued by government spokespersons—and I would include presidents in this club—is studiously couched in bland, optimistic, woolly prose. Comely abstractions echo from the electronic platforms: Democracy, Freedom, Peace, Liberty. We hear the words, but we—the great listening public—have become deaf to what we hear. The moral debacle of Vietnam and a succession of scandals, such as Watergate and Iran-contra, have had one positive effect: the American people rarely believe anything their political leaders tell them. The problem is that they feel drained of power to resist or even protest.

Walter Lippmann—the American journalist and commentator—once noted the special importance of propaganda in a situation in which the national narrative is relentlessly at odds with the facts. What he called the "manufacture of consent" becomes terribly important in this situation. Edward S. Herman and Noam Chomsky, in *Manufacturing Consent* (1988)—the title echoing Lippmann—offer a systematic analysis of the propaganda system in the United States. They outline rather starkly how bias is created and maintained by the media:

> Institutional critiques such as we present in this book are commonly dismissed by establishment commentators as "conspiracy theories," but this is merely an evasion. We do not use any kind of "conspiracy" hypothesis to explain mass-media performance. In fact, our treatment is much closer to a "free market" analysis, with the results largely an outcome of the workings of market forces. Most biased choices in the media arise from the preselection of right-thinking people, internalized preconceptions, and the adaptation of personnel to the constraints of ownership, organization, market, and political power. Censorship is largely self-censorship, by reporters and commentators who adjust to the realities of source and media organizational requirements, and by people at higher levels within media organizations who are chosen to implement, and have usually internalized, the constraints imposed by proprietary and other market and governmental centers of power.

To be sure, within the system there will always be disagreements. One gets used to seeing dignified men in suits (and a few women) sitting around a table before TV cameras to discuss which of several options might be chosen to promote a certain end. But do they ever challenge real premises? Or even note them? Does the language of debate move outside the most prescribed and narrow circles? When, for instance, the subject of a debate is terrorism, what would happen if one debater simply assumed that the United States, in its activities—past and present—in Central America or the Middle

221

East, might be guilty of state terrorism? The case can be made; indeed, it is often made in marginal journals and books, but how often is it argued in the mass, or mainstream, media? The question does not require a response.

For the most part, the people who are chosen to conduct public discourse are carefully self-selected; they know what—in a free market society—will upset a sponsor. They realize that certain kinds of argument will not even be heard by the audience, which has been subtly educated to screen out certain kinds of analysis. Cultural power devolves on those, it seems, who are willing and able to reinforce the assumptions already shared by those in power. These men and women are intellectuals, of course; they are people trained in discourse of a particular kind, and many of them are experts in some field, such as economics or sociology or international politics. But we cannot safely look in their direction for a discourse that is free of cant, that is fully imagined, and where the grain of a unique voice is heard. Here is where the artist—the imaginative writer—comes in.

There is something almost painfully practical about literature. It provides what Kenneth Burke once called "equipment for living." Literature is, as Czeslaw Milosz, the Polish poet, has said, "as essential as bread." Wallace Stevens, again, put it beautifully at the end of his greatest poem, his *Notes Toward a Supreme Fiction* (1942), which ends:

> Monsieur and comrade,
> The soldier is poor without the poet's lines,
>
> His petty syllabi, the sounds that stick,
> Inevitably modulating, in the blood.
> And war for war, each has its gallant kind.
>
> How simply the fictive hero becomes the real;
> How gladly with proper words the soldier dies,
> If he must, or lives on the bread of faithful speech.

This bread of faithful speech is what we all ask of our writers, and sometimes it seems in short supply. But to what exactly does this speech owe fidelity? To truth, of course, as the writer imagines that truth. And writers must have the freedom to imagine that truth in their unique way: "What is a writer's freedom?" asks Nadine Gordimer. "To me it is his right to maintain and publish to the world a deep, intense, private view of the situation in which he finds his society. If he is to work as well as he can, he must take, and be granted, freedom from the public conformity of political interpretation, morals, and tastes."

A complex negotiation always exists within the writer—and within the work of art itself—between politics and the imagination. Stevens, as a poet, understood the pressures exerted by the external world, the world of reality, and he coveted the inward pressure of the imagination, which pushes outward, which confronts and subverts, which reinscribes and reinvents, which seduces and transmogrifies the cruelty and stupidity of the unimagined world, the world reduced to fact.

Everyone has felt the degradation of the world, which in the 1990s seems hideously bleak. We cannot escape reality, with its large and small cruelties, injustices, exploitations. André Brink, in a fierce little book called *Writing in a State of Siege* (1983), contemplates the parched landscape of this century and asks,

> Is there anything new in this condition? Has there not always been suffering and injustice and oppression? Of course. But until recently the condition of the world was not wholly intolerable—because the full measure of the truth was not known. . . . Mass communications have propagated these events around the world.

In some ways, the twenty-first century is going to present a challenge beyond anything we have yet encountered. With satellite communications, fiber optics, and the proliferation of the media, we may find ourselves lost in a wilderness of mirrors. Everywhere we look, a ragged face will stare back at us. We will see everything: the ruined forests of the Amazon, the tumultuous human dumps that ring Mexico City, Lima, Buenos Aires, and Bogotá. African children with swollen stomachs will stand lifesize in our living rooms in Los Angeles and London and, through interactive video, beg for bread. The civilian victims of mass bombing raids will point their fingers at us in our sleep. We will smell the dead rivers of the world as we listen to the radio. There will, I think, be no way to escape the atrocities that our collective histories have brought to a head.

The great cynicism that has, in the United States, swamped the masses and turned them away from electoral politics has a great deal to do with the technological revolution, which has brought about a dramatic change in the means of representation. For instance, it was much easier during World War I to conceal the horrors of war. The British government in the days before TV and radio could exercise a terrifying lockgrip on the public imagination. Railway stations and other public places bore posters of handsome blond English soldiers fighting off brutish Huns, who were pictured as wolves with sharp teeth and pointed ears. This was how the government invented reality for hapless consumers, who paid for these images with the blood of their sons.

Perhaps maintaining control of public imagery is a little harder now. In the Gulf War, for instance, George Bush knew that he could keep the thing going for a very limited time before the reality of bombed Baghdad leaked through, especially with CNN carrying the bombing live. One does, indeed, look back now with astonishment at Desert Storm, that brutal little war, to contemplate how revoltingly complicit and weak the press actually was (despite Peter Arnett's brave dispatches from Baghdad for CNN) in reporting what really happened or challenging the government's demand for control. The Pentagon manipulated the networks into presenting their version of the war, and by the time it was all over, everything was pretty much forgotten.

But the government can control only so much and for so long. Reality presses back in: the statistics about the number of political prisoners, the spread of AIDS, the tides of violence that wash our shores so regularly that we believe they are part of nature. In his preface to *The Portrait of a Lady* (1881), Henry James notes that "the real" is that which "we cannot not know." James was, as ever, aiming well. But he could hardly guess what was coming: so much horrific reality and so little chance to escape it. But we must imagine in order to understand.

The mind quite naturally wants to move outward, to absorb facts and reimagine them to the level of truth. The question becomes, then, one of strategy. How do we do it? Poets often go inward again, dive into strange depths and find there a kind of reality. Pablo Neruda, Adrienne Rich, Anna Ahkmatova, and Octavio Paz are among the handful of contemporary poets who have managed to imagine, to press back successfully, to find a language adequate to their experience. "The poem," says Paz in *Alternating Current* (1973), is "a transformation mechanism." Through the use of metaphor, inner and outer realms are reconciled and balanced. "History," he says, "is a daily invention." And poetry plays an inestimable role in this invention. Let me quote Paz at length (in Helen Lane's translation):

We fight to preserve our souls; we speak so that the other may recognize our soul and so that we may recognize ourselves in his soul, which is different from ours. The powerful conceive of history as a mirror: in the battered faces of others—the insulted and injured, the conquered or the "converted"—they see their own face reflected. This is the dialogue of masks, that double monologue of the victimizer and the victimized. Revolt is the criticism of masks, the beginning of genuine dialogue. It is also the creation of our own faces.

Paz, of course, speaks as a Mexican, a Latin American. And each geographical region bears the marks of its own, highly distinct, often tragic history. The forms that repression takes, and liberation, will vary. And revolutions will be more or less bloody. What remains constant is what Paz calls "the dialogue of masks," that often unvoiced drama in which the powerful, less powerful, and powerless fulfill the forms inherited from the previous revolution. In the ideal political poem, the poem of conscience, these inherited masks are exchanged, mocked, replaced.

Neruda, in a beautiful poem called "The Poet's Obligation" (the poem has been translated into English by Alastair Reid), explains the role of imaginative writing in a repressive society (and, I would argue, each unhappy society is oppressive in its own way):

To whoever is not listening to the sea
this Friday morning, to whoever is cooped up
in house or office, factory or woman
or street or mine or harsh prison cell:
to him I come, and, without speaking or looking,
I arrive and open the door of his prison,
and a great fragment of thunder sets in motion
the rumble of the planet and the foam,
the raucous rivers of the ocean flood,
the star vibrates swiftly in its corona,
and the sea is beating, dying and continuing.
So, drawn on by my destiny,
I ceaselessly must listen to and keep
the sea's lamenting in my awareness,

225

I must feel the crash of the hard water
and gather it up in a perpetual cup
so that, wherever those in prison may be,
wherever they suffer the autumn's castigation,
I may be there with an errant wave,
I may move, passing through window,
and hearing me, eyes will glance upward
saying "How can I reach the sea?"
And I shall broadcast, saying nothing,
the starry echoes of the wave,
a breaking up of foam and of quicksand,
a rustling of salt withdrawing,
the grey cry of sea-birds on the coast.

So, through me, freedom and the sea
will make their answer to the shuttered heart.

Neruda was the complete political poet, working simultaneously from the inside and outside. From the inside, as in the poetic credo quoted, writers become a voice for those who otherwise cannot or will not speak. They speak for those in prisons, in tedious jobs or marriages, for those outside the system. They speak as well for a flower, a stone, a bird, a window. The texture of the world is summoned, named, bodied forth, within the world of their text.

But Neruda also worked from the outside, involving himself in overt politics. He ran for the presidency of Chile, bowing out to Salvador Allende, who later made Neruda the Chilean ambassador to Paris. He sat on committees, signed petitions, appeared at public demonstrations. And although few writers ever actually run for public office—Mario Vargos Llosa and Vaclav Havel are the important exceptions—a large number of our best writers have in overt ways connected to political movements: Graham Greene, for instance, lent crucial public support to the Sandinistas in Nicaragua. Gárcia Márquez has been an ally of socialists throughout Latin America. Solzhenitsyn and other dissident writers found the imaginative wherewithal to oppose the monolith of the Soviet state. In South Africa, Gordimer, Brink, Dennis Brutus, Breyten Breytenbach, and Athol Fugard, among others, fought apartheid. In Israel, Amos Oz, David Grossman, Nathan Zach, and others have brought nuance to a political situation desperately in need of complex thought and representation. In the United States, Toni Morrison and Alice Walker—to name only the obvious examples—have worked to reclaim the history of African American people. The imagination of politics is complex, various, and unconfined to simplistic dichotomies, such as right versus left or liberal versus conservative.

Walter Benjamin, one of the original critical minds of this century, distinguished between the "operating writer" and the "informing writer." Of the latter, he wrote, "his mission is not to report but to struggle; not to play the spectator but to intervene actively." This distinction, although useful in sorting out kinds of writers and approaches to politics, has its invidious aspect. Writers who may not seem political on the surface, who would never dream of intervening directly in the political process of their country, may be crucial in providing the imagined reality that is a prelude to all political change.

Perhaps more so than any other form, the novel has played a genuine role in the imagination of reality. "The novel," writes Edward Said, "is not only selective and affirmative but centralizing and powerful." It is indeed a major instrument in the creation of culture, an instrument for plucking out and naming as valuable certain aspects of reality, for choosing this fact over that one, for ushering these chosen facts into a relation. "History," as Lytton Strachey said, "is not an accumulation of facts but a relation of them." The novelist, like the historian, looks for the relations among things, identifying and selecting certain "good" things, forms, practices, and ideas. If novelists choose—as most do—to ally with those in power, the result can be highly visible. The British imperialists needed Rudyard Kipling to imagine their politics, and those in opposition to that empire needed their Conrad and Forster, both of whom provided subtle critiques of empire by setting many of the same facts in a different relation.

One can hardly overestimate the power of the realistic novel to organize reality, to authorize it, to make it susceptible to ordinary politics. A novel—*Uncle Tom's Cabin* and *The Grapes of Wrath* are two obvious examples—can force a disruption, rearrange priorities, shift consciousness in significant ways. When W. H. Auden said that "poetry makes nothing happen," he engaged in wishful thinking of a particularly destructive kind. Auden, at this point in his life, wanted to believe in the poem as a hermetically sealed preserve of intellect and feeling. As a homosexual, he already felt excluded; he wanted a place to call his own, and the poem was that place. But poetry and fiction make things happen. The poetry of Yeats, for

227

example, played a terribly important role in the formation of the Irish Free State.

One of the best examples of political writing in our time is Steinbeck's *Grapes of Wrath* (1939), which dramatically affected the nation. Between 1933 and 1937, more than 200,000 homeless migrants were driven along California's Central Valley, desperate for work, like grasshoppers scattered before a storm. They lacked medical care, food, shelter, or hope. The locals hated them, refusing to let them enter their towns or camp on their farmlands. Squatters' camps, which were unsanitary and unorganized, arose along the valley. The response of the federal government was minimal: it set up a few demonstration camps, but they were underfunded and barely touched the need.

One of the worst aspects of this situation was that these migrant workers were utterly ignored. In a 1938 article on the crisis in *The Nation*, Steinbeck concluded with these words:

> Next year the hunger will come again, and the year after that, and so on, until we come out of this coma and realize that our agriculture for all its great produce is a failure. If you buy a farm horse and feed him only when you work him, the horse will die. No one complains at the necessity of feeding the horse when he is not working. But we complain about feeding the men and women who work our lands. Is it possible that this state is so stupid, so vicious, and so greedy that it cannot feed and clothe the men and women who help to make it the richest area in the world? Must the hunger become anger and the anger fury before anything will be done?

The answer, alas, was yes to every question. But *The Grapes of Wrath*, both the novel and the subsequent film, was incendiary. *The New Yorker* reviewer, Clifton Fadiman, found that it dramatized "so that you cannot forget it the terrible facts of a wholesale injustice committed by society." Edward Weeks, writing in *The Atlantic Monthly*, called it "the summation of eighteen years of realism . . . a novel whose hunger, passion, and poetry are in direct answer to the angry stirring of our conscience these past seven years." John Chamberlain in *Harper's* found it "a wise and tender and moving book as well as a social document of the first order." Within a year, the book had sold 430,000 copies in hardback. Consciousness of the plight of the migrants was indeed raised, and money flowed in to them from around the country. The federal government dramatically increased its efforts in the region, and the locals—many of whom were shamed into it—began to work with rather than against the migrants. Of course, the Second World War soon added a further dimension: the armed forces absorbed a vast number of farm laborers, and the need for live bodies to plant and harvest increased in California as it did elsewhere.

We can never really quantify the effects of a novel, play, or poem. It's not even easy to say which works of art are political, although I am suggesting here that writers who can imagine—or reimagine—reality are ipso facto political. These writers do not impose an ideology: that is the naive view of political writing. They find a relation, a true relation, among facts. As Wallace Stevens puts it so well in *Notes Toward a Supreme Fiction*,

> But to impose is not
> To discover. To discover an order as of
> A season, to discover summer and know it,
>
> To discover winter and know it well, to find,
> Not to impose, not to have reasoned at all,
> Out of nothing to have come on major weather,
>
> It is possible, possible, possible.

This last phrase is the ultimate imagining of the political: "It is possible, possible, possible." The political writer dwells in possibility. A writer must have the ability to listen forward, to imagine an audience and a time when the text written in the present will find, or create, the conditions for its reception. Virginia Woolf, for example, had a tiny audience in her time, often selling fewer than five hundred copies of a novel. Decades later, she became a major voice in the creation of the women's movement, in the imagination of a politics of sexual liberation. The same may be said for dozens of other women writers of the past, such as Mary Wollstonecraft and Kate Chopin.

My point is that good writing often does not find its most sympathetic readers for decades; it may be censored or suppressed, or it may have a conceptual basis in advance of the time or a style that cannot yet be absorbed.

I go back to Wallace Stevens: It is possible, possible, possible. The writer has to keep saying this. The word is a seed planted invisibly in the mud; the imagination of a fully grown and blossoming tree, three or four or five decades into the future, makes the act of planting possible. Writers must imagine a reality that is always down the road, must work (where possible) without allegiances to power: their job is to afflict the comfortable, to unmask authority, to confound and conflict the status quo, to imagine a politics of redemption.

LITERARY THEORY AND THE
CULTURE OF CREATIVE WRITING

Literature faculties in the United States usually have two camps: the critics and the writers. The critics have, if they are younger than forty, been schooled in theory, and they have access to a formidable (some would say jargon-ridden) language and, in most cases, a half-dozen critical approaches, which they have mastered to some degree. The writers live and work apart from the critics, ignoring their journals and bad-mouthing their books. They may see their critical counterparts at department meetings or cocktail parties, but there is rarely much conversation. Their private bibliographies of favorite books rarely coincide.

This wasn't always the case, of course. The shortlist of major poets from Ben Jonson to T. S. Eliot is more or less coincident with the shortlist of major critics of each dis-

231

tinct period. Jonson—perhaps the first modern critic—was also a formidably talented playwright and poet. John Milton, the central figure of the late Renaissance in England, also possessed a critical mind of astounding power (as in the *Areopagitica* or, even more tellingly, his defense of eloquence in the *Apology for Smectymnuus*). John Dryden defined the particular forms of irony one associates with his period, as did Samuel Johnson, the critic's critic, whose *Lives of the English Poets* might be thought of as the finest collection of short stories published in the eighteenth century. (Johnson was not, I should add, an insignificant "creative" writer, as *Irene* and "The Vanity of Human Wishes" prove). The litany continues: William Wordsworth, Samuel Taylor Coleridge, Matthew Arnold, Eliot: all writers of sufficient strength as poets and critics to articulate and embody their cultural moments.

Eliot, a founder if not the founder of critical inquiry as we know it today, is fascinating to read on the subject of the writer-as-critic. His influential book of essays, *The Sacred Wood,* appeared in 1919; it begins with a review-essay of a book by Arthur Symons on Elizabethan drama; typically, Eliot scarcely mentions the book under review. Instead, he ruminates on the then-popular controversy over whether the twentieth century would be an age of creativity or an age of criticism: "It is fatuous," he writes,

> to say that criticism is for the sake of "creation" or creation for the sake of criticism. It is also fatuous to assume that there are ages of criticism and ages of creativeness, as if by plunging ourselves into intellectual darkness we were in better hopes of finding spiritual light. The two directions of sensibility are complementary; and as sensibility is rare, unpopular, and desirable, it is to be expected that the critic and the creative artist should frequently be the same person.

This seems both astute and deeply relevant to the current literary scene, but it just so happens that in the very next essay in *The Sacred Wood,* "The Imperfect Critic," Eliot overturns his previous arguments rather abruptly, concluding, "The creative artist in England finds himself compelled, or at least tempted, to spend much of his time and energy in criticism that he might reserve for the perfecting of his proper work: simply because there is no one else to do it." This grumpy, somewhat pretentious, sentiment assumes (contrary to what Eliot has argued earlier) that criticism is a secondary, parasitical, and boring task that has to be done by somebody, and because no one else is apparently willing to help, the writers had better get on with it.

With the emergence of English as a distinct academic field (it was only just taking root in the universities of Great Britain and the United States in the years after the First World War), there was suddenly a group of able and willing critics who were not, at least not primarily, poets: I. A. Richards, F. R. Leavis, William Empson, and Cleanth Brooks were paramount among them—the post-Eliot group first called the "New Critics" in 1941 by John Crowe Ransom (himself an influential critic and brilliant, if self-consciously minor, poet). Many of the more prominent New Critics were themselves poets, of course: Richards, Empson, Yvor Winters, Ransom, Robert Penn Warren, Allen Tate, and Randall Jarrell all worked both sides of the fence. But the bulk of criticism on both sides of the Atlantic was now being written by nonpoets.

The New Criticism arose in part as a defense of literary modernism, as Jonathan Culler suggests in *Framing the Sign* (1978): "It made it easier for critics to discuss modernist poetry such as Eliot's, while situating it in the tradition of English literature. Cleanth Brooks's *Modern Poetry and the Tradition* (1939) helped make the New Criticism indispensable. Moreover, the authority of New Critics such as Ransom, Tate, and Penn Warren came in part from their accomplishments as poets." Culler argues, in essence, that the modernist writers attempted to create a critical climate that would be hospitable to their work and, to a fantastic degree, succeeded.

The problem in the postmodern era has been, as much for critics as for writers of poetry and fiction, a sense of belatedness—a subject Harold Bloom and others have examined with much hand-wringing. A sense of futility, a lack of empowerment, an urge toward parody and pastiche: these are the fatal signs of belatedness. A poet like John Ashbery is thus able to fashion an entire career of poems that read like high modernist false starts, leftovers from Wallace Stevens's wastebasket. In novels like *Snow White* (1967), *The Dead Father* (1975), and *The King* (1990), Donald Barthelme created a corpus of corpses: works exhumed from an imaginary cultural boneyard where Faulkner, Walt Disney, and Sir Thomas Mallory were scattered uneasily in the same dirt. Even the critics struggle with belatedness. Jacques Derrida and Paul de Man wrestled (unsuccessfully, in most cases) with the ghost of Martin Heidegger, much as Sartre had done before them.

The situation of belatedness, then, affects writers and critics alike, especially those working in reaction to modernism on the one hand and the New Criticism on the other. But the situation is more complicated than this, involving the institutionalizing of literature and criticism. The great poet-critics of the past had almost nothing to do with the academy as such. Right up to, say, midcentury, a significant part of the literary community had few "contact hours" with students; indeed, Edmund Wilson, Dwight MacDonald, Lewis Mumford, Mary McCarthy, Paul Goodman, Kenneth Burke, and Malcolm Cowley flourished largely outside academe. In this extra-academic culture, "creative" writers and critics mingled freely, enlightening or, often, bashing each other. It was a heady and productive swell.

The aftermath of this epoch goes something like this: the expansion of universities in the postwar era led to the proliferation of creative writing programs and the expansion of English generally as a field of academic study. "Creativity" was, and remains, fashionable, especially in the wake of the 1960s. But it started much earlier: Robert Frost was hired by President Alexander Meiklejohn of Amherst College in 1917, as a "poet-in-residence." By the 1940s, it was becoming not unusual for colleges to have a writer in their midst: Kenyon had John Crowe Ransom, Louisiana State had Robert Penn Warren (who moved on to Minnesota, then Yale), Penn State (and later, Bennington and the University of Washington) had Theodore Roethke. Saul Bellow was at Minnesota. By the 1950s, the proliferation had begun, and one came to expect most elite colleges and universities to house a poet or novelist.

At first, the writers mingled freely with the more traditional scholars. By the mid-1970s, however, the explosion of creative writing programs led to the ghettoization of writers. Programs offering masters in fine arts began to multiply too—indeed, the situation went out of control in the 1980s as one saw writers migrating from program to program, and "schools" of writing began to emerge: minimalism, the new surrealism, the new formalism. Students were "taught" how to write in certain styles and what to value in a poem or story. In fiction, one saw a fatal separation occur between the larger audience of readers and serious writers; Donald Barthelme, William Gass, Thomas Pynchon, John Barth, and others became popular within the academy walls, but they did not have what Gore Vidal has called "voluntary readers." Their stories and novels were written for classroom study. Many of these writers, influenced by the French nouvelle roman of Alain

Robbe-Grillet, Claude Simon, and Philippe Sollers, produced novels that bored the common reader to death; the sense of narrative compulsion that one finds in Tolstoy, Dickens, Gabriel García Márquez, or Graham Greene was temporarily lost in the shuffle of signs and symbols.

Meanwhile, the invasion of the French continued in the field of criticism. The last of the New Critics, transmogrified into die-hard humanists, fought a losing battle in the 1970s and '80s. Poststructuralist theory, with its decidedly antiauthoritarian roots in the international cultural revolution of the '60s, came to dominate the academic village. Although deconstruction (which came and went rather quickly) had few purist adherents, aspects of the deconstructive method permanently changed the ways we think about literature. In his sweeping analyses of the Western metaphysical tradition, begun in the late '60s, Derrida questioned the foundational center or "origin" of human knowledge. In an original essay called "Structure, Sign, and Play in the Discourse of the Human Sciences" (1966), he suggests that it "has always been thought that [this] center, which is by definition unique, constituted that very thing within a structure which governs the structure, while escaping structurality."

Derrida's baroque, often impenetrable, style was coupled with a method whose aim was finally the disruption of all traditional notions of authority, including the institution of authorship itself. By calling into question the hierarchical oppositions of Western culture, such as truth/error, health/disease, male/female, nature/culture, philosophy/literature, speech/writing, or seriousness/play, Derrida revealed—more convincingly in some places than others—the essentially fictive nature of what we commonly take as fact. In Derrida's votaries, the marking of oppositions, followed by their reversals and "reinscriptions," often seemed like a trick anybody could learn; the deconstructive method became, at its worst, a kind of cultish cliché whose moves (and conclusions) were predictable. But the purpose of these reversals was not merely to question value systems; Derrida hoped to "explode" the original opposition, laying bare the ideological origins of terms one might have taken for granted as fundamental. He argued that the critic must challenge interpretations that seek "a truth or an origin which is free from freeplay and the order of the sign."

Derrida influenced a wide range of critics who fell under the larger aegis of poststructuralism, including feminists, neo-Marxists, reader-response critics, Lacanians, and New Historicists—all critical approaches that continue to flourish. These schools remain highly permeable, of course; I doubt that many serious critics in the late 1990s even want to identify with a particular school or be yoked to a single method. What these critical approaches have in common, however, is a desire to unmask authority, whether that authority resides in patriarchal formations, capitalist economics, or ego psychology.

The *post* in the term *poststructuralism* alludes to a general drift against all totalizing formations, which are seen to be arbitrary and tainted by unacknowledged ideology. Indeed, a notable aspect of poststructuralist criticism has been its unwillingness to let bias stand unquestioned—an aspect that has opened it up to a good deal of mockery in the neoconservative press, where the shout of "political correctness!" is heard whenever anyone questions the status quo.

To the dedicated poststructuralist, even common sense is the product of a layer of prejudice acquired early in childhood. We so easily assume that reality formations are given, fixed, like constellations in the heavens. In a self-revealing moment in *The Anatomy of Criticism* (1957), the North American bible of structuralist criticism, Northrop Frye meditates on the almost sacred notion of a philosophical center:

> Unless there is such a center, there is nothing to prevent analogies supplied by convention and genre from being an endless series of free associations, perhaps suggestive . . . but never creating a real structure. . . . If there are such things as archetypes at all, then, we have to take yet another step, and conceive the possibility of a self-contained literary universe. Either archetypal criticism is a will-'o-the-wisp, an endless labyrinth without an outlet, or we have to assume that literature is a total form.

This "endless labyrinth without a structure," as Frank Lentricchia points out in *After the New Criticism* (1980), is a perfect figure for what Derrida means by a decentered structure, for what he refers to as "the structurality of structure." A sense of liberation swept through the ranks of many critics in the wake of Derrida's critique of structuralist and formalist theory, with its uncritical acceptance of a whole range of tantalizing forms. A revolution was underway, one that continued along different lines, and it was as often as not a fairly apolitical revolution, as in the critical work of Roland Barthes, J. Hillis Miller, and Geoffrey Hartmann—all of whom have sought "the pleasures of the text," delighting in the free play of signs, what Derrida calls "a joyous affirmation of the freeplay of the world and without truth, without origin."

The world, however, does seem to exist, so the rather bourgeois activity of delighting in the free play of signs was bound to come to an end. Wallace Stevens is the embodiment of this belated aestheticism, with its painful recognition, as he says in "Yellow Afternoon," that "It was in the earth only / That he was at the bottom of things / And of himself." Time and again, Stevens bumps his windy head against the rock, what in another context he calls "the necessary angel" of reality, just as anti-Derridian critics repeat, almost tiresomely, Samuel Johnson's stubborn refutation of Bishop Berkeley. One of these critics, Terry Eagleton, says in *Literary Theory* (1983), "One advantage of the dogma that we are the prisoners of our own discourse, unable to advance reasonably certain truth-claims because such claims are merely relative to our language, is that it allows you to drive a coach and horses through everybody else's belief while not saddling you with the inconvenience of having to adopt any yourself."

Eagleton, like all critics with a Marxist bent, brings everything back to politics, which is his necessary angel. But poststructuralists (even those with no interest in Marxism) are in general agreement that no critical writing, or writing at all, is without ideology. This insistence on ideology has felt threatening to many old-style humanists, who still believe that any recognition of a specific ideological content somehow negates the artistic quality of a given artwork. "We all want politics not to exist," says Lionel Trilling sadly in *Beyond Culture* (1968), one of his irascible late volumes. Trilling was merely expressing a resistance to certain progressive social movements that many older critics felt and still feel. The purpose of art, in Trilling's formulation, was to free us from politics, to raise us above the taint of ideology, to inject us into the ozone of aesthetic bliss where all the ironies and paradoxical motions of a given text are finally harmonized.

One critic who has sharply criticized this position, which might be called the aesthetic position, is Richard Ohmann; in *English in America* (1976), he marshals a fascinating, if naively Marxist, argument against the New Critics and their supposedly disinterested form of critical activity—a critique that can be traced back to Mikhail Bakhtin, who in 1926 attacked what he called "the fetishization of the artistic work artifact," a formalist heresy that continues through the New Critics and, to some extent, their deconstructive heirs.

One hesitates to chart the relations among reactionary politics, social quietism, and a particular school of criticism—although poststructuralist critics have rarely hesitated to do so, often falling into a generational game that, in sixties fashion, pits us against them. (I know a number of fifty-year-old hippies who still don't trust anyone over thirty!) It is worth recalling that there was indeed an intensely political streak in those critics associated, in the mid-1950s, with *The Partisan Review,* such as Philip Rahv and Trilling himself. These critics were, to an extent, influenced by the technical advances associated with the New Criticism, but this hardly quelled their ardor for reform or their dislike of the status quo. As Richard Ohmann notes, "Bourgeois culture rests on the idea of freedom," and New Critical methods— which supported a kind of intellectual freedom—were drafted into the service of a prevailing bourgeois liberalism. Ohmann says, "The ideologue settles on freedom of thought as fundamental, and he is willing to allow everyone that freedom so long as it does not lead to 'disruption.'"

By contrast, recent theory has become—at least in theory—willfully disruptive, deliberately focusing on race, income, and gender issues. Critics like Frederic Jameson, Terry Eagleton, Frank Lentricchia, and Michael Denning (of the younger generation of neo-Marxists and cultural critics) have boldly situated texts in the world of power relations. Indeed, a kind of general discourse theory has emerged since the mid-1980s, a hybrid discipline that cuts across departmental lines as well as high and popular culture; it has, in fact, something in common with the ancient discipline of rhetoric.

It is, I believe, at this juncture—rhetoric—where literary theory and creative writing meet. Why did people study rhetoric in the first place? Not because, like Mount Everest, it was there. They worked for knowledge: knowledge of the most productive ways of "making" language, of creating meaning, and eliciting responses within the bounds of predictability. Likewise, critics in the poststructuralist mode are interested in "reader response," the affective realm; they want to know exactly how a given text works its magic, becomes persuasive. Interestingly, it is the critical essay (which often takes a highly personal turn) that has come to dominate the world of criticism. An essay—like a poem or story—is an attempt (*essai*), a setting forth, a journey toward an end perhaps only dimly sensed at the outset. "Creative" writers join with the critics here in seeking what Stevens has called "The poem of the mind in the act of finding / What will suffice."

The relative ignorance of most poets and novelists with regard to literary theory strikes me as profoundly unhealthy. This is true even of writers who work in academic settings—where suspicion on both sides often impedes communication between writers and theorists of writing. The detrimental effect of this impasse has been considerable. In the world of current fiction, even our best writers seem hopelessly convention bound and limited by worn-out theories of genre (which they don't even know are theories). They repeat empty formal experiments of yesteryear or (more commonly) naively reproduce "realistic" novels that neither challenge the assumptions of their society at large nor push toward the limits of discursivity.

On the other side, critics—especially those with a theoretical bent—have been largely out of conversation with the culture of poets and fiction writers. This was not the case, for example, in the bohemian culture of the twenties, where clusters of poets, novelists, critics, and revolutionaries gathered in the street cafes of Paris, Greenwich Village, Prague, Berlin, Frankfurt, and Vienna. The modern university, with its mania for specialization, has isolated the community of writers, dividing them into "creative" and "critical" writers. One of the many consequences of this isolation is the technocratic, needlessly obscure language in which so much contemporary theory is couched: a language fatally separated from the general reader (which includes most novelists, playwrights, and poets).

The possibility of reintegration exists—a faintly burning light on the horizon. After all, we are all storytellers in the end, whether the story we tell is, as in a poem, the story of an emotion's rise and fall, or—as in a critical work—the story of a reading. The world is a confusing spray of signs that must somehow be brought into a narrative flow if understanding is to occur. After all, the root of *fiction* (*fictio*) involves a shaping voice, the voice that raises itself above other voices by the campfire and begins its "Once upon a time." It is, inevitably, a biased voice, necessarily informed by ideology, by politics; fortunately, it is only one voice among many (even, at times, within the same writer's work), so that a countermanding voice can rub against it, give the culture its grain and texture.

FACT OR FICTION
Writing Biographies Versus Writing Novels

The relationship between fact and fiction is vexed. It's also a hot topic, as they say, and one that's bedeviled literary theory in particular, turning that once rather placid land into a charred battlefield where what is at stake is the nature of truth itself. The general drift of postmodern theory runs something like this: although truth may be in some sense objective, most attempts to reconstruct or reflect that objectivity, whether in fiction or nonfiction, history or biography, are tainted by both the medium itself—language, and ideology, that matrix of assumptions and preconceptions that underlies every gesture in the direction of signification. The extreme (if by now boringly commonplace) observation by Derrida, *"Il n'y pas de hors texte"* [There is nothing outside the text], has become a kind of poststructuralist mantra.

Like all revolutionary, or quasi-revolutionary, movements, poststructuralism served as a corrective, bending the proverbial board perhaps a little too hard in the opposite direction in the attempt to straighten it out. I suspect that few of us would be willing to posit an easy or (as they say) "unproblematic" relation between language and truth or, in the fields of literature and history, between narration and objective reality.

The assumption today is that the writer of any text—a critical essay, novel, biography, historical study—speaks from a particular point of view and that this viewpoint colors and to some extent shapes the content of the work. This is even, in important ways, true of science, as Stephen J. Gould points out in his reflections on natural history, *Eight Little Piggies* (1973). Gould spent a week with Richard Leakey at his field camp on early Miocene sediments near the western shore of Lake Turkana in Africa's Great Rift Valley, and he was present when the skull of *Afropithecus*—a new genus in the ape family—was discovered. Gould notes that try as he might, he could not see bone fragments or a skull anywhere in the sedimentation. What he could see, however—and this startled Leakey and his colleagues—was snails. Gould remarks:

> All field naturalists know and respect the phenomenon of "search image"—the best proof that observation is an interaction of mind and nature, not a fully objective and reproducible mapping of outside upon inside, done in the same way by all careful and competent people. In short, you see what you are trained to view—and observation of different sorts of objects often requires a conscious shift of focus, not a total and indiscriminate expansion in the hopes of seeing everything. The world is too crowded with wonders for simultaneous perception of all; we learn our fruitful selectivities.

I would argue that poems and novels, biographies and works of history, might also be thought of as "fruitful selectivities." To say that something is subjective, or (more properly) that it contains a "subjective element," is not to dismiss it. The subjective element is a product of necessary selection: we choose among the crowd of wonders, seeing what we are trained—or disposed—to see. Whether we like it or not, we have each been educated—trained, if you will—differently. We have read many of the same books but many different ones. Our experiences in life have shaped us too and so that we react differently to the same phenomena. It would be odd if we didn't. And rather boring. Furthermore, it is downright useful in the end for some of us to see skulls and others to see snails.

What interests me is how the poststructuralist shift toward subjectivity affects a novelist or biographer. I've written several historical or biographical novels, including *The Last Station* (1990), which looks at the last year in Tolstoy's life from several viewpoints. More recently, I've written a straight, that is, nonfictional life of John Steinbeck. As I worked on these books, my mind often turned to the relation of fact to fiction, and I want to share some of this thinking.

Not long after I began my research on the Steinbeck biography, my subject's widow, Elaine Steinbeck, told me that she had had a dream in which Steinbeck was sitting in heaven at dinner beside Leo Tolstoy. The famous American novelist told the great Russian writer that Jay Parini was about to write his biography. "Good luck, old man," Tolstoy exclaimed. "Have you seen what he did to me?"

This was funny but also not so funny. I take it for granted that all writers, in whatever genre, are trying to get at what we nervously call the truth. But how to do this?

I doubt whether anyone—even Tolstoy himself—could verify the reality summoned by me in *The Last Station*. Nevertheless, my method in that book still strikes me as a plausible one: I approached the story of that tumultuous last year at Yasnaya Polyana from a half-dozen viewpoints, hoping that by layering voice on voice something like the truth would emerge. I based those chapters on the actual voices of friends or relatives who were living with Tolstoy during this year; luckily for me, it happened that most of these people kept an intimate diary, so I had access to what my characters, who were after all real people, actually thought and felt. I did, however, take the novelist's option of invention when it seemed necessary. For instance, Tolstoy's young amanuensis, Valentin Bulgakov, mentions in his diary that he had a romantic affiliation with a young Tolstoyan woman; he alludes to her several times, intriguingly but unspecifically. I decided to invent her myself. I called her Masha—a typical Russian name—and had a wonderful time imagining her relationship with Bulgakov and making up their correspondence. In fact, I was quite pleased when an extremely well-known Tolstoy scholar wrote to me to say, "I thought your use of those letters between Bulgakov and Masha were particularly effective. I have indeed always admired those letters."

But did I get close to the truth about Tolstoy? Could I have come closer in a work of straight biography? What is indeed the relationship between the Yasnaya Polyana imagined in that book and the real place and lives that criss-crossed, often so tragicomically, in that house in 1910? Was it utterly corrupt of me to blur the distinction between fact and fiction so willfully? Instead of answering these questions directly, let me circle the subject like a fox around the henhouse. If the farmer is asleep, I may take a chicken or two.

It is interesting that, in modern Hebrew, no formal distinction exists between the genres of fiction and nonfiction. If you go into an Israeli bookstore, there is simply one category—*siporet*—which means 'prose narrative.' Although I would hate to lose the license to invent granted by the word *fiction,* I find it useful to dwell on the immense common ground shared by all forms of prose narrative. The areas of fiction and nonfiction overlap in suggestive ways, creating a kind of wild zone in which disbelief is suspended and the narrative itself becomes all consuming.

The term fiction, of course, has its origins in the Latin *fictio,* which means 'shaping.' The term, in this sense, suggests a process of selection and arrangement. Reality—that ongoing hail of sensation that pelts us from cradle to grave—is formless and, in its unmediated condition, without meaning. Random facts are not intrinsically interesting—rather like the sediment in Richard Leakey's dig. It takes a certain frame of reference, a shaping point of view, and, yes, an ideology, to make a fruitful selectivity.

One always begins, of course, with this thing called Fact or, as we say, "the agreed-upon facts." These are the bricks from which we must erect our house of fiction—or nonfiction. But what are facts?

The Bible is as good a place as any to search for truth, and one finds an early instance of the word *fact* in the Gospel of John. "And the word was made flesh" is a translation from the Vulgate: *verbum caro factum est.* The phrase "factum est" is, of course, not nominal but verbal in its construction. It wasn't until the late Middle Ages that, in Latin, factum began to creep slowly toward its modern, positivistic denotation. Even during the late Renaissance, the word fact retained a certain verbalness, as in the French *fait* or the Italian *fatto.* As late as the early nineteenth century, Jane Austen could describe a character as "gracious in fact, if not in word" and mean *deed* when she refers to fact. (It is at least intriguing to note that the Greek equivalents of the Latin *facio* would be *poieo,* 'to make', or *drao,* 'to do'— words that, as it were, evolved into *poetry* and *drama,* two of our main genres in the general category of fiction.)

244

In the nineteenth century fact was transformed into an ideal and thoroughly nominal category. So Thomas Carlyle would note with a lovely twang of irony: "How impressive the smallest historical fact may become as contrasted with the grandest fictitious event." Indeed, writers of the day were loathe to handcuff themselves to the mast of literalness that seemed to dominate the new ship of mental state. Dickens protested grandly and in *Hard Times* (1845), invented the schoolmaster from hell, Thomas Gradgrind, who has forever stood as the worst example of demonic adherence to mindless factuality. Oscar Wilde, that angel of wit, remarked near the turn of the century: "The English are always degrading truths into facts." Giving the aphorism that extra twist, he added: "When a truth becomes a fact it loses all its intellectual value." Lytton Strachey, the black prince of biography, observed wisely that history is "not an accumulation of facts but a relation of them."

Few except perhaps the most stalwart deconstructionist or philosophical idealist along the lines of Bishop Berkeley would go so far as to deny altogether the existence of a concrete reality: a world antecedent to both language and thought. Dr. Johnson, in his famous refutation of Berkeley, merely kicked a stone by the side of the road and said, "I refute it thus." Science, history, biography, and—yes—fiction, depend on the agreed-upon facts, and there is no point in denying that Napoleon was defeated at the Battle of Waterloo, that water is composed of two parts hydrogen to one part oxygen, or that sexual intercourse leads, in some instances, to pregnancy. It is the relation among facts that matters. So what the imaginative writer does is try to imagine Napoleon having sexual intercourse during the Battle of Waterloo while drinking a glass of water.

This relation among the facts assumes not only a narrative of events or repetition of facts but an imaginative revision and rearrangement—a mosaic that is, in effect, an interpretation. And so we return to fiction as shaping, a process that involves the manipulation of language and relies on similar tropes, turns, techniques, and sleights of tongue. This will be true, as I've learned, for the biographer as well as the novelist.

The task of the writer of biography (which is really a subgenre of history) is, I think, similar to that of the novelist and poet: to construct a version of reality, a *fictio* of events. And any construction involves a selection from the myriad parts of reality and then the creation of a relation of those selected parts to form a new whole. This is the crucial act of intellection as well as creation. "We compare, contrast, abstract, generalize, connect, adjust, clas-

245

sify, and we view all our knowledge in the association with which these processes have invested it," wrote Isaac Newton, emphasizing the associative nature of intellectual construction.

In his essay on the metaphysical poets, T. S. Eliot wrote what, for me, has always been a memorable description of the process of imaginative construction. Eliot is commenting on Donne in this passage, comparing Donne's verse to those of Tennyson and Browning, neither of whom Eliot especially liked. "A thought to Donne was an experience," he said, "it modified his sensibility. When a poet's mind is perfectly equipped for its work, it is constantly amalgamating disparate experience; the ordinary man's experience is chaotic, irregular, fragmentary. The latter falls in love, or reads Spinoza, and these two experiences have nothing to do with each other, or with the noise of the typewriter or the smell of cooking; in the mind of the poet these experiences are always forming new wholes."

The obvious source of Eliot's notion is Coleridge, who in his wonderfully ramshackle grammar of the creative mind, the *Biographia Literaria* (1817), distinguished between what he called the Primary Imagination and the Secondary Imagination. "The primary IMAGINATION," he wrote, "I hold to be the living Power and prime Agent of all human Perception and as a repetition in the finite mind of the eternal act of creation in the infinite I AM. The secondary Imagination I consider as an echo of the former . . . differing only in degree, and in the mode of its operation. It dissolves, diffuses, dissipates, in order to recreate." In another passage, Coleridge said, "Facts, you know, are not truths; they are not conclusions; they are not even premises, but in the nature and parts of premises."

Thus the primary act of perception involves facts: seizing the object by the senses, gripping it literally. It is an active motion, one of possession. It is a deed. And each time we see something and seize it and make it over into our own, we are repeating the eternal act of creation, participating in what Wallace Stevens in "A Primitive Like an Orb" calls "the essential poem at the center of things." And this essential poem is not any specific poem or story or novel or essay or biography, it is the sum of these acts. Stevens writes,

> One poem proves another and the whole,
> For the clairvoyant men that need no proof:
> The lover, the believer and the poet.
> Their words are chosen out of their desire,

The joy of language, when it is themselves.
With these they celebrate the central poem,
The fulfillment of fulfillments . . .

Stevens's clairvoyants of the imagination—and I would include biographers and historians here as well as lovers, believers, and poets—take the image in the mind's mirror and shatter it, then reconstruct it. And so falling in love, reading Spinoza, listening to the clack of the typewriter, and smelling the garlic as it wafts in from the kitchen all enter into a new relation, and they become parts of a new creation, one that comments on and, ideally, informs the old creation. The writer's job, thus construed, is to take what God has given and to give back better.

Wallace Stevens is a useful poet for me, because he took as his main subject the complex negotiations between reality and the imagination that concern everyone who puts pen to paper. Stevens repeatedly paid homage to what he called "the necessary angel" of reality. Dr. Johnson may have kicked a rock to verify its existence, but what happens to that reality when we evoke it with a word? A subtle, almost invisible, textual maneuver occurs when we say "rock" and the hearer conjures the illusion of a specific rock. The better the poet, the firmer the sense of this reality. "How simply the fictive hero becomes the real," as Stevens says at the end of *Notes Toward a Supreme Fiction* (1942), in which the poet anticipates and out-deconstructs the deconstructer to the tenth power. But the reality of the imagined rock is not really real, not in the same way that the thing we lie down on by Otter Creek to enjoy a bit of sunbathing is real. A rock is a rock is a rock. But the word *rock* in Wallace Stevens's last great poem, "The Rock," is another thing. It takes its place in a grand procession of linguistic differentials.

What all this means for biographers or historians has interested many recent theorists, Foucault chief among them. He folds history into the realm of textuality, which brings it ever closer to fiction. In *The Archaeology of Knowledge* (1972), he writes that once we understand the true nature of history as a text, "the entire field is set free. A vast field, but one that can be defined nevertheless: this field is made up of the totality of all effective statements (whether spoken or written) in their dispersions as events and in the occurrence that is proper to them." Here I would simply call attention to the phrase "in their dispersions as events." These are the facts still in their active verbal phase: *verbum caro factum est*. Reality transmogrified into language and by language.

247

This view of history as textuality has seemed dazzling to some, though a moment's serious reflection suggests that little that is called new ever really is. The ancient Greeks, who seem at times to have understood everything, did not confuse facts with truth. Nor did they distinguish between fiction and nonfiction as we do. Their assumption was that narrative works contained elements of myth and legend, poetry, and fact. The *Iliad* was, in this regard, a fine prototype for later Greek historiography, represented by the imaginative, even fictive, histories of Herodotus and Thucydides.

Students of modern historical narrative often find Herodotus frustrating. There is no pretense to linearity in his work, for example. Herodotus was an early cubist, juxtaposing stories and points of view with artistic abandon, taking a scissors to the time line and rearranging events for dramatic purpose. He adored digressions too. There is a long digression, for example, about wildlife in Egypt in the middle of his history of the Persian Wars, and he intersperses this meander with gossip about Egyptian religious and social customs. He even includes a wonderful story-within-a-story about Helen of Troy and her supposed stay in Egypt during the Trojan War: a passage that assumes that both Helen of Troy and the Trojan War should be regarded with the same degree of historicity as the Persian Wars themselves.

Where did Herodotus get all his arcane information about the Egyptians and their beliefs and practices? In case we should wonder excessively, he tells us that he visited Egypt and interviewed a number of Egyptian priests. These priests, alas, talk about rival systems of Greek philosophy in explicitly Greek terms. They chat fluently about Greek culture with an awareness of nuance unlikely to be found in an Egyptian priest of that time, however learned. When Herodotus writes about the Persians, he plays similar tricks. At one point, for instance, he reconstructs a debate between Persian noblemen in 521 B.C. on the subject of whether the Persian Empire should remain a monarchy or try its hand at oligarchy or, even more shockingly, Athenian-style democracy. The debate is charged throughout with familiar Greek rhetoric about the pros and cons of the three rival systems, and the whole debate begins with these words: "A debate was held which some Greek readers may find hard to believe: but it was indeed held." Indeed.

Perhaps we should simply call Herodotus the father of the New Journalism. Like Tom Wolfe and others, he is constantly making up conversations between historical characters. So are we to assume that the Ionic-reading audience of this history of the Persian Wars actually believed that these conversations took place? Did the historian's readers really believe that Helen of Troy existed and had gone to Egypt—an account of the legend deeply at variance with that of Homer? Though I can't answer this question, I would like to assume that his audience simply regarded this history as a fiction—a well-shaped if somewhat idiosyncratic narrative that was open to debate. Indeed, future Greek historians would take issue with Herodotus and challenge him, as would generations of classical historians. But nobody in his or her right mind would accuse Herodotus of trying to deceive anyone. He was merely selecting and arranging his material in a pattern that seemed to him to be true.

The relationship between history and fiction is complex, and it would be churlish of me to suggest there is no difference. Fiction is in fact part of history. It both reflects and occasionally makes history. It is not, I suspect, for nothing that the rise of modern history parallels the rise of the novel. The Göttingen school of modern historiography and the novel were both flourishing by the 1770s, and the nineteenth century was pretty much the Age of History, for both history as a practice and the novel. The great novelists of that era—Scott, Dickens, Balzac, Flaubert, Stendhal—were all historians of a sort. Dickens's *Barnaby Rudge* (1841), for instance, provides an account of the Gordon riots more detailed and analytical than any yet produced by an historian. Stendhal's account of the Battle of Waterloo in *The Charterhouse of Parma* (1839) is superb military history. And Balzac's *Comédie humaine* (1841) offers a detailed social history of France between the years 1792 and 1840.

More so than any previous form of literature, fiction is history. But the story it evokes is not some remote idealized past; in a good novel, the past is not only our present but our future as well. We look to history for examples, for instances of what went wrong or right. And although some novels specifically ally themselves with the traditions of historical fiction, an argument can be made that any novel is by its nature historical, even those written in the present tense. Anything processed by memory is fiction. That is to say, anything that has been shaped and reconstructed is fiction.

Whereas only a few years ago any self-respecting novelist would cringe at the epithet *historical,* this seems to have changed. Writers have seized historical, often biographical, subjects and for good reason. In the old-style historical novels, such as *War and Peace* (1864–1869), history was a pictorial backdrop against which fictional characters played out their lives. We may catch a glimpse of Napoleon at the Battle of Borodino, but Napoleon is not the subject of the fiction. Recently, novelists have been foregrounding history and historical figures, thus redefining the genre. I have in mind here novels like *The General in His Labyrinth* (1990), García Márquez's study of the dying Simón Bolívar, or Peter Ackroyd's *Chatterton* (1987) or *Hawksmoor* (1985).

Novels are about lives, after all: about pieces of lives or whole lives. Traditionally, these lives have been made up, with half-believable disclosures at the outset that read, "The characters in this novel are entirely fictitious and any relation to persons living or dead is entirely accidental." I would prefer that novelists of the future write: "Everything in the following pages is authentic, which is to say it is as true as I could make it. Take it or leave it." One peculiarity of contemporary life, of course, is that so-called real lives often seem less true than the lives in novels. Could anyone have made up David Koresh, O. J. Simpson, and Newt Gingrich, for instance?

Prose fiction in the form of biography precedes the novel by centuries, gathering into its narrative streams the lives of great warriors, saints, and statesmen. Many of these biographies followed in the mode of Suetonius, who felt relatively free to imagine what he could not empirically know. It was taken for granted that what mattered was the story itself and that truth revealed itself in the process of narration. In *Dubin's Lives* (1979), Bernard Malamud's novel about a biographer and his problems, Dubin says, "There is no life that can be recaptured wholly, as it was. Which is to say that all biography is ultimately fiction."

The most fictitious form of biography from ancient times to the present is clearly autobiography, that mode of "true confessions" that begins with St. Augustine and proceeds through Rousseau and Erica Jong. The art of fiction has its origins there, I suspect, in a genre where subjectivity is, at least by the reader, simply assumed. (I once introduced Gore Vidal to Erica Jong, and Vidal asked what she was writing. "My memoirs," she said. Vidal replied, "At last, you're trying your hand at fiction.")

The autobiographical aspect of contemporary fiction could almost be called its defining feature. Saul Bellow, John Updike, and Norman Mailer, for instance, have been self-consciously autobiographical to the point of embarrassment. Updike's *Problems and Other Stories* (1979) is a searing example. This portrait of a family torn apart by divorce begins with an autobiographical preface in which Updike notes that the book describes "the curve of a sad time" in his personal life. The reader is thus invited to read the book as autobiography. *Problems* tells us what it's like for a family to go through a divorce, and one might argue that people can learn more by reading here about the infinitely complicated tensions, cross-purposes, and mixed feelings involved in such a crisis than by actually going through it. For mysterious reasons, it is hard to get a grip on what is happening in our lives while it is actually happening. We apparently need the mirror of fiction to see what lies in front of our noses. In a sense, we learn what our lives are like by reading about them as well as by living them, which is why fiction matters.

We read biographies for a similar reason: to find out how other people got through their lives. I, for instance, love to read about writers to see how they managed to get their work done in the course of busy lives. It's not easy to sit down to write when there are bills to be paid, children to ferry from one place to another, classes to teach, phone calls to answer, letters to respond to, and so forth. How did Dickens do it? Or Scott? Or Nabokov? In a good biography, one learns about a given subject's job difficulties, sexual conflicts, money problems, dental troubles, everything. If I'm interested in a writer, almost nothing about her or him can bore me.

Let me return to my novel, *The Last Station.* My longtime obsession with biography naturally spilled over into my fiction. Having read the diaries of the dozen or so people closest to him, I thought briefly about writing a straight biography of Tolstoy; I quickly, however, began to feel the limitations posed by conventional biography as a genre. One can describe events on the surface, but one can't get into them and under them in the same way that novelists can. What interested me in the case of Tolstoy was not the facts themselves—a half-dozen sound biographies already existed—but the emotional resonance of those facts. As I wrote, I found myself freely inventing, of course: how else can one write a novel? But I was working within the bounds of fact. Fact was the landscape and fiction the weather that played over that landscape and gave it color, texture, and mood.

I knew, for example, that Sofya Tolstoy on the night of July 23, 1910, threw herself into a pond with the intention of committing suicide. The "straight" biographer is stymied here by the fact that she did not mention this extremely significant act in her diary. Her husband merely notes it, rather dryly, as did a half-dozen other people. The agreed-upon facts are sparse. But these facts were productive for me as a novelist. I felt at liberty to enter her mind, to imagine her feelings. The conventional boundaries of biography may have prevented me from trying to put myself so fully into Sofya's shoes, although I was always keenly aware that if Sofya Tolstoy were to read this particular scene, she would say, "Give me a break, Parini. It was nothing like that." I would counter, "My dear Sofya, it never is."

Having written the Tolstoy novel and two other semifictional narratives, I began to wonder what it would feel like to write straight biography. No sooner had I begun to speculate along these lines than the chance to write John Steinbeck's life presented itself. I decided to go with it, and the experience of writing this book only confirmed what Malamud's Dubin asserts, that "all biography is ultimately fiction." The biographer, like the paleontologist, must reconstruct the extinct creature from a few scattered bone fragments; unless one wishes to erect a massive crate of air, one has no choice but to invent. Perhaps *invent* is the wrong word. To *envision*. Like the novelist, the biographer must summon the weather, the feel of a landscape, the texture of the subject's skin. A social fabric must be woven, made dense with conflicting motives, expectations, and anxieties. All the while, one realizes that the life of the biographical subject is not life at all: we do not live our lives in chapters, for example. The billion-faceted thing called human motivation must be simplified, often guessed at. One must choose a particular story from perhaps dozens of stories one could tell, which is why no single biography is ever definitive.

Elaine Steinbeck's dream about her husband's meeting with Tolstoy in heaven got me thinking. What follows is an interview I did recently with John Steinbeck himself, in heaven:

As I walked, ankle-deep in cloud, across the cool floor (heaven is rather like a geisha parlor that way: they make you take your shoes off), I could see Steinbeck sitting at a gilded table, reading. As I got closer, I saw the name of Charles Fourier, the Utopian socialist, on the cover.

"I never read this while alive," he said, without so much as introducing himself. "I should have. My notion of the 'phalanx'—you know, the idea that people act differently in group situations than they do on their own—it's all here."

Against my better judgment, I could not resist teasing him. "You were wrong about the etymology of the word, Mr. Steinbeck."

"Call me John," he said.

"Thank you . . . John. You see, it derives from a Greek word meaning 'spider', not a Latin word meaning 'turtle', as you thought."

"Does it matter?" he asked, rather wanly. I felt petty and, yes, pedantic. For a hideous moment I thought he was going to get up and go.

"You've come a long way," he said.

"There are some in Oxford," I said, "who would not agree with you."

He seemed mildly bemused. "I've read your book," he said. "Or most of it. I never like reading about myself. It never, you know, seems quite real."

"Was the book inaccurate in any way?"

"Look, son. May I call you Jay?"

"Of course."

"The point is, it only matters to a limited extent how 'accurate' a book like yours is. I picked up one or two mistakes, maybe half a dozen. This kind of thing is mostly irrelevant."

"Did you recognize yourself?"

"Sometimes,"he said, scratching his darkly tanned scalp. "But it's not really me there. Biographies are always caricatures. It's why I don't like them."

"Can you be specific? I tried very hard to picture things as I imagined them."

"Ah, imagined! There you are! Your book is a fantasy of what you thought my life was like."

"What did you expect," I countered, "a videotape?"

"I suppose my quarrel is with the genre itself, not you. Biographies are really novels in disguise, aren't they?"

"Just as novels are autobiographies in disguise," I said. "I remember that letter to your editor, Pat Covici, where you said you always identified with one of the characters in each novel, and you called this the 'author-character.'"

He squinted at me through the bright haze. "Did you 'identify,' as they say in high school English classes, with me as you wrote your book?"

"Let's say I sympathized," I said, rather nervously. "You made it difficult for me at times."

"What upset you?" he asked. "That thing with Carol?"

He was referring to his first marriage, to Carol Henning. She wanted children, but he didn't. When she got pregnant accidentally, he insisted that she have an abortion. The procedure went wrong, and Carol could never again have children. Not long after, he insisted on a divorce—much to her chagrin.

"You behaved badly," I said. "Carol loved you. She typed your books, pushed you in all the right directions as a writer. She even gave you a title for *The Grapes of Wrath*."

He was scowling now. "You think your job as biographer is to sit in judgment, is that it? I didn't like your little asides about that marriage, in fact. You weren't there. You couldn't possibly know what went on between us."

He was right, and I felt horribly small.

"At least you uncovered that affair she had with Joe Campbell. Even I was shocked to read his diary. My God, the man was a cad."

"You tended to idealize women," I said, perhaps too boldly for someone in my position. "It was inevitable that you would be disappointed so many times in love."

"In life!" he said.

"I hope I didn't go overboard in attacking your mother," I said.

"Again, you simplified. But in general you got the right idea. She was a perfectionist, and I wasn't perfect. She used to say I'd either be president of the United States or go to jail. But you made my father into a weaker man than he really was. There was a quiet strength there: you'd need that videotape to see it. Even then, if you weren't inside me, you might have missed the exchange of energies between us."

"Perhaps I should have written a novel about you, not a biography," I said.

Wisely, he ignored my remark and leaned toward me now, his breath sweet with ambrosia. "I don't think my mother was half so upset with my academic failures as you made out. That was your mother you were writing about, not mine!"

I sat back, horrified. Perhaps in conjuring John Ernst and Olive Steinbeck I had really summoned the ghosts of my own parents! Biographers, like scientists, are subject to the phenomenon of "search image" as well. We see what we have been conditioned to see.

"You made one other big mistake," Steinbeck said gravely. "Like many of your colleagues in the field, you assume that oral testimony is accurate. You often try to prove points with quotations, forgetting that a dozen people have a dozen different versions of the same event. You were uncanny in ferreting out Carol's friends, and Gwyn's."

"Did they lie to me?"

"*Lie* isn't the word. These people didn't like me. They thought of me as somehow responsible for the misery of my wives."

I thought he was being awfully touchy. For the most part, my book is deeply pro-Steinbeck. The book is laced with quotations from his admirers.

"The people who could have really said something useful about me were Ed Ricketts and Dook Sheffield," he added. "And Pat Covici."

"They were all dead when I began my research," I said. "I'm not really one for seances."

He looked at me skeptically.

"Look," I said, feeling suddenly aggressive. "I knew quite a few things about you that I didn't say."

"I know, I know," he said. "I'm at least glad you were discreet. So many of your colleagues aren't. But I must complain about one thing. Your readers may well get the impression that I went all haughty and pompous at the end—that stuff about my staying in fancy hotels and owning a yacht and attending the theater in a top hat and tails. That stuff meant nothing to me."

I listened and inwardly acknowledged the truth of what he was saying. I think I had looked in some corners a little too hard for a story. It's not that what I said was untrue: Steinbeck had changed over time, and his values shifted. But everyone changes. Given Steinbeck's great financial success, he might well have gone over the top.

"And that stuff about the Vietnam War. You were one of them, weren't you? That antiwar gang?"

"I was," I said.

"You people really let down the side," he said. "There was no need."

I decided against rehearsing the arguments for and against the Vietnam War just now. Some issues are never resolved. "Was there anything about the book you liked?" I asked, feeling a bit let down by this interview.

He laughed that barrel-chest laugh of his. "Poor man," he said, "I've been rough on you, have I?" He looked at me warmly. "You must realize that no book is ever satisfactory. What was it Paul Valery said? 'A poem is never finished, only abandoned.' A biography is an invention, more or less true. You got some of it right. Tolstoy, you should know, is not especially happy about what you did to him. He was not nearly as bad to Sofya as you suggest."

I bit my lip. It still seems to me that I went easy on Tolstoy when it came to his marriage. The man was a dreadful husband in most respects: a bully and, in his most idiosyncratic way, a puritanical snob.

"I can assure you, however, I didn't like Jack Benson's biography any more than I liked yours. And I will probably dislike the next one as well."

The archangel who had escorted me through the gates was suddenly waving in the distance, and I knew I must go or forfeit my evening meals at Christ Church. "It was good of you to agree to this meeting," I said, standing.

"Fourier," he said, utterly ignoring my remark. "I was grateful to you for one thing: the tip on Fourier. He understood the phalanx better than I did. He was there way ahead of me, in fact."

I left him reading. I could see that no book I could have written would ever seem, to him, an accurate version of his life. A biography, like a novel, is simply one version of reality, more or less true depending on the depth of the author's knowledge and the extent of his or her imagination and sympathy. The "agreed-upon facts" in any given life are relatively few and fairly stable; what one makes of them is, as it were, another thing entirely.

POETRY AND SILENCE

A poem is a gesture into silence, an attempt to reclaim the
stillness and clarity broken by the fall into language.
When the Gospel writer claims, "In the beginning was
the Word," he opens a rich vein of metaphysical specula-
tion about the relation of word to fact, of language to
logos. It was, and will remain, an uneasy correspondence:
the bird rising in flight and whatever zoological term we
summon to name that bird will never meet exactly. A
cognitive lag, the sense of a rupture plastered over some-
what poorly, always exists; language inevitably becomes
what Derrida has called a "mode of temporalizing," one
that "puts off till 'later' what is presently denied, the pos-
sible that is presently impossible."

Derrida should have said "the seemingly possible that
is always impossible." The gap between word and thing is

257

fatal, and there is no recovery except in silence. And this is where poetry becomes crucial as a spiritual aid; it assists us in the recovery of silence, leading us toward the crystal pond and, at its best, allowing us to bathe there. The refreshment in the silence that a good poem organizes may be considered a primary function of poetry. "The poem," as Wallace Stevens says in *Notes Toward a Supreme Fiction* (1942), "refreshes life so that we share, / For a moment, the first idea. . . . It satisfies / Belief in an immaculate beginning." This beginning is, of course, a place before sound, the silent ground in which language takes root.

Silence is a condition that may be likened to William Blake's category of Organized Innocence: a state radically different from mere ignorance or, for that matter, mere experience. It involves a plunge into the depths of what Blake in his provocative myth making calls Generation, that bonfire of human vanities. This is no place for a weak soul. In *The Book of Thel* (1789), he describes the impulse toward innocence, suggesting that Thel will not enter, as it were, into the hard work of Generation because of a lack of courage; she is eternally poised on the brink of embodiment, resisting incarnation, preferring "airy nothings" to "a local habitation and a name." The poem opens with a motto that is meant to lead Thel in the right direction:

> Does the Eagle know what is in the pit?
> Or wilt thou go ask the Mole?
> Can Wisdom be put in a silver rod?
> Or love in a golden bowl?

The fall of man is the fall into Generation, hence the phallic rod (a variant of the silver cord in Ecclesiastes 12:6) and the obviously vaginal bowl, which remain quite useless in this idealized (hence silver and gold) state in which Thel would live in Unorganized Innocence, in a silence that has not been sieved by the experience of physical embodiment.

The fall of man is, again, the fall into language. Adam and Eve did not need to speak; indeed, they should probably not have spoken. But Adam could not resist, and it was he who committed the original sin, which was naming. Why call the powerful bronze beast with the shaggy mane *lion*? Why give in to that irresistible longing to get up and say "I love you" to another person? Because this is our Adamic flaw; it defines our humanity: People are, as Aristotle and Hesiod both said, creatures of the word. Exactly how this came to be remains a riddle, as Socrates suggests in *Cratylus*. But this riddle, like a Zen koan, is a goad to fuller consciousness. The end of all our efforts, and of poetry as a form of meditative practice, is to waken into silence.

The Buddhist tradition assumes that truth lies beyond linguistic borders. What the Buddha discovered after sitting for six years under the bo tree could not be spoken. "The One who knows does not speak," cautions a Buddhist text. "The one who speaks does not know." This self-canceling aphorism embodies, within its tragic ironies, the riddle of language. And it damns all poets from the start; indeed, as T. S. Eliot observes wryly in "East Coker" (1943), "one has only learnt to get the better of words / For the thing one no longer has to say, or the way in which / One is no longer disposed to say it."

These marks on a page and sequential grunts, which are supposed to waken "meaning," are necessarily doomed. They are stones lining the path to the pond. They point to the moon, but they are not the moon. And those of us who speak or write or even listen are like the dog who, when shown the moon by his master, barked at the master's finger.

"Art," as D. H. Lawrence has said, "is an act of attention." Poetry too, as the supreme linguistic art, is best understood as a kind of attention, one that uses language to move beyond language into silence. The poet's eye is fixed resolutely on the object. The image, when properly composed, pulls the reader downward into a spiral of attention and through it—out in the blank space of silence.

The Zenso Mondo, a series of dialogues by Zen masters, contains a memorable anecdote:

> One day a man of the people said to Zen Master Ikkyu:
> "Master, will you please write for me some maxim of the highest wisdom?"
> Ikkyu immediately took his brush and wrote the word "Attention."
> "Is that all?" asked the man. "Will you not add something more?"
> Ikkyu then wrote twice: "Attention. Attention."
> "Well," remarked the man rather irritably: "I really don't see much depth or subtlety in what you have just written."
> Then Ikkyhu wrote the same word three times again: "Attention. Attention. Attention."

> Angry now, the man demanded: "What does the word
> 'Attention' mean anyway?"
> And Ikkyu answered gently: "Attention means attention."

In the world of Blake's Experience, the mind is frazzled, fragmented, fixed on ideas of things. Ideally, suggests William Carlos Williams, the poet's mind is not fixed on ideas but on the thing itself: the concrete object. This refocus of attention is the turn that enables the mind to move into the realm of Organized Innocence and toward an achieved silence. The image becomes, in a sense, a mantra that provides a focus; the poet and reader can look through, listen through, the image toward the blank, the silence, with exhilaration as in Emerson's *Nature* (1836), where he argues for that moment of vision in which the axis of vision is "coincident with the axis of things" and therefore we become "a transparent eyeball." Or with despair, as in Coleridge's *Dejection: An Ode* (1802), where he cries, "And still I gaze—and with how blank an eye."

Poets describe the visionary goal in so many different ways. Perhaps the supreme moment of vision in Western poetry occurs in the thirty-third canto of the *Paradiso* (1321). Dante's traveler arrives before the face of God after climbing through hell and purgatory, and he is utterly transfixed:

Oh abbondante grazie ond' io presu. . . .
ficcar lo viso per la luce etterna,
Tanto che la veduta vi consunsi!

[O, abounding grace in which I presume
to fix my gaze through eternal light
so far that all my vision is consumed by it.]

He is led to a further point in which all language is consumed: *"Oh quanto é corto il dire e come fioco / al mio concetta!"* [How limited speech is, how inadequate to my conception!] The reality of language breaks down and is absorbed into the reality of silence. This remains, I think, the goal of poetry.

But the steps along the way are endless, and they are terrifying. Pascal spoke of "the infinite spaces between the stars" with breathlessness, reverence, and fear. The space between the words, between the lines, of a poem can be terrifying. The margins of the page, which form a kind of amniotic fluid of white space containing and supporting the verse line, beckon the reader away from language itself. The ideal poem is altogether blank, a white page, but it must be achieved, written through. Just as Freud says one must "remember the past to burn it up," the poet uses language to destroy language. The innocence of the uninscribed page is like the great wall that the Bodhidharma—a giant of Buddhist spirituality—faced while sitting in perfect silence for nine years before experiencing enlightenment. "Only through time time is conquered," writes Eliot in "Burnt Norton" (1943). One cannot move from innocent or unorganized silence to achieved silence except through language, in time:

> Words move, music moves
> Only in time; but that which is only living
> Can only die. Words, after speech, reach
> Into silence.

A poem arranges the silence, makes poet and reader aware of its presence. In a poem called "A Lesson in Music," Alastair Reid develops this conceit rather hauntingly:

> Play the tune again: but this time
> with more regard for the movement at the source of it
> and less attention to time. Time falls
> curiously in the course of it.
>
> Play the tune again: not watching
> your fingering, but forgetting, letting flow
> the sound till it surrounds you. Do not count
> or even think. Let go.
>
> Play the tune again: but try to be
> nobody, nothing, as though the pace
> of the sound were your heart beating, as though
> the music were your face.
>
> Play the tune again. It should be easier
> to think less every time of the notes, of the measure.
> It is all an arrangement of silence. Be silent,
> and then play it for your pleasure.

261

Play the tune again; and this time, when it ends,
do not ask me what I think. Feel what is happening
strangely in the room as the sound glooms over
you, me, everything.

Now,
play the tune again.

Reid, by suggesting that meaning in music (and, by extension, in poetry) is "an arrangement of silence," moves toward the paradox at the center of literary representation. Language may be thought of as a kind of ivy that covers and, in so doing, makes visible an invisible wall. One has to see the wall to tear it down. This is, perhaps, the same wall before which the Bodhidharma sat all those years, plucking the leaves of ivy one by one till nothing was left and satori became possible.

The ancient Chinese poets of the T'ang dynasty tended, stripped, and pruned this wall of ivy rather carefully, and they produced a body of poetry of austere simplicity and power, a verse rooted in silence. The white space on the page seems wonderfully pure, the silence arranged to perfection, in "I Stand Alone," a poem by Tu Fu:

A hawk hangs on the edge of heaven.
A pair of gulls is drifting up the river,

buffeted by wind that buoys them up;
they coast and glide.

The dewy grass below them shimmers
with a spider's web.

Nature's way is my way, too.
I stand alone among a thousand arrows.

Or in this poem, by his friend, Li Po, called "Summer in the Mountain":

Too indolent to fan myself or even breathe,
naked to the waist in leafy woods,
my headband left beside a wall or lost,

I let the pine winds dry my scalp.
I dream of oceans.

The rhetoric of such a poem is clipped, consciously spare, self-limiting. One does not expect a profusion of detail. The image itself is pressed into the poem like a watermark, dug into the paper's soft rag to steady the poem, to pull everything toward its still center. The spaces between the lines are wide and white, and there is silence in the snowy fields of either margin. The lines of the poem are rooted in silence and derive their strength from its rich emptiness.

Li Po and Tu Fu work at the opposite pole from Walt Whitman, in whose poetry language crowds to the fore and the silence on which it feeds seems willfully occluded. The lines thrash and writhe, twisting free of the silence that seems to threaten at every moment; in *Song of Myself* (1855), the poet confronts his existential fear of silence directly:

> Dazzling and tremendous how quick the sun-rise would kill
> me,
> If I could not now and always send sun-rise out of me.
>
> We also ascend dazzling and tremendous as the sun,
> We found our own O my soul in the calm and cool of the
> day-break.
>
> My voice goes after what my eyes cannot reach,
>   With the twirl of my tongue I encompass worlds and
>   volumes of worlds.
> Speech is the twin of my vision, it is unequal to measure
> itself,
> It provokes me forever, it says sarcastically,
> *Walt you contain enough, why don't you let it out then?*
>
> Come now I will not be tantalized, you conceive too much
>   of articulation,
> Do you not know O speech how the buds beneath you are
>   folded?
> Waiting in gloom, protected by frost,
> The dirt receding before my prophetical screams,

Whitman positions himself before the wall in a different posture from Li Po's or Tu Fu's, but silence is nevertheless essential to the production of his voice, whose lineaments become visible only in contrast to the blank spaces, the pauses, the chinks of white light that blaze through the blinds of each stanza. At the end of each breathless line, a pause occurs; in this gasp, as in the spaces between the planks of a scaffolding, one glimpses the air of reality, shimmering, in which he has suspended the poem.

It may be worth pausing over Whitman's key observation: "Speech is the twin of my vision." I have already made the synesthetic analogy of silence and a blank space, but there is a level on which I was cheating there (in the way that, as Aristotle noted, all metaphorical thinking is a kind of cheat, because one thing is not another thing). Voice and vision are not the same thing, but the link between them, in poetry, is especially close. "Description is revelation," says Wallace Stevens, edging close to an understanding of this link. Language, used descriptively in poetry, becomes a mode of vision; we see through words to a world beyond words. We attune ourselves to hear the silence.

Stevens's famous line occurs in one of his lesser known but more interesting poems, "Description Without Place," in which he expands on what he meant in an earlier poem, "The Creations of Sound." There he insists that "speech is not dirty silence / Clarified. It is silence made still dirtier." This antimimetic theory of language flowers in the later poem:

> Description is revelation. It is not
> The thing described, nor false facsimile.
>
> It is an artificial thing that exists,
> In its own seeming, plainly visible.
>
> Yet not too closely the double of our lives,
> Intenser than any actual life could be,
>
> A text we should be born that we might read,
> More explicit than the experience of sun
>
> And moon.

Stevens's rather Coleridgean complication is worth bearing in mind: language taints reality, drenches it in its own subjectivity, and this is a good thing too. A "false facsimile" may be good enough for a trompe l'oeil painter, but it's not the stuff of genuine art, which departs from reality and reaches for Reality. Along these lines, the poem does not imitate speech; it elevates and distorts, heightens and (as Stevens suggests) makes dirtier still the dirt of speech. The poet, as it were, tosses a stone into the clear pond of silence; this stirs up the mud, and the reader watches as the particles filter through the translucent water, caught in a pillar of clouded sunlight. The water clears eventually, but this is not the usual state of affairs. Life is noisy, dirty, confused: the audial equivalent of a Jackson Pollack painting. The poet's job, therefore, is to unsay what has been said or (in Roland Barthes's phrase) "to unexpress the expressible."

Poetic language is not in the familiar sense a language of communication. There is, in fact, something oddly intransitive about the way poets use language. A poem is not, in the terminology of analytic philosophy, a "speech act." The philosopher John Searle, for instance, believes that the purpose of human language is "to produce a certain illocutionary effect in the hearer." Although the rhetorical aspect of poetry is well worth contemplating and, in poetry with a political aim, crucial to the poem's success in the world, it is not and can never be the primary aspect of the art. The poet writes from a deep compulsion to make visible something previously hidden by the dense undergrowth of nonpoetic language.

In this sense, Noam Chomsky's view of language as the embodiment of some innate or prelinguistic reality seems, to me, a helpful way of thinking about poetry as well. In his 1975 essay "On Cognitive Capacity," Chomsky writes,

> A human language is a system of remarkable complexity. To come to know a human language would be an extraordinary intellectual achievement for a creature not specifically designed to accomplish this task. A normal child acquires this knowledge on relatively slight exposure and without specific training. He can then quite effortlessly make use of an intricate structure of specific rules and guiding principles to convey his thoughts and feelings to others, arousing in them novel ideas and subtle perceptions and judgments. To the conscious mind, not specifically designed for the purpose, it remains a distant goal to reconstruct and compre-

hend what the child has done intuitively and with minimal effort. Thus language is a mirror of mind in a deep and significant sense.

The poem also is a mirror of sorts—a metaphor explored in rich detail by M. H. Abrams in *The Mirror and the Lamp* (1953). The mirror metaphor is infinitely suggestive, however complex and potentially misleading (as Richard Rorty has argued in *Philosophy and the Mirror of Nature* [1979]). The mirror of language naturally distorts the world it perceives, but it offers at least a version of the external world; for Chomsky, language also provides a way into the mind's steep caverns, an inner geography of the kind summoned by Gerard Manley Hopkins when he cries (in "'No Worse, there is none'"),

> O the mind, mind has mountains; cliffs of fall
> Frightful, sheer, no-man-fathomed. Hold them cheap
> May who ne'er hung there.

Andrew Marvell evokes a less ferocious inner landscape in "The Garden" (1681):

> The mind, that Ocean where each kind
> Does straight its own resemblance find;
> Yet it creates, transcending these,
> Far other worlds, and other seas;
> Annihilating all that's made
> To a green thought in a green shade.

This annihilating instinct of the imagination is what returns us, the reader and the writer, to silence as a condition of nonbeing, that terrifying and preexistential abyss contradicted by Wallace Stevens with post-Cartesian confidence when he declares, "I am but that I am and as I am I am." But the abyss, with its profound silences and labyrinthine ways, exists, and many poets—from San Juan de la Cruz to Hopkins and Eliot—have been tempted down the via negativa. As Emerson, in his late sixties, wrote in his *Journal* (1866): "There may be two or three of four steps, according to the genius of each, but for every seeing soul there are two absorbing facts,—I and the Abyss."

266

In an essay called "The Object of Inquiry" (1975), Chomsky notes that what we normally think of as language has many components, and many of these are invisible. "Thus an actual language," he writes, "may result only from the interaction of several mental faculties, one being the faculty of language." Among the least understood of these mental facilities, the one upon which all language is founded, is the capacity to absorb silence and, ideally, to organize it. The poet, as the primal language maker, has a huge capacity to soak in this silence, to create the margins that, like a photographic negative, form a kind of inverse visibility.

Language is endlessly protean, fragile, impermanent, provisional, even in its written form; it is fatally bound to time. And just as time is nature's way of preventing everything from happening all at once, language is a temporalizing medium that bridges us from thought to thought and moment to moment. It feigns presence, masking the absence that lies—like Marvell's mental ocean—beneath the glittering surface. It is a way of postponing the ultimate silence of death.

When Milton, in a fit of naming in *Paradise Lost* (1667), summons "Rocks, moss, stonecrop, iron, merds" (a line wonderfully recast by Eliot in "Gerontion") one senses the unreclaimable distance between words and things. More to the point, one feels the hollowness at the center of things themselves: the rock, broken, yields a silent empty core. The lake, drained, is a barren field. "Where man is not, nature is barren," argues Blake. Humankind, which cannot bear much reality, deflects reality through art, as in the shield of Perseus, the Greek hero who understood that the Gorgon Medusa could be slain only if viewed by reflection.

Poetry, then, provides a slantwise means of confronting something intolerable, a way of looking into what Eliot called "the heart of light, the silence" in that unforgettable moment in *The Waste Land* (1922) followed by the plaintive lines from *Tristan und Isolde: "Oed' und leer das Meer."* This is Marvell's oceanic mind swept clean of spindrift language and the froth of chatter. In the dark cosmology of this century, it is Heidegger's *Nichtigkeit,* reinterpreted as *le néant* by Sartre; it is the point made with chilling wryness by Gertrude Stein when she observed, "There is no there there."

The theory of poetry that emerges from these considerations is almost necessarily antimimetic and, in the last analysis, gnostic. Modern philosophers from Wittgenstein and J. L. Austin through Richard Rorty and his neopragmatists have pulled us away from all simplistic notions of "picturing" or "mirroring" in language; the correspondences between word and world have been broken, and we are left with the self-reflexive word incarnate of Eliot and the Gospel of John or, perhaps more beguilingly, that vision of poetic incarnation that appears in the final stanza of Hart Crane's "Voyages" where he approaches the almost oxymoronic position of visionary skepticism:

> The imaged Word, it is, that holds
> Hushed willows anchored in its glow.
> It is the unbetrayable reply
> Whose accent no farewell can know.

The willows in Crane's poem are hushed because they are anchored in the "imaged Word." The stillness of the poetic image, when properly resolved, is rooted in silence, the silence of the desert or the mountain hut, the silence of meditation, the silence that follows struggle for knowledge, the famous "peace that passeth understanding."

Emerson, the father of American poetry, was (as Carlyle once said) "the aid and abettor of all who would live in the spirit." Poet and philosopher, shaman, preacher, counselor: he rejected all forms of received religion, but he assembled from the broken shards of world mythology a form of thought that "linked back" (*religio*) to what Paul Tillich, writing a century later, would call "the ground of being." From a mystical point of view, the link is to the One, an ecstatic (as in *ekstasis*) leaping from body to spirit, from sound to silence. In his *Journal* of 1838, Emerson writes about this sublime state in an interesting way:

> In the highest moments, we are a vision. There is nothing that can be called gratitude nor properly joy. The soul is raised over passion. It seeth nothing so much as Identity. It is a Perceiving that Truth and Right ARE. Hence it becomes a perfect Peace out of the knowing that all things will go well. Vast spaces of nature—the Atlantic Ocean, the South Seas: vast intervals of time, years, centuries, are annihilated to it; this which I think and feel underlay that former state of life and circumstances, as it does underlie my present, and will always all circumstance, and what is called life and what is called death.

As usual, Emerson takes us in unexpected directions and away from sentimental notions of gratitude or joy. Even passion is dismissed. In the "moment of vision," we see nothing and hear nothing. Identity is all: a union of subject and object, body and soul, mind and nature. Space and time—the conveyer belt on which we turn—dissolve. A gnostic awareness akin to the "Peace that passeth understanding" comes into our possession: "this knowing that all things will go well."

The work of the poet is the recovery of silence, but there is no way of doing this except through language, and this is difficult, as Eliot notes in "Burnt Norton":

> Words strain,
> Crack and sometimes break, under the burden,
> Under the tension, slip, slide, perish,
> Decay with imprecision, will not stay in place,
> Will not stay still.

If, for the critic, all readings are misreadings, and meaning (as Terry Eagleton says) "a kind of flickering of absence and presence together," imagine how difficult it is for poets to work, situated precariously as they are between absence and presence, darkness and light, unsaying and saying. All truth claims dissolve in the fragile web of textuality, as language itself undoes the meanings that seem, briefly, to harden into words.

Of course poetry is not about truth claims, not in the philosophical sense of that term. La différence makes no difference when it comes to unsaying what has been said in the way poets do. Poets feed language like scraps of driftwood into the bonfire of consciousness and listen as it crackles and burns; a pale smoke rises; the fire flakes drift to the ground, spent. The poet, in making the darkness visible, makes the silence audible. And meaning is, after all, "an arrangement of silence."

One of the most terrifying poems on the subject of language and silence is Frost's "The Most of It," in which a man stands on a "boulder-broken shore" and shouts across a mountain lake from a "tree-hidden cliff":

> He would cry out on life, that what it wants
> Is not its own love back in copy speech,
> But counter-love, original response.

Alas, nothing comes of his hopeful call across the water, "Unless it was the embodiment that crashed / In the cliff's talus on the other side, / And then in the far distant water splashed." What makes this noise is a great buck emerging from the wilderness, a raw but noble embodiment of nature's inarticulate presence.

The poet addresses the universe and does not want his "own love back in copy speech." The *vox clamantis in deserto* [voice crying in the desert] is the poet alone with the silence, raging against its almost willful challenge to human sanity. It marks one stage on the way toward marshaling the silence, letting it wash over, warp, and ultimately wean the speaker from speech itself. Poets, like every person in the face of extinction, discover their original (as in the root sense of the word) and intimate relation to the silence. In *Nature*, Emerson says, "Our age is retrospective. It builds the sepulchres of the fathers. It writes biographies, histories, and criticism. The foregoing generations beheld God and nature face to face; we, through their eyes. Why should we not also enjoy an original relation to the universe?"

Perhaps the greatest irony of poetry, and language itself, is that the most complete expression involves a total erasure of the medium as the speaker arrives at a condition of understanding so complete that speech becomes superfluous. There is no "counter-love, original response" unless we call *other* that which comes from within. What we all seek is the silence of the perfect poem, the poem that crackles, flares in the darkness, then fades, consumed by the silence that was always its goal.

ACKNOWLEDGMENTS

Quotations from the poems of Alastair Reid are used by permission of the author.

Quotations from the poems of Robert Penn Warren are from *New and Selected Poems, 1923–1985.* Copyright © 1985 by Random House. Used by permission of the William Morris Agency.

Quotations from the poems of Wallace Stevens are from *Collected Poems of Wallace Stevens.* Copyright © 1942 by Wallace Stevens and renewed 1970 by Holly Stevens. Used by permission of Alfred A. Knopf.

Quotations from Charles Wright are from *Country Music: Selected Early Poems.* Copyright © 1982 by Wesleyan University Press. Used by permission of University Press of New England.

"California Dreaming" and "Year of the Ox" are from *The World of the Ten Thousand Things: Poems, 1980–*

1990. Copyright © 1990 by Farrar, Straus and Giroux. Used by permission.

Quotations from Robert Frost are from *Complete Poems of Robert Frost.* Copyright © 1936, 1945, 1956 by Robert Frost. © 1964, 1970, 1973, 1975, 1977 by Leslie Frost Ballantine. © 1928, 1947, 1949, 1969 by Henry Holt and Co. Reprinted by arrangement with Henry Holt.

Quotations from Seamus Heaney are from *Selected Poems, 1966–1987.* Copyright © 1990 by Farrar, Straus and Giroux. Used by permission of Farrar, Straus and Giroux and Faber and Faber, Ltd.

Quotations from Theodore Roethke are from *Collected Poems of Theodore Roethke.* Copyright © 1962 Beatrice Roethke for the Estate of Theodore Roethke. Used by permission of Doubleday and Company, a division of Bantam Doubleday Dell Publishing Group.

Quotations from T. S. Eliot are from *Collected Poems, 1909–1962.* Copyright © 1963, 1964 by Harcourt Brace and Company. Used by permission of Harcourt Brace and Faber and Faber, Ltd.